Guide
to
Good
Speech

Guide
to
Good
Speech

James H. McBurney

Ernest J. Wrage

SECOND EDITION

Dean, The School of Speech, Northwestern University

Director, The Basic Course in Speech, Northwestern University

Englewood Cliffs, New Jersey

PRENTICE-HALL, INC.

Guide to Good Speech

SECOND EDITION

McBurney and Wrage

c

© *Copyright* 1955, 1960 *by* PRENTICE-HALL, INC., *Englewood Cliffs, N. J.*

*Illustration credits: Bahnsen from Monkmeyer, 20-21;
British Information Services, 96-97, 240-241, 296-297;
City College of New York, 280-281; Ewing Galloway, 2-3, 228-229, 258-259;
Fujihira from Monkmeyer, 60-61; Hays from Monkmeyer, 34-35, 76-77, 110-111;
National Broadcasting Company, 178-179;
New York University, 126-127, 212-213, 314-315; Standard Oil Co. (N. J.),
142-143; Stern from Monkmeyer,
44-45; Wide World Photos, 10-11, 160-161, 198-199.*

*The cartoons on pages 13, 27, 29, 41, 47, 69, 78, 106, 112, 138,
154, 164, 188, 207, 223, 233, 262, 289, 301, and 307 are reproduced
by permission of the publishers, The Vanguard Press,
from* Louder and Funnier *by Burr Shafer. Copyright, 1951, by Burr Shafer.*

Sixth printing .... *July, 1963*

Designed by Harry Rinehart

Preface

This edition of GUIDE TO GOOD SPEECH is a thorough revision of the original text. The aim is the same: To present a concise statement of the basic principles of good speech with emphasis on clarity, usefulness, and economy. But the principles have been restated and reinterpreted in light of suggestions from the many instructors and students who have used the book.

We have tried to write a practical, readable manual that students will respect and enjoy. And, so far as possible, we have tried to keep in mind the different commitments and arrangements faced by teachers, ourselves included. But in no instance have we intentionally compromised our primary purpose—to make available a book that will guide young men and women to good speech in all their personal and public relations.

We appreciate the many constructive criticisms from unidentified sources provided by our publishers, and we are again indebted to Dr. Naomi Wrage (formerly Instructor in Public Speaking, The School of Speech, Northwestern University) and Everett M. Sims (of Prentice-Hall, Inc.) for their help with this revision. The cartoons we use here and there in the book are the work of Burr Shafer, whose drawings first came to our attention in the *Saturday Review*.

James H. McBurney
Ernest J. Wrage

Contents

vi

Guide
to
Good
Speech

CHAPTER ONE

Your
Speech

Helen Keller tells how she learned to speak after the years of unbroken silence she had endured since early childhood: "My soul, conscious of new strength, came out of bondage, and was reaching through those broken symbols of

speech to all knowledge and all faith." [1]

Those of us who have never lived without speech are likely to hold a much less exalted view of its power. In fact, we take speech for granted—like the air we breathe

[1] *The Story of My Life.* New York: Doubleday, 1947, p. 60.

or the ground we walk on. We simply accept it as one of nature's gratuities.

The typical reader of this book has from seventeen to twenty years of speaking experience to draw on. He can make known his more obvious wants; he can communicate with his parents and friends; he can hold up his end of a social conversation fairly well; in general, he can make himself understood.

What more can you ask? Much more. This chapter invites you to appraise your own speech, and suggests what you should expect from your speech—what your speech can do for you and what you can do with your speech.

Does Your Speech Limit You?

For Helen Keller, learning to speak was a release from "the prison of silence." Might this same figure of speech apply to many of us, who have the gift of speech but who fail to realize its worth? Are we imprisoned by poor speech habits that deny us self-expression and full access to others' ideas?

Let's assume that you could make a film and sound record of all the talking you do in a typical day—everything from early morning until late night. What would such a record tell you about your successes and failures in communication?

Of one thing you may be certain: This record would give you dramatic proof of the heavy reliance you place on speech and the many purposes to which you put speech in a single day. But it might also give you some disquieting evidence of a bondage more limiting than you had ever realized.

Your record *might* present you with a profile of slovenly habits: monotonous or unpleasant voice, blurred sounds, lumbering language, tired words, and grammatical mistakes. You might wish desperately for the editor's privilege of correcting copy: deleting a half-hundred banal comments, clarifying a murky set of instructions, toning down ill-founded statements made with an air of complete certitude, withholding the ill-considered remark and the offending comment. But you might be pained even more by the record of clues to wasted opportunities—the times when ideas struggled within you for expression while you sat mute, a prisoner of your self-concern and apprehensions.

Does this picture seem exaggerated? Could it possibly apply to your own speech habits? Before you answer, read what one experienced observer has to say:

> Most children soon learn to talk the language of the people around them. Yet few of them continue their verbal maturing throughout life. Few of them, in adulthood, are so able to say what they want to say—with confidence, precision, beauty, and a sensitive awareness of what is fitting in the situation—that the communicative experience holds more of success than of failure. In no area of our maturing, in fact, is arrested development more common than in the area of communication. It is so common that it is not even noticed; it is taken for granted as natural. The person who is mature in his communicative powers is noted as an exception to the rule. The person who is immature—halting, clumsy, obscure, rambling, dull, platitudinous, insensitive—is the rule.[2]

What Can Speech Do for You?

Most of our speech consists of conversation. We exchange pleasantries, report events, tell stories, and give advice. Through this everyday communication, we maintain a kind of fellowship with the people around us. This fellowship—call it rapport, community of interest, friendly understanding—is important to us. Often it is more important than we care to admit.

Much of our speech is aimed at discussing the problems we face

[2] H. A. Overstreet, *The Mature Mind*. New York: W. W. Norton & Company, Inc., 1949, pp. 54-55. Reprinted by permission.

in our daily lives: Should I take this course? Why major in history? Is Professor Jones the best bet in math? Should I take that summer job? What are the opportunities for women in journalism? Does the foreign language requirement make sense? How should I meet my military obligations? Should I plan a career in teaching?

These are serious questions worth serious discussion. You can go it alone or you can invite the counsel of others. The choice is not difficult once you feel confident of your ability to use speech for this purpose.

Speech is also part of our professional equipment. The modern world demands special skill in speaking from those who hold places of responsibility. Success in some fields, such as law, politics, teaching, and preaching, has always demanded this skill. More recently, motion pictures, radio, and television have opened careers that require highly developed speaking skill from thousands of men and women. The tremendous growth and complexity of business and industry have made the telephone, conference room, and convention hall nerve-centers in the production of goods, services, enlightenment, and pleasure. Medical practice makes wide use of the team approach in which specialists pool their knowledge and skills. Science and technology are vast cooperative enterprises faced with the constant need to report and interpret their findings. Members of the professions gather to make speeches and read papers, and are called upon to speak to community organizations. Sooner or later, if you follow the road to success, you will discover that it often leads to a platform or conference table.

What Can You Do with Your Speech?

In large part, we have already answered this question. What speech can do for you suggests what you can do with your speech. Most speech is shared experience. You give as well as receive. And what you get out of speech is likely to bear a very close relation to what others are able to get out of your speech.

In the kind of society in which we live, social action stems from public deliberation. A democratic society is no stronger than the people who make its decisions. You have the opportunity and the obligation to bring your best resources to bear on these deliberations. And you will soon discover that this obligation requires speaking skills of the highest order.

Democratic society is served by talk, but only if that talk leads to understanding, thoughtful reflection, and rational behavior. Of course we must admit demagoguery and we must expect license—these are the price we have to pay for our guarantee of free speech. But the great danger is that our tolerance may lead to indifference, that a surfeited and cynical public may lose faith in the value of deliberation.

What happens when our lawmakers and statesmen fail to talk sense? When their hours of debate fail to lead to action? Many people—too many—become impatient, throw up their hands, and turn to their private interests, letting the world muddle along as best it can. And yet one person, skillful in speech and in human relations, is enough to swing a meeting from a chaos of frustration into channels of productive talk. When many members of a group have that skill, discussion generates effective action based on the pooled wisdom of the group.

Education for speaking is education for democratic living. Here is how T. V. Smith puts it: "Not less talk but more—more debate and better debate—that is the manner in which the very principle of revolution is peacefully preserved in our American institutions and the spirit of evolution is made the deepest law of our land." [3]

Points to Keep in Mind

1. Poor speech habits limit self-expression and deprive us of full access to the ideas of others.

2. Good speech can help you win the comradeship of others,

---

[3] T. V. Smith and Robert A. Taft, *Foundations of Democracy*. New York: Alfred A. Knopf, 1939, p. 47.

can help you share the counsel and guidance of your fellows, and can open up professional opportunities to you in the years ahead.

3. Good speech enables you to make a larger contribution in all democratic councils—in your home, your community, and in your state and nation.

Exercises

1. Introduce yourself to the members of the class. Include just enough biographical data to identify yourself and then tell the class in what field you are majoring or plan to major. Give them the reasons for your choice.

2. Every city, town, village, and neighborhood in America has some local institution, tradition, custom, or identifying characteristic that distinguishes it from all others. One of these places you call home. Tell the class about your home town in terms that identify it in a meaningful, interesting way.

3. Most people have a hobby of some kind—maps, stamps, old cars, dogs, dancing, records, fishing, boats, guns, books, cooking, gardening, or sports. Tell the class about your hobby, how you got started, some of your experiences with it, and why you find it interesting.

4. Divide the class into groups of five or six members on the basis of major fields of study or professional, occupational, or career interests. Select a leader for each group to guide a panel discussion. Phrase a question for discussion that will give you an opportunity to discuss the field in which you are interested and its values and limitations for the individual and society. Seat the group in front of the class and explore the question through panel discussion.

The leader will introduce himself in a few sentences and ask each member of the panel to do the same. Then the leader will open the discussion with a question he has planned in advance. Members of the group will reply, leading into whatever considerations serve best to bring out the thinking of the group and to develop the subject in interesting, stimulating ways.

5. Select an editorial or short article from the editorial page of a newspaper or magazine. Read it to the class and interpret the meaning and implication of the opinions expressed. Do three things in presenting your talk: (1) Identify the subject and source of the editorial; (2) read it aloud in ways that will do full justice to the author; and (3) interpret the meaning as you see it.

CHAPTER TWO

What Is
Good
Speech?

Whenever we try to evaluate speech, we must unavoidably make certain assumptions about the nature of speech. Our own conception of speech has already been suggested by the values we assigned to speech in Chapter 1.

10

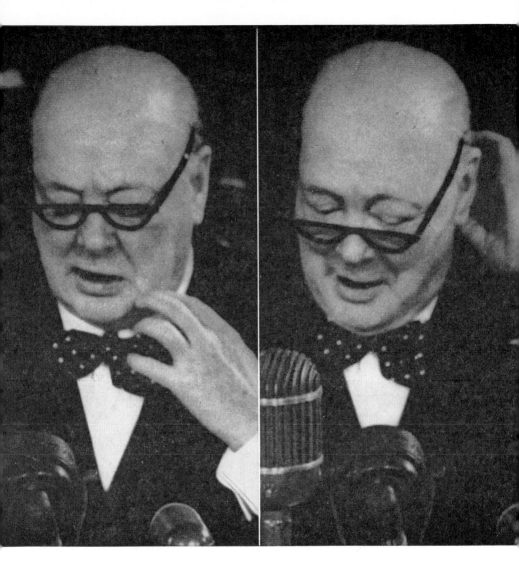

In this chapter we shall try to make this conception more explicit by raising two questions that are of basic concern to all students of speech: First, what is speech? Once we have answered that question, we can go on to the second one: What is *good* speech?

What Is Speech?

Speech is *the communication of ideas and feelings by means of visible and audible symbols originating in the speaker.* Speech is *all* oral communication—original and interpretative, public and private. It deals in ideas, for speaking and thinking go hand in hand.

Speech uses symbols—sounds, words, inflections, and gestures. Whether or not the speaker's ideas get through to his listeners depends on his skill in using these symbols, and on the skill of his listeners in interpreting them. In speech, unlike written language or any other form of communication, these symbols originate in the speaker—they are the products of his muscles, nerves, and glands. Speech may be amplified by loudspeaker systems, carried across the nation by radio and television, reproduced on film and sound track, or supplemented by scenery, properties, and lights. But helpful as these devices are, they are not essential to speech, and most speech takes place without them.

The purpose of all speech is *response.* The speaker uses visible and audible symbols to stir up meaningful reactions in his listeners. Stimulus and response are the essence of communication through speech.

What Is Good Speech?

Through the centuries, critics have given four different answers to this question. Speech may be judged: (1) by its results—the nature of the response, (2) by the truth—the soundness of the speaker's position, (3) by the motives and intentions of the speaker, or (4) by the principles of the art of good speech. What is the best answer?

Let's begin with the theory that speech is good if it gets results and poor if it fails to get results. We ask: Did the campaigner get elected? Did the lawyer win his case? Did the salesman sell his product? Since we always speak to get a response, it might seem logical to judge speech by the speaker's success or failure in getting the response he is after. This plausible theory, however, suffers from one fatal defect: In any speech, many factors influence the outcome. Some of these factors are beyond the speaker's control, and may be so stacked against the speaker that not even the most brilliant performance will win him the response he seeks. In other cases, these outside factors may work automatically for the speaker, with no effort on his part. In short, a "good" speaker may fail to get results through no fault of his own; and a "poor" speaker may win a favorable response in spite of his weaknesses.

The results theory is a perfect example of the old fallacy of attributing an effect to a single cause where many causes are operating. This mistake, of course, produces false evaluations of speech and misleading counsel to students of speech.

Other critics have tried to judge speech by its *truth,* or by *the character and motives of the speaker.* There is no question whatsoever that any speaker who sticks with the truth as he sees it is on sound moral grounds. And there is no question that speakers of good character and high motives are preferable to scoundrels. Unfortunately, however, these theories get us into new difficulties.

We have all seen the best causes—the truth—suffer at the hands of poor speakers. And we have seen speakers with the finest character and most worthy motives fail to perceive the truth or defend it poorly if they do see it. Good causes and worthy motives help the speaker, but they can seldom do the job alone.

There are further difficulties: Truth is often relative to time,

"Before I introduce our speaker, I must say that due to the slowness with which membership dues are coming in we have been forced to fall back on cheaper talent—so, fellows, how about coughing up and . . ."

place, and circumstances, and motives are always personal and elusive. We cannot always be sure we know the truth nor can we be certain of the speaker's motives. Judging speech by these standards is precarious at best.

How *can* we judge speech then? The only adequate answer is to judge speech as an *art* based on established principles. We hold speech to be good when it conforms to these principles and poor when it does not. But what are these principles? How are they derived? And how reliable are they?

Since stimulus and response are the essence of all speech, we must search out the principles of good speech by identifying the stimuli that have proved successful in getting desired responses. And if we are to avoid the mistake of judging by results, we must isolate the influence of outside factors from the stimuli that are provided by the speech itself. In short, we must rely on controlled experimental studies and on careful investigations of speakers and the circumstances under which their speeches are given.

As Aristotle put it over 2,000 years ago, ". . . When the practised and the spontaneous speaker gain their end, it is possible to investigate the causes of their success, and such an inquiry, we shall all admit, performs the function of an art." [1] For centuries, men have been recording their observations on speaking and speakers. And these observations are still being checked and refined in an effort to provide directives for speakers and bases for evaluating speech. These are the principles that give us the most reliable answer to our question, "What is good speech?"

Principles of Good Speech

There are ten basic principles of good speech that you can apply both in learning how to speak more effectively and in evaluating speech—your own and that of others.

---

[1] *The Rhetoric of Aristotle*, I.1.

■ 1. GOOD SPEECH IS SOCIALLY RESPONSIBLE. Speech is one of our chief means of influencing others. Since we are beneficiaries of freedom of speech, we are also under an obligation to exercise it wisely. A socially responsible speaker is aware of his potential influence on attitudes, values, traditions, and institutions, and he reveals his awareness by his respect for facts, sound reasoning, and informed judgments. In short, speech is responsible to the degree that a speaker comprehends the social context of his remarks, strives valiantly to make intelligence prevail, and is accountable for the consequences of his discourse.

■ 2. GOOD SPEECH REVEALS A SPEAKER WITH GOOD PERSONAL QUALIFICATIONS. The speaker with strong personal qualifications is better equipped for his job, and is in a better position to command the respect of his audience. Listeners always size up a speaker, and their judgment of his personal qualifications influences their attitude toward what he says.

■ 3. GOOD SPEECH IS DIRECTED TO SERVE A SPECIFIC PURPOSE. The specific purpose is simply the response that the speaker is seeking, the objective toward which he directs all his efforts. Without purpose, speech is random and aimless. And if the speaker without a purpose gets any response at all from his audience, it is not likely to be one that he values.

■ 4. GOOD SPEECH DEALS WITH WORTH-WHILE SUBJECTS. Good subjects for speech tap the best resources of the speaker and make demands on the best resources of the listener. We talk about countless things—experiences, events, problems, hopes, aspirations, joys, sorrows, and fears. Some of these subjects are so urgent that they cannot be denied. They *must* be talked about. Others are tempting simply because they seem to be worth exploring. And still others find their way into speech merely because we need *something* to talk about. The *subjects* people talk about affect the level and quality of speech. If you want to learn more about someone, find out what he chooses to say and hear.

■ 5. GOOD SPEECH IS BASED ON THE BEST AVAILABLE MATERIALS. No responsible speaker can afford to ignore the best materials at his command. Without content, no amount of attention to form will rescue speech from the fate it deserves. And any speaker equipped with good ideas will find it much easier to discharge his other responsibilities graciously and efficiently.

■ 6. GOOD SPEECH IS ANALYTICAL. *Speech always takes place in a context—a setting.* This setting is created by the subject, the audience, the occasion, and the speaker himself. *Analytical speech is speech that takes these factors into account.*

Good speakers are sensitive to every element in the setting. They "size up the situation." If you make a poor analysis of your *subject,* you will deceive both yourself and your audience. If you make a poor analysis of your *audience,* your speech will miss its mark completely. If you make a poor analysis of the *occasion,* you may stumble into improprieties of the worst kind. And if you make a poor analysis of *yourself* in relation to all the other factors, you may display attitudes that will block communication.

Analysis is launched when you outline your speech, and is brought to perfection as you deliver your speech.

■ 7. GOOD SPEECH IS BASED ON SOUND METHOD. The method of the speaker is his plan of attack. It is dictated very largely by his purpose and by his analysis of the situation. There are four primary purposes of speech and four basic methods to serve these purposes —inquiry, reporting, advocacy, and evocation. We shall explain these purposes and methods in later chapters. Suffice it to say here that a good speaker knows *when* and *how* to use the appropriate method. It is a fair test of any speech to ask: Has the speaker used the method best designed to accomplish his purpose?

■ 8. GOOD SPEECH CLAIMS THE ATTENTION AND INTEREST OF THE LISTENER. Communication stops when attention is lost. And attention will not persist for very long unless the audience's interest is engaged. The best speech is rewarding to both speaker and listener, for then the speaker is motivated to give his best and the audience is motivated to get the most out of what he says. This kind of motivated speech is realized only when the speaker analyzes and adapts to his audience, and when the listeners analyze and adapt to the speaker.

■ 9. GOOD SPEECH MAKES EFFECTIVE USE OF VOICE AND BODILY ACTION. Without voice and bodily action there can be no speech, for they carry the symbols out of which all speech is fashioned and the symbols to which listeners respond. The human voice and body are flexible instruments with enormous potentialities for sensitive communication far beyond the relatively simple demands of making oneself heard and seen. Good speakers have complete command of these instruments.

■ 10. GOOD SPEECH USES GOOD DICTION, LANGUAGE, AND STYLE. The selection, arrangement, and pronunciation of words are dictated by generally accepted standards of convention and good taste. Any speaker who violates these conventions does so at his own peril. A good speaker uses diction, language, and style to give his speech added precision, vigor, and beauty. Properly conceived, these are not ends in themselves, but they are essential ingredients of effective communication.

A Note to the Reader

These ten basic principles represent our analysis of the art of good speech. They are derived from our conception of the nature of speech and our interpretation of the evidence bearing on the sources of good speech. For the most part, these are time-tested principles sanctioned by the authority of tradition. But there is no reason in the world for you to accept them at face value. You will find them far more meaningful if you test them for yourself. The chapters that follow are designed to help you make this test, both in your speech class and in all the years of speaking that lie ahead of you.

Don't expect to find a one-to-one relation between principles and chapters, for many of the principles appear and re-appear in several chapters. As you come to understand the principles, you will have no trouble identifying them when you meet them.

Points to Keep in Mind

1. Speech is the communication of ideas and feelings by means of visible and audible symbols originating in the speaker.

2. There are four ways of evaluating speech: by its results, by its truth, by the motives of the speaker, and by the principles of the art of good speech. Judging by the principles of the art is the best way.

3. There are ten basic principles of speech that will guide you in improving your speech and in judging the speech of others.

Exercises

1. Choose a subject of genuine interest to you and prepare a short talk on it. Your purpose is to put into practice *one* of the ten principles of good speech. Choose the one that you think may give you the most trouble. Actually, of course, you will try to follow all ten principles, but give special attention to one of them. After your speech, tell the class which principle was uppermost in your mind. Ask the class members to discuss how well they think you may have succeeded in putting it into practice.

2. Think of a speaker you have heard whose speech exemplifies in strikingly effective ways any one of the basic principles of speech. Give a talk in which you explain the principle and then describe as vividly as you can how the speaker gains special strength through the application of this principle.

3. Make a short talk on a pleasant experience you have had. Your purpose here is to interest your listeners enough so that they will try it for themselves. Use the why-not-try-it? approach, but without stating the question outright. Emphasize those aspects of your experience that will mean the most to your listeners. Here are some ideas:

An enjoyable radio or TV program.

A trip you have taken.

A course you have taken.

A product you have used.

A church you have attended.

A play or movie you liked.

A magazine you read regularly.

4. Read to the class a short passage that you feel has literary merit. Choose one you enjoy enough to want to share with others. Let the strength, beauty, and impact of the language and ideas come *through you*, as the writer's agent. When you have finished reading, give your own interpretation of the passage: What message does it carry? What points does it make? What are the sources of its strength and beauty?

5. Divide the class into groups of from eight to twelve people. Appoint a leader for each group and carry on a discussion for 40 to 50 minutes on a question of campus policy. Here are some suggestions:

Should your college adopt the Honor System for all examinations?

Should attendance be required at chapel?

On what basis should scholarships be awarded?

Should students be permitted to operate automobiles?

CHAPTER THREE

Talking
with
People

A ll the principles of speech are brought into play either directly or indirectly in the delivery of speech—in your vocal and bodily behavior during the presentation of speech. You can talk *with* people or you can talk *at* people—

20

that is, you can choose between good delivery and poor delivery.

Good delivery is never an *end* in itself. But it is one of the more important *means* for achieving successful communication.

What Is
Good Delivery?

You can talk *at* the four walls of an empty room, but you can't talk *with* them. The walls have no way of showing interest or talking back. True, people can be almost as unresponsive as inanimate objects if they are merely talked *at*. But talking *with* people provokes a stimulating exchange of attitudes and ideas and a rewarding interaction between speaker and listener.

Have you ever watched listeners who seem to be hanging on a speaker's words? Perhaps you can recall some physical signs of the bond that joined speaker and audience. You sensed the listeners' quick responses in their postures, facial expressions, bursts of laughter, and spontaneous applause. And as the listeners manifested their attitudes, the speaker's words and actions revealed sensitive adaptations to their developing responses. What you witnessed was a dramatic instance of speaker-audience empathy and rapport.

Empathy is the mental entering into the thoughts and feelings of another. When both speaker and listener project themselves imaginatively and sympathetically into the mind and emotion of the other, the resulting interaction constitutes *rapport*. In a sense, rapport is two-way empathy. The physical evidences of this interaction vary with time, place, and circumstances, but rapport is the goal of all effective delivery. Without it, communication is truncated and incomplete.

The Conversational Norm

Good conversation provides a useful norm for all speaking. Here you are acting as speaker one moment and listener the next. Conversation invites an interchange of interests and close rapport that are subtly reflected in vocal and bodily behavior. At its best, conversation is lively, spontaneous, and, above all, sensitive to the response of the participants. These are desirable qualities in all speech.

If you can talk easily, directly, and responsively to a few friends in conversation, you can do the same in more public communication. Good conversation, then, is a useful norm for public speech. But remember that not *all* conversation is good conversation. To base public speech on the dull, rambling conversations that we all overhear (or engage in) every day of our lives would be an unforgivable affront to our audience.

Public speech differs from conversation in several obvious ways, however: The speaker does all or most of the talking, the response of the audience is largely covert rather than overt, there are more people present, and the speaker usually stands in front of the audience, often on a platform. The public speaker needs to adapt his delivery to these special conditions, but he can and should create the *sense of communication* that we all recognize in good conversational speech.

How to Talk with People

Here are some suggestions that will help you strengthen your delivery in both conversation and public speech:

EXHIBIT A DESIRE TO SHARE

The first requisite of good delivery is an evident interest in what you are saying and in the people with whom you are talking. Given this interest in your subject and your listeners, many of the most common problems in delivery will simply vanish. Even a highly polished delivery will seem false and empty unless you are motivated by a desire to share your ideas and feelings with your listeners. As soon as you make delivery an end in itself, your speech becomes an artificial, devitalized act.

THINK OF WHAT YOU ARE SAYING
WHILE YOU ARE SAYING IT

Mental and emotional drifting can be spotted in a second, for the speaker's manner and voice will give him away. You have listened to people talk from memory or from a manuscript who obviously didn't have their minds on what they were saying—and no one else did either.

An extemporaneous speaker, of course, has no choice but to keep his wits about him. He must think as he talks and talk as he thinks. We expect talk to go forward with fluency, but not at the expense of thoughtful reactions on the speaker's part to his own remarks. Don't be distressed if you have to pause now and then to pick out the right word. Listeners regard occasional hesitations, on-the-spot revisions, or short digressions as signs of an active mind at work. Rattling glibness often betrays a rattling mind. No speaker is really communicating unless he is in touch with what he is saying as he says it.

RESPOND TO YOUR AUDIENCE

Think about what you are saying while you are saying it, but *think about it in relation to your audience*. Every audience sends out signals. Tune in on them to see if they carry messages of understanding, puzzlement, interest, boredom, weariness, or disapproval. Ask yourself: "Am I making myself heard? Would another example help? Am I spinning this out unnecessarily? Did this sound too flippant?"

Most audiences will go more than halfway in giving you a fair hearing. But if you see that the audience is backing off or slipping away, take positive steps then and there to re-establish contact. Perhaps you need to change pace, or increase or decrease the force of your delivery. Don't hesitate to break in and underscore items with remarks like these: "The point I'm trying to make is this. . . ." "I want this to be perfectly clear. . . ." Throw out some questions: "Have you ever had this experience?" "Have you ever thought of it in this light?" Pointed remarks and questions help to retrieve wandering attention.

A good audience is a stimulus; and a difficult audience is a challenge. But speech without any audience at all is a fiasco. Hold on to your listeners by talking things over *with* them instead of just talking *at* them.

USE YOUR VOICE
TO CARRY MEANING AND FEELING

The greatest value of the conversational norm is that it guides you in the use of your voice. Listen to the ordinary conversations around you. You will hear good and bad voices, clear and slovenly enunciation, good and poor diction—dialectal differences, mispronunciations, and grammatical errors. But through it all will come remarkable purposefulness and vitality. There will be exceptions, to be sure. But people do have a way of making their voices work for them. A student asks a question, and an instructor replies; a foreman directs the workman on a job; a girl explains to an anxious house-mother why she got in late; the cast talks over the play after rehearsal. These people are not thinking about their voices, but they have important business on their minds. Accordingly, their voices are remarkably flexible and expressive.

One of the most common problems among beginning speakers is learning to use their voices with this same flexibility when they are speaking to larger groups. Why do train conductors and sight-seeing guides lapse into sing-song speech? Why do radio and TV announcers, extravagantly extolling lawn fertilizer in one breath and skin balm in the next, speak in souped-up tones? Why do old-time political orators intone? Why do so many beginning public speakers talk in flat, dull monotones? Speech has become routinized for the conductor and guide; announcers who cannot coax enthusiasm from the heart must rely on an artificial pump; the political orator has established bad vocal habits that he thinks are good; and the beginning speaker is inhibited and nervous. In all these cases, *the speaker has lost contact with his ideas and feelings.* In short, his voice has been cut off from its supply of vital energy and has been rendered lifeless. This is the principal cause of breakdowns in voice communication.

Put your mind and heart into the job of reaching your audience. Your voice is likely to follow along.

SPEAK WITH PHYSICAL ANIMATION AND DIRECTNESS

Speaking is action in which mind and body cooperate. Bodily action supplements and reinforces words; it energizes thought; it reveals you as a person who is self-confident rather than self-conscious. A listless person fails to sustain interest for very long; an anxious, distracted person communicates his distress; an over-wrought person wears us out by trying too hard. A nice balance between relaxation and tension contributes to poise and directness.

People like personal attention. When you look your audience straight in the eye, you are taking notice of them. You are saying, "I invite you to share this information or observation." This simple gesture contributes to good human relationships. It also helps you to adapt sensitively to the reactions of others.

If you are talking to a large group, you cannot focus your attention on everyone at once. Simply shift your attention unobtrusively from one segment of the audience to another so that no one is excluded. You can do this easily and naturally without swinging your head back and forth like a busy airport beacon. Usually there is no need to single out individuals unless you happen to be especially interested in their reactions. Even then, be careful not to fix them with your eye until they squirm in their seats.

AVOID ANNOYING MANNERISMS

You have seen speakers shift uneasily in their chairs or pace restlessly up and down the platform. You have seen some who rock back and forth on their heels, who jangle coins in their pockets, who aimlessly take their glasses off and put them on again. You have been distracted by speakers who induce little artificial coughs, who clear their throats every few seconds, and who clutter their

"And now are there any stupid questions?"

speech with stray sounds such as *ah, uh,* and *er.* These mannerisms call attention to themselves and distract listeners from what the speaker is trying to say. If fellow members of your speech class make you aware of such mannerisms, welcome their criticisms and take steps to eliminate the offending habits.

OBSERVE THE COURTESIES OF THE OCCASION

When you are introduced to a stranger, you acknowledge the introduction in a warm, courteous manner. Similarly, when you are introduced to an audience, you acknowledge the chairman's introduction and greet the audience with a friendly salutation and remarks appropriate to the occasion.

Good rapport with listeners calls for respect for their feelings. If someone asks a question, don't brush him off or punish him for his audacity. Assume that he is asking his question in good faith. Pugnacity, sarcasm, and defensiveness repel listeners, even when they know you are being goaded by a boor. A friendly, urbane manner helps win them over to your side.

Methods of Presentation

THE EXTEMPORANEOUS METHOD

Most of the speaking occasions you will face have certain things in common: (1) they are relatively informal; (2) they are flexible; (3) questions and replies are expected; (4) several people are present who take their turn at speaking and listening. The best preparation for meeting situations of this sort is practice in extemporaneous speaking.

Extemporaneous speaking is simply unmemorized speaking that has been prepared in advance. You investigate, analyze, select, and outline your material so that you know beforehand what you want to say and the order in which you will say it. But you supply the language for your speech at the time you deliver it. Extemporaneous speech is not "canned." At its best, it combines the rigor gained from your study with freedom, flexibility, and spontaneity when you face a live audience.

■ SHOULD I PRACTICE EXTEMPORANEOUS SPEECHES BEFORE DELIVERING THEM? Yes. This will give you a chance to test your ideas, fix the outline in mind, and develop a "feel" for the sound and swing of your talk. Think out your speech and then talk it out. If you hit upon some especially good words and phrases along the way, make a mental note of them, but don't come to depend on them. The really good ones will probably stick with you and turn up when you deliver the talk to an audience. There are exceptions to this rule, of course. For example, you may want to plan a good sentence or two as insurance against a fumbling start and an inconclusive conclusion.

Practice beforehand, and space your practice sessions, so that the speech you finally deliver will be the best you are capable of making. It is painful and wasteful to spend class time criticizing poor delivery that could have been remedied by preliminary workouts.

■ MAY I USE NOTES? Use them by all means to report complicated information or extended quotations. Such notes insure accuracy and eliminate the strain of memorizing. Usually there is no reason why you shouldn't use prompting notes, such as a skeleton outline, if your speech is technical or long, and if you use them both sparingly and unobtrusively. You will have some assignments, however, in which notes are unnecessary and inadvisable. In any event, your instructor will let you know whether notes are an aid or a hindrance to your progress. When you need notes, these suggestions may help you:

1. Make your notes simple.

2. Put them in proper sequence before you speak.

3. Write your notes legibly. (It's best to type them out in double-spaced lines.)

4. Place your notes on the desk or speaker's stand where you can consult them easily.

5. Resist the impulse to retreat into your notes. Use them only to jog your memory and to keep you on the track.

6. If you read quotations or other material, hold up your card, sheet, or book. Look up and out at your audience from time to time while reading.

IMPROMPTU SPEAKING

Impromptu speech is speech that we have had no opportunity to prepare beforehand. Much of our conversation, in fact, is nothing more than a series of short, impromptu talks.

Suppose you are attending a get-together along with twenty or thirty other people. You are all set to sit back and listen to someone else. Suddenly the chairman turns to you and asks you to say something to the group. As you get to your feet, you must swiftly decide on the substance, purpose, and plan of your remarks. In short, you have to compose and deliver your talk at the same time.

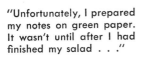

"Unfortunately, I prepared my notes on green paper. It wasn't until after I had finished my salad . . ."

There is no magic formula to help you become a skillful impromptu speaker. Actually, the best preparation for impromptu speaking, whatever the circumstances, is preliminary experience in extemporaneous speaking. The facility you acquire in finding subjects for extemporaneous speech, in analyzing and organizing materials, and in adapting your language to the occasion, will immeasurably increase your readiness to deal with impromptu speeches.

SPEAKING FROM MANUSCRIPT

With a manuscript clutched firmly in your hands, you are free from the fear of making slips of the tongue, from relying on catch-as-catch-can language, from the danger of running overtime or being cut off before you have finished. Sometimes these advantages are compelling. Yet few people read a manuscript with enough skill to communicate successfully. They plant themselves behind a lectern, bury their faces, and then lapse into a sing-song recital of words while their minds wander off into unknown realms.

If your material or the situation demands that you use a manuscript, then make a sincere and serious effort to get your ideas across despite the barriers. Here are some suggestions that will help you avoid glaring mistakes when speaking from a manuscript:

▪ WRITE YOUR SPEECH FOR THE EAR AND NOT FOR THE EYE. Make sure it represents your best oral style. Keep your sentences short and simple. Weed out the long, complex ones. Favor colloquial words. Use the active voice rather than the passive. In short, write the talk in your most direct, personal, and graphic style, just as if you were talking person-to-person without a manuscript. Try it out on a friend and ask if it sounds like you.

▪ AFTER YOU HAVE FINISHED WRITING YOUR SPEECH, DON'T TOSS THE MANUSCRIPT ASIDE AND FORGET ABOUT IT. Return to it from time to time. Review, re-think, and revise your ideas and language. Make your speech a living, growing thing. You will develop a richer feeling for it. This is the best way to keep your writing from turning cold and to keep your delivery from becoming mechanical.

▪ MAINTAIN CONTACT WITH YOUR AUDIENCE WHILE SPEAKING. If you prepare well, you will be free to talk directly with your audience. You will find it easy to catch at a glance the sweep of a sentence, even a paragraph, and to concentrate on getting it across. And if you have your speech well in mind, you can work in on-the-spot comments that will keep it geared to the developing reactions of your listeners.

SPEAKING FROM MEMORY

Memorizing a talk frees you from the manuscript and preserves the advantages of a carefully written speech. Special events, such as a formal ceremonial occasion, sometimes call for speeches that exhibit finesse in composition. If reading a manuscript seems out of place, you may decide to commit your speech to memory.

One hazard of a memorized talk is that it often leads to mechanical delivery. Some people become so engrossed in recalling words and in behaving elegantly that they lose touch with the sense and sentiment that prompted the speech in the first place. Listeners quickly detect a "canned" speech and are likely to dismiss it as a schoolboy performance. A second hazard is that you may forget your speech. The fear of forgetting may itself make your mind go blank.

But you can reduce these hazards. You will discover that skill in extemporaneous speaking will help you when speaking from memory. In extemporaneous speech, you acquire the habit of first focusing your mind on a basic outline of points. Extemporaneous speaking also promotes habits of flexibility and directness that will help you to improvise when necessary and to preserve the conversational norm.

If you memorize a speech, avoid memorizing in rote fashion, line by line. Instead, begin by studying the pattern of ideas you worked up in your preliminary outline. Fix in your mind a picture of the talk as a whole, then take up the separate units as part of a logical structure. You will memorize with greatest efficiency if you spread your study sessions over a period of time.

Points to Keep in Mind

Talking with people is two-way transmission. Sensitize yourself to the reactions of your listeners and respond to them. This is the key to rapport between you and your audience.

1. Preserve the qualities of conversational speech at its best.

2. Genuine enthusiasm, friendliness, and sincerity on your part will evoke similar responses from your audience.

3. Think of what you are saying while you are saying it. Don't let your mind drift.

4. Alert yourself to your listeners' reactions and adapt to them.

5. Let your voice be governed by honest convictions and feelings.

6. Speak with energy and directness.

7. Invite others to help you spot and overcome annoying mannerisms in speech.

8. Never neglect the courtesies expected of you. They facilitate good speaking relationships.

9. Skill in extemporaneous speaking is basic. Use other methods—impromptu speaking, speaking from manuscript, or speaking from memory—when there is a special reason for doing so.

Exercises

1. A series of open-forum assignments on controversial subjects stimulates good delivery. Each talk should be extemporaneous. Reserve half

of the period for questions and answers. Appoint a chairman to preside. In the open-forum period, insist that each person stand when he speaks and that no one speak for more than one minute. Allow time for a critique of all the aspects of delivery covered in this chapter.

2. Make a short, extemporaneous talk. After the other speakers scheduled for the day have spoken, you will be recalled to expand on the points of your talk or to offer additional ones. Invite the rest of the class to comment on your poise and communicativeness in your two appearances. Were there any differences? Analyze the differences.

3. Divide the class into three or four groups and have members of each group investigate independently a general topic of interest to the group. Appoint a leader for each group. On a scheduled day, have the leader open the discussion of the general topic in an easy, informal way. As the discussion proceeds, the leader will invite each member to rise and speak briefly to some point on which he is prepared to speak extemporaneously.

4. Each member of the class contributes two non-technical subjects that are suitable for short impromptu talks. Then each person draws two subjects other than his own. After thinking them both over, he rises and speaks briefly on the one he chooses.

5. Choose a subject, investigate it, and write out your talk word for word. Test your writing on someone who knows you well to see if it is in keeping with your best oral style. Be as communicative as you can when you read the speech to the class.

6. Prepare a short talk that will be largely extemporaneous. Write out and memorize only short passages of it. After you have delivered it to the class, find out if your listeners were able to detect the portions you memorized. If they were, try to find out how they managed to spot them.

7. Choose a passage of prose or poetry. Prepare a short introduction and a conclusion that enforce the point of your passage. Read communicatively as if you were talking with people.

CHAPTER FOUR

Speaking
with a
Purpose

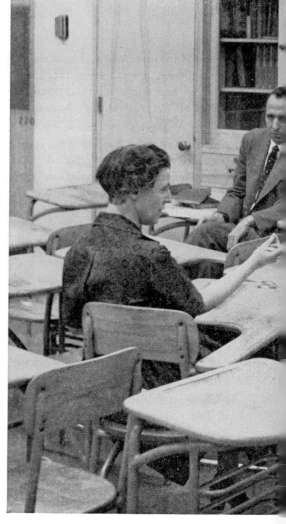

The efficiency with which you perform any task depends on your having a clear objective in mind and a definite plan of attack. Your speech is no exception. In this chapter we shall set down the basic purposes of speech and sug-

gest the best methods for achieving each purpose. Making a clear-cut decision on the purpose of your speech will help you choose an appropriate subject, will help you investigate that subject, and will help you develop a soundly structured speech around that subject.

Primary Purposes

The universal purpose of all speech is to get a *response*. When we communicate with others, we translate ideas and feelings of our own into symbols that others can see and hear, in the hope that they will react to them in meaningful ways. In short, we seek a response of some kind from someone.

At first sight, the conceivable purposes of speech seem too numerous to classify. After all, anybody can talk about anything for any reason under the sun. But if we look more closely, we find that there are four primary purposes that encompass all the important objectives of speech. These basic purposes will guide you in identifying and accomplishing your specific purpose, whatever it may be.

INQUIRY

Much of our speaking is a search for information or insights that we lack, or about which we are doubtful or uncertain. We may simply ask someone a question in the hope that he can give us a helpful answer. Or we may try out our ideas on another person to see what he thinks of them. Or we may join with a group of people to discuss a common problem in the hope that we can solve it, or at least understand it better.

The common denominator in all speech of this sort is *inquiry*—or call it exploration, problem-solving, investigation, or discovery. The occasion may be private conversation or public deliberation, but the purpose is always this searching for knowledge and understanding. In a sense, when we speak to inquire we are doing what the scientist does in his search for facts and hypotheses. The laboratory and the conference table may have little else in common, but both can yield new insights of great social significance.

REPORTING

Most of you will be called on to make reports—reports in class, reports to business associates, reports to clubs to which you belong, and innumerable informal reports to friends and other people you meet in your daily activities. Here you are presenting information to your listeners. In your capacity as a reporter you are not searching for information—you already have it or think you have. Your purpose now is to inform or to instruct others who hope to learn from your report. What they do with this report may be of real concern to you, but your job as a reporter is well done if you have conveyed your information clearly, accurately, and in ways that sustain the interest and attention of your audience.

Reporting to inform or to instruct, like inquiry, is one of the four great purposes of human discourse. In fact, most speakers will find themselves cast in the role of reporter more frequently than in any other. Like inquiry, reporting involves special skills and methods that every speaker must master.

ADVOCACY

The speaker who seeks to convince or persuade is an advocate. The advocate is not content just to provide his audience with information. He wants his listeners to adopt a specific attitude toward a proposition or to take action on it. He marshals arguments and appeals in support of a predetermined position—a position to which he is committed because he believes in it or simply because he has chosen to support it.

Advocacy is the third important purpose of speech. We practice it every day in selling, advertising, promoting, campaigning—in representing and defending causes that are important to us. Much of the practical decision-making in our society is accomplished by advocates who defend competing ideas and yield to majority votes.

EVOCATION

The fourth primary purpose of speech is to inspire or to entertain. Here the speaker's intent is to evoke an emotional response—to intensify or allay feelings. You inspire people to greater efforts, comfort a friend in distress, tell a story to get a laugh, call for faith, reminisce, give encouragement, share your fears, stir up anger and resentment, express affection.

Such emotional experiences may be deeply moving, exciting, and exhilarating to the listener. Or they may be quieting and consoling. They may be pleasurable and entertaining, or stern and demanding.

All good speaking contains emotional elements, of course, but in evocation the speaker's *central* purpose is to induce an emotional experience. It is an end in itself, to be enjoyed or valued in any way the speaker and his listeners see fit.

Secondary Purposes

One of these four primary purposes should dominate every speech, but secondary purposes may enter in along the way. In fact, even the primary purposes that we have mentioned may serve as secondary purposes when they operate in supporting roles.

We have just seen that emotional factors enter into all speaking. This is simply another way of saying that a funny story or an emotional appeal may be used to make a point or clinch an argument. Similarly, a speaker whose primary purpose is inquiry will almost always do some reporting, and may occasionally slip into the role of advocate. Advocates often use the reporter's approach in developing their case, and they have been known to use the techniques of inquiry for persuasive purposes. In short, any primary purpose, and the methods associated with it, may be used as a secondary purpose.

If secondary purposes are admitted, however, they must be kept subordinate to the primary objective. If a speaker's primary purpose is inquiry and he succeeds only in advocating his own point of view, his inquiry has failed; if his primary purpose is reporting and he succeeds only in entertaining, he has failed as a reporter.

The Specific Purpose

Your specific purpose is your immediate goal in speaking to a particular audience. You should be able to state your specific purpose in a way that will point up your central idea and make clear precisely what you hope to accomplish. This statement should also indicate your primary objective. If inquiry is your primary purpose, you might put your statement of specific purpose this way: "How may we establish more efficient study habits?" or "We intend to investigate capital punishment as a deterrent to crime." If reporting is your primary purpose, your statement of specific purpose might be: "My object is to recount the highlights of the national Delta Sigma Rho Congress," or "I wish to explain the essential differences between boogie and cool jazz." If advocacy is your primary purpose, you might express your specific purpose this way: "My purpose is to urge the abolition of spring football practice," or "We must organize to oppose universal military conscription." If evocation is your primary objective, your specific goal might be expressed this way: "I wish to entertain my audience with an account of the rise and fall of Jenkins' Corners," or "I wish to stimulate appreciation for the poetic qualities in the sermons of John Donne."

Always phrase your specific purpose beforehand for your own guidance in preparing and presenting your speech. If you are to investigate a subject efficiently and organize your speech effectively, you need a clear and concise statement of purpose.

When, where, and under what circumstances you should disclose your specific purpose to your audience is quite another matter. Most often, perhaps, it is wise to state your purpose at the outset so that your listeners will know precisely what you are trying to do from the very beginning. Sometimes, however, it may be wise to withhold your purpose until later in the speech. And there are even times when you may decide never to state it at all. If your objective is controversial and likely to arouse a hostile reaction, pave the way for your proposition before submitting it directly. If you are after an emotional response of any kind, it would probably be naïve to spell out your purpose for your audience. Your purpose and your development of it can be implicit rather than explicit in any speech.

Stating
Your Specific Purpose

Your *statement* of specific purpose should meet the following three tests.

■ 1. IT SHOULD BE A COMPLETE SENTENCE. Usually a question is the most satisfactory form for speeches of inquiry. A declarative sentence is suitable for reporting, advocacy, and evocative speaking.

> *Inquiry:*   "Are telephone operators becoming obsolete?"
> *Reporting:* "There are four basic procedures to be mastered to qualify for a position as telephone operator."
> *Advocacy:* "Telephone operators should receive a ten-cent-an-hour pay hike."
> *Evocation:* "Your telephone operator may be your life line."

■ 2. YOUR STATEMENT OF YOUR SPECIFIC PURPOSE SHOULD CONTAIN ONE CENTRAL IDEA. It must present one idea, and only one. Many speakers find it difficult to compress their purpose into a unified sentence. They confuse supporting arguments or other lines of development with their specific purpose. Notice the confusion in this statement: "I want to acquaint my audience with Franklin D. Roosevelt's message to Congress in 1941 asking for a declaration of war against the Japanese Empire, because the step he was proposing was an important one in modern history, and it literally affected the entire world." Only the first part of this statement, ending with the word "Empire," expresses intention or purpose. The rest of the sentence is a justification for talking about Roosevelt's message. These reasons should appear later on as part of the speaker's development of his talk.

■ 3. YOUR STATEMENT OF SPECIFIC PURPOSE SHOULD BE CLEAR AND CONCISE. Be as terse and explicit as you can. Avoid ambiguity and vagueness. The statement, "The best way to check inflation is to increase income taxes," is far more precise than "Something ought to be done about high prices."

"Tell him to keep talking.
It's still raining outside."

Ulterior Purposes

A speaker may have a purpose in the back of his mind that he never reveals to his audience—that is, he may have an *ulterior* purpose. This is some indirect end toward which the speaker is moving but which is unrelated to the form and substance of his talk. A candidate for a job might present a report on novel methods in advertising, but with the ulterior purpose of impressing his prospective employers. Speaking contests are good examples. Each speaker hopes to win the contest—that is his ulterior purpose. But each speaker tries to achieve this success by speaking to some specific purpose that is completely unrelated to winning or losing. Similarly, in your speech class your ulterior purpose may be to win a good grade. But your speeches will be planned to inquire, report, advocate, and evoke in order to secure a specific response that is unrelated to the grade you get.

A Final Observation

We have stressed the value of having firm goals or purposes in speaking. We wish to add this suggestion: *Make your purposes worthy ones.* It's one thing to have a clear target, and it's another thing to have a target worth shooting at. The worthiness of your purpose brings several of the basic principles of speech sharply into focus: subjects that are worth talking about, speech that is socially responsible, and purposes that reveal you as a worthy person. Good speech is marked by worthy purposes as well as by clear-cut purposes.

Points to Keep in Mind

All speech seeks some kind of response. You will have a better chance of winning the response you want if you define your objectives carefully.

1. Decide on your primary purpose. The one you choose will indicate the kind of response you seek and the best methods for winning it. Make one of these your primary purpose: to inquire, to report, to advocate, to evoke.

2. Decide on your specific purpose. This will be your central idea and will be in keeping with your primary purpose.

3. State your specific purpose in a clear, concise, complete sentence that contains only your central idea.

Exercises

1. Prepare a short talk based on (a) one of the four primary purposes set forth in this chapter and (b) a full and precise statement of your specific purpose. Speak to these purposes but withhold any statement of them when you deliver your talk. After your speech, have your listeners write statements of what they understood your primary purpose and specific purpose to be.

Are your listeners in agreement? Now read to them the statements of your intentions. Did any of the listeners fail to recognize your intentions? What reasons do they offer for possible failure to understand your primary and specific purposes? How do you explain the discrepancies, if any? What conclusions may you draw from this experience?

2. Assume that you are to prepare a five-minute talk on each of the "statements of purpose" below. Is each an acceptable statement? If not, revise it to make it an acceptable statement of specific purpose. Then

identify each specific purpose with some primary purpose that it might serve.

    a. The best way to keep down weight is to push yourself away from the table.

    b. College students are taller today than they were a generation ago.

    c. The owners of a big business are the American public.

    d. Something needs to be done about high prices and extravagance and lack of self-discipline.

    e. Radio and television have made "whistle-stop" presidential campaigns an anachronism.

    f. How should we study for the final examination in this course?

    g. Making assets out of our liabilities.

    h. Evansdale needs a public library and a swimming pool.

    i. The British Monarchy.

    j. There are many satisfactions in owning your own home, and you can finance it as cheaply as you can rent a house.

    k. Our vanishing forests and Indians.

3. Pick out a big, inclusive subject such as theater, fashion, door-to-door selling, Texas, trains, chemistry, automobiles. Break this large subject down into four sub-topics, each of which is suitable for a short class talk. Formulate a primary purpose and a specific purpose for each. Now prepare a speech on one of the topics. Have the class evaluate your talk in light of your avowed purposes.

4. Analyze the printed text of a speech that you find in a newspaper, in *Vital Speeches of the Day,* or in an anthology. Prepare and present a report that answers these questions:

Who gave the speech? When? Under what circumstances?

What is the speaker's primary purpose?

What is the speaker's specific purpose? If it is not stated explicitly, what do you believe it to be?

Is there any evidence that the speaker had an ulterior purpose? If so, do you regard it as commendable or justifiable?

5. Have four members of the class choose a single topic that is of interest to all of them. One will use this topic as the basis for a speech of inquiry. A second will use this topic for a report; a third for a speech of advocacy; and a fourth for an evocative speech.

CHAPTER FIVE

Choosing Subjects

Our days are filled with talk—shop talk, conferences, telephone conversations, comments on public issues, casual exchanges. Many subjects spring naturally from our everyday living. When you take your car to a mechanic, you don't have to ask yourself what to talk about. But there are also times when you have to initiate

subjects yourself and evoke interest in what you say. This is true in your speech class. Here you will acquire training and resourcefulness in choosing subjects that will carry over into other experiences.

Subjects are the pivots of discourse. They control the orbit through which discussion swings. The value of our discourse turns on the subjects we choose to talk about.

Finding Subjects:
A Perspective

The catalog description of a course offered by a certain university ends with this requirement: "The only prerequisite is a persistent curiosity." Add to persistent curiosity the thoughtful probing of yourself and your reactions to your environment and you have a working principle for finding subjects. Environment means total environment. Think of it in concentric circles, beginning with intimate, first-hand experiences and moving out to events, people, and ideas of widespread interest.

The key factor in your search for subjects is *reaction*. A subject for speech is not simply an event you have read or heard about. Neither is it a book, a memory, an acquaintance, or a concept. The subject lies in your *reaction* to the book, event, person, or idea. Finding subjects is not like picking up rocks or seashells. It is a creative process in which experience sets your mind in motion. It is a search that leads you to perceive, probe, wonder, and judge.

PROBING PERSONAL EXPERIENCES
AND EXPECTATIONS

Nothing you say has meaning for others until it first has meaning for you. What's it like to travel the Trail Ridge Road in the Colorado Rockies at an elevation of over twelve thousand feet? Better ask the person who has made the trip. Does Boris Pasternak's *Doctor Zhivago* have the stature of a Tolstoy novel? Who can attempt to answer the question unless he has read both Pasternak and Tolstoy? How effective is the Woman's Judiciary Board in handling disciplinary problems on campus? A member of the Board can offer facts that outweigh the opinions of the casual observer.

Oddly, students with special abilities and enthusiasms often dismiss rewarding subjects because of a mistaken notion that only fellow-specialists are interested in them. Here is a ski enthusiast, a collector of antiques, a cartoonist, an accomplished gardener. Here is some one wrapped up in thermodynamics, automation, puppetry,

"Mr. MacNulty, believe it or not, will speak on flower arrangement."

theater-in-the-round. Often your best subjects are your special interests. These are the things you can speak about with authority and enthusiasm. Through them you open a world only dimly known to others.

Examine your life as an unfolding process. Each of you has gone through infancy, childhood, adolescence, and into adulthood. Looking back over the years provides new insights, and looking ahead thrusts forward new questions and goals. A college student takes a retrospective view of his high-school days that helps himself and others to revise their study habits. A boy looking forward to a career in law may be either dismayed or stimulated when he attends police court for the first time. Both experiences contain the raw materials for speech. Stretching out before you are a career, travel, marriage, parenthood, and active citizenship. Clustered around these experiences are scores of questions—real questions that open subjects for talk.

REACHING OUT TO THE WORLD AROUND US

The drama of modern life unfolds before our ears and eyes. We have only to look, listen, read, and think. Whatever indictments may be leveled against life in the twentieth century—"the terrible twentieth century," as Winston Churchill calls it—it is not dull or prosaic, except to the dumpling. The supersonic speed of our age makes Lewis Carroll, writing in the nineteenth century, a prophet of our times:

47

Where Life becomes a Spasm,
And History a Whiz:
If that is not Sensation,
I don't know what it is.

But not all worthy subjects are world-shaking. Often we are blind to good subjects right before our eyes: the rising price of food, the condition of our hospitals and schools, the roads we travel and the billboards that block our view. A commuter once complained he had nothing to talk about because he missed out on all the campus activities. Encouraged to inspect his immediate environment more closely, he asked himself, "What do I look at each day without really seeing it?" Among the things he listed were three used-car lots, each covering a city block. He took new interest in these car lots, asking questions such as these: Why do people dispose of cars that still have years of service left in them? Who buys these cars? What special sales pitch is used to sell them? Is there any other country in the world where you would find acres of used cars in a large city? What does the used-car business say about our economy? Does it mean that we are an enterprising or an extravagant people? Out of these questions grew the subject for an extremely interesting class talk: cars as a status symbol in our society.

REACTING TO THE IDEAS OF OTHERS

Be alert to possible subjects for speech as you scan the newspapers, listen to lectures, dinner conversations, or talks in your speech class. Jot down the ideas that turn up. A conversation on hypocrisy in religion may suggest a talk on hypocrisy in education, the law, or the home. A student who explained the theory of majority rule prompted a classmate to explain the doctrine of consensus practiced by the Society of Friends. A critic of the social ethics of advertisers aroused a member of the class to champion the advertising industry as essential to a free economy. A creative listener uses what he hears as a springboard to related topics.

USING THE FOUR PRIMARY PURPOSES OF SPEECH AS GUIDES TO SUBJECTS

■ INQUIRY.   All of us carry in our heads unresolved questions that may perplex others too. When there is so much pressure to get into college, why do some students cut classes once they are admitted? Why does mononucleosis seem endemic to college students? You go with some friends to see a play. Some find it obscene, others don't. You decide to make a speech of inquiry on the question, "How does one judge whether or not a dramatic work is obscene?" You attend an evening lecture and discover that the audience is largely made up of townspeople and faculty. Why do so few students turn out for these lectures? You ask, "Should the university calendar be cleared of all extracurricular activities one night each week, to be known as Cultural Activities Night?" You cringe when you read the morning's headline: "Convicted Murderer to be Executed Tonight." You are aroused to revive the long-standing question, "Should capital punishment be abolished?"

Use your speech opportunities, in class and outside, to state valid questions, to think them through with others, and to make some approach to satisfactory answers.

■ REPORTING.   Here are just a few subjects that students have used successfully in making reports: "Reactions to crisis: bailing out of an airplane." "The proposed honor system." "My life on a dude ranch." "Uses of classical mythology in our modern world." "Forerunners in the Presidential sweepstakes." "How the Secret Service protects the President." "The life history of a bank check." "Susie: a case study of a cerebral palsy victim." "A new development in automation."

Make a list of things you have done, seen, heard, or read that might be worked up into speeches you would enjoy making and that would add to the information of others.

■ ADVOCACY.   Consult your convictions; speak up in behalf of causes you deem worthy. Here are several sample propositions used by students in speeches of advocacy: "Labor unions should be stopped from contributing to election campaigns." "Everyone ought to take a vocational aptitude test before his last two years in college." "A student judiciary system should replace the faculty-student disciplinary committee." "The library stacks should be opened to undergraduates as well as graduate students." "One foreign language should be required for graduation." "Balance the national budget in the next fiscal year." "We need uniform traffic signs and signals throughout the nation."

Not only do your convictions open prospects for subjects; they also furnish you with strong motivation for speaking and get you off to a strong start in your early speeches.

■ EVOCATION.   You may admire the personality and career of great humanitarians such as Charles Dickens, Helen Keller, Wendell Phillips, and Jane Addams. You may wish to make an inspirational talk on a theme, such as Albert Schweitzer's "Reverence for Life." Or you may want to work up a light-touch speech on subjects such as "What is 'funny'?" "The secret language of women." "How I tell my friends from apes."

Reflect on people, deeds, events, and sentiments that move and entertain you. You will find many subjects for speech that will stimulate others too.

Finding Subjects:
Some Common Misevaluations

All this advice on how to find subjects will be wasted on a person who habitually misevaluates himself and his responsibilities in speaking. What are some of these misevaluations?

■ "I'M NOT AN AUTHORITY ON ANYTHING."   Being an authority is a relative matter. It depends on the situation and the problem at hand. If you have had first-aid training, you will be able to perform useful service at the scene of an accident, but you will give way when the doctor arrives. Similarly, if you have served as a counselor at a summer camp, you don't have to be a psychologist or a sociologist to report on how unruly children were changed into socially cooperative youngsters.

Know what you are talking about. The more you know, the better; but it's wise to indicate the limits of your knowledge on a topic. Authoritativeness is never absolute. We might as well sew up our mouths if we have to know everything there is to know before we speak.

■ "NOTHING I CAN SAY WILL INTEREST MY AUDIENCE." This concern arises from the comparisons a person makes between himself and those around him, always to his own disadvantage. Burt complained that all he had ever done was to help his father keep their small grocery store alive in a neighborhood that had been almost taken over by chain stores. Reluctantly, he decided to talk on the threat of big business to the small businessman: The favorable reactions to his speech convinced Burt that audiences respect ideas and attitudes gained from direct experience. And they also taught him to stop belittling himself. Audiences will give you a hearing if you respect yourself and your ideas.

■ "I HAVEN'T ANY BURNING ENTHUSIASMS." The subject you choose doesn't have to make the blood pound at your temples. You aren't expected to set off a crusade or campaign in a five-minute talk. True, some people have more excitement in them than others. But all of us have interests that lead to subjects for class speeches. What's more, as free men and women we are under an obligation to strengthen our interests in social problems and to think and talk on these matters.

■ "NOBODY HAS SUGGESTED ANYTHING THAT APPEALS TO ME." This clinging-vine attitude is rooted in the false notion that our own education is always somebody else's responsibility. You may pick up some good leads from something somebody else said or wrote. But in the final analysis, your own mind needs to reach out, take hold, and make the selection. You will never be able to speak convincingly until you can claim the subject as your own.

■ "I HAVE PLENTY OF TIME TO THINK UP A SUBJECT. I DON'T SPEAK FOR A WEEK." You may have met up with the grab-bag specialist. The night before he is scheduled to talk, he scans a newspaper for the first time in days, gives an ear to a radio commentator, glances at some predigested magazine articles, or prowls through the dormitory badgering anyone on the loose with a "Hey, I've got to make a speech tomorrow. Know any good topics?"

A last-minute speech is a talk of desperation—a batch of jumbled, pointless remarks on a topic chosen at random. There are no shortcuts to good speech. You have to live with an idea long enough to get acquainted with it. Select your subject early so that you will be on familiar terms with it before you introduce it to others.

Staking Out Your Topic

Some topics are just too big and shapeless for short talks or discussions. Others box you in so tightly that you can't move. The big topics need to be pared down to size, and the undersized ones need to be enlarged.

LIMITING YOUR SUBJECT

To limit your subject, move from the general to the specific. At first, you will probably cast about among general fields of interest, such as international relations, politics, science, art, literature, travel, and so on. Having chosen a general subject, break it down into smaller, more specific ones. For example, international relations may be broken into units such as the history of our foreign policy, treaties, alliances, international tribunals and peace organizations, programs for international understanding. Then let's say that international understanding strikes you as particularly appealing. But this is still too broad a topic; so you break it down into seven factors that promote or block understanding.

Any one of these seven subjects may be further subdivided. For instance:

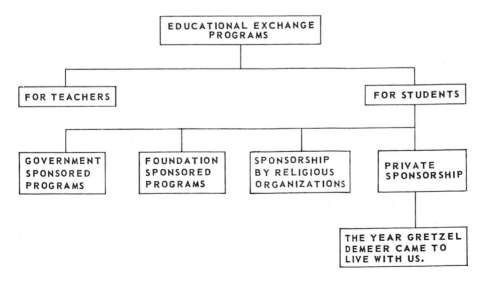

Of course, you won't always have to follow such an elaborate procedure. Once you pick up the trail of "Educational Exchange Programs," your mind might jump immediately to "The Year Gretzel DeMeer Came to Live with Us." The important thing is to grasp the principle behind the schematic device.

EXPANDING YOUR SUBJECT

Sometimes you may be attracted by a subject on which you have strong feelings and opinions, and then decide to drop it because it seems too restricted and personal for others to be interested in it. But before you do, see if you can detect certain implications in the subject that can be used to give it wider appeal.

Here's an example. A commuter is regularly late for his nine o'clock class because he can never find a parking place. His annoyance deepens every day, but he feels that a classroom is no place to air a personal gripe. Gradually, however, his annoyance gives way to inquiry and reflection. The building and grounds department tells him that the university has no more space for parking areas. The city officials tell him the same thing. Then the student comes to see that his private problem is part of a critical problem in urban transportation. He also perceives that his personal grievance leads directly to urgent questions of general concern. Here, for example, are some of those questions:

> Should the university grant parking privileges only to students who can prove a legitimate need for an automobile in residence?
>
> Should the city undertake construction of subterranean and skyscraper parking areas?
>
> Are automobile manufacturers doing all they can to redesign cars to meet mounting traffic and parking problems?
>
> What are the prospects for redesigning and modernizing rail transportation to meet urban needs?

Subjects for conversation, discussions, and speeches often originate in a personal experience which, when explored thoughtfully, proves to have wide interest and application.

Testing Your Subject

■ Is MY SUBJECT LIKELY TO YIELD SOLID VALUES FOR ME AND MY AUDIENCE?   Some occasions call for small talk, but people who talk only about trivial things betray trivial minds. They cheat themselves and others. Discriminating listeners judge us by our interests. What you choose to talk about reveals how well you live up to your social responsibilities.

■ AM I ABLE TO DEAL WITH THIS SUBJECT COMPETENTLY?   Ask yourself, "Do I already know enough about this topic to discuss it responsibly?" If not, "Do I know how and where I can find the information I need?" If so, "Do I have the background to understand and interpret the material?"

■ DOES MY SUBJECT FIT THE INTERESTS AND BACKGROUND OF MY AUDIENCE?   An archeologist returning from excavations in Egypt may hold fellow archeologists spellbound with an account of complicated techniques for excavating and preserving remains. The same subject would probably fall flat in a speech to a woman's club. Here the archeologist might be well advised to talk about tastes in home furnishings during various periods of Egyptian history.

■ Is MY SUBJECT APPROPRIATE TO THE OCCASION?   A church group in a college town wanted to promote understanding and good inter-faith relationships among students of different religions. Invited to a dinner meeting were Mohammedans, Hindus, Brahmans, Christians, and Jews. As it turned out, everything was off-key: The main course included ham; the only prayer was to the Christian God; the only song was a Christian hymn; and the speaker topped it all off by extolling the Christian missionary spirit. As you can imagine, the whole session was an embarrassing failure.

A blunder that offends the sensibilities of individuals and groups

—their rituals, conventions, taboos—cuts off lines of communication.

■ IS MY SUBJECT MANAGEABLE?   Beginning speakers often make the mistake of choosing subjects of almost unlimited scope for a five-minute talk. They try to take a cross-continental trip instead of a short excursion. Instead of talking on "advertising" in all its phases, confine yourself to one specific aspect of the subject: ethics in advertising, artistic television commercials, scenery and sign-boards, hidden persuaders in our supermarkets.

Points to Keep in Mind

1. When prospecting for subjects, make use of:
   a. Your personal experiences.
   b. Your interactions with your social and physical environment.
   c. The four primary purposes of speech as guides to your resources.

2. Unfortunate attitudes toward speech may impair your search for a subject. Don't cripple yourself by misjudging your responsibilities.

3. Limit or enlarge your subject beforehand so that you can handle it successfully in the time at your disposal.

4. Apply the five tests of suitability to your subject before you finally adopt it for a speech.

Exercises

1. Start now to build a classified list of potential subjects for speeches. Be alert to possibilities—in the classroom, while reading a newspaper or magazine, while watching TV, in conversations, while studying, while listening to your classmates speak.

2. Think of three people you know well, and think of one subject you would like to hear each one talk about. Now apply the same test to yourself. Of all your experiences and interests, what might the class most enjoy hearing you talk about? If you still have doubts, ask your friends for their opinions. Prepare a short extemporaneous talk on the subject you choose.

3. Prepare a short talk on an occupation. Your speech should answer questions such as these: What is the nature of the work? What qualifications are required? How useful is it? What future is there in it? How interesting is it likely to be? What are some of its disadvantages? Here are some suggestions:

Playwright	Teacher	Radio and TV commentator
Landscape gardener	Farmer	Professional football
Personnel director	Clergyman	player
Electrical engineer	Salesman	Space pilot
Commercial artist	Psychiatrist	Nurse
Novelist	Fashion model	Architect

4. The lives of famous or infamous men and women—their ideas, pursuits, and deeds—serve as good subjects for speech. Choose someone who interests you greatly, then phrase a question or two you would like to ask him or her. From the writings by or about the person, figure out the answers he or she might give to your questions. Prepare a talk based on your questions and answers. Here are some examples of questions:

Albert Einstein: "Does a scientist have a social responsibility with respect to his specific research?"

Albert Schweitzer: "Why did you choose to pursue your philosophic, medical, and musical talents in an African jungle?"

Abraham Lincoln: "Did you have your eye on the Presidency when you engaged Douglas in debate during the Illinois senatorial campaign of 1858?"

George Bernard Shaw: "Which of your plays do you regard as the best?"

Here are the names of other people to whom you may wish to put a question:

Frank Lloyd Wright	Edward R. Murrow	Conan Doyle
Ralph Waldo Emerson	Franklin D. Roosevelt	Karl Marx
Winston Churchill	Benedict Arnold	Mark Twain
Robert E. Lee	Adolf Hitler	Aldous Huxley
Dwight D. Eisenhower	Jonas Salk	Emily Dickinson
Charles Darwin	Van Cliburn	Charles Lindbergh
Eleanor Roosevelt	Babe Ruth	Robert Frost
Leonard Bernstein	Ernest Hemingway	Adlai Stevenson

5. Listen thoughtfully to all speeches given in class. Would you like to challenge the positions taken by some of the speakers? Did any of them suggest questions you would like to pursue? Did some speaker discuss an event or place (such as an educational experiment in high school) that calls attention to something you might like to take up in a future talk? Keep a running list of the subjects that occur to you.

CHAPTER SIX

Exploring
Your
Subject

Let's assume that you have a purpose and subject in mind. Now you ask, "How do I get rolling on the speech itself?"

Exploring a subject calls for brainwork, imagination, and grubbing. There are no short-

60

cuts. Two thousand years ago the great Roman teacher Quintilian satirized the antics of lazy speakers who ducked painstaking effort. His thrusts at the charlatans of his age expose one of the basic causes of vapid discourse in our age as well:

. . . Owing to their contempt for method, when they are meditating on some future effusion, they spend whole days looking at the ceiling in the hope that some magnificent inspiration may occur to them, or rock their bodies to and fro, booming inarticulately as if they had a trumpet inside them and adapting their agitated movements, not to the delivery of words, but to their pursuit. Some again settle on certain definite openings long before they have thought what they are going to say, with a view to using them as pegs for subsequent snatches of eloquence, and then after practicing their delivery first in silent thought and then aloud for hours together, in utter desperation of providing any connecting links, abandon them and take refuge in one formula after another, each no less hackneyed and familiar than the last.[1]

The way to get on with the job is to stop rocking to and fro and to launch into an orderly, step-by-step program of analysis and investigation.

Preliminary Survey and Analysis

MAKE A PRELIMINARY INVENTORY

First take stock of what you know or think you know about your subject before you scout out the "authorities." This kind of concentrated brain-cudgeling will jog your memory and stir up some original thinking. Talk that draws slavishly on the ideas and material of others sounds bookish and smells of somebody else's ink.

Make a list of your discoveries—key factual items, ideas, hunches, and questions that you can either use as they stand or else investigate further. What you turn up will probably look like a housewife's grocery list. No matter, there are solid reasons for beginning this way. If you were to turn this list over to someone else, it probably

[1] *The Institutio Oratoria of Quintilian*, trans. by H. E. Butler. London: William Heinemann, 1920, I, 281-283.

wouldn't mean much to him. After all, this is a strictly personal record of self-investigation that may both please and dismay you. Some of your insights may excite you as genuine discoveries, but you will probably find some gaping holes in your background of information that need to be filled.

ANALYZE YOUR AUDIENCE IN ITS SETTING

When working up a speech, don't plunge ahead guided exclusively by your private interest in the subject, or by what you consider to be the logical dictates of your material.

Visualize your audience in their setting before you meet them. For example, if you are getting ready for a ticklish conference, think of the people who will be there. Consider the range of their information, interests, and prejudices. Which points are urgent? Which points need to be mentioned without laboring them? Which points have to be introduced gingerly, or dropped altogether? Keep the time limits in mind.

Here is an actual case in which a little preliminary analysis of the audience and the occasion would have saved the day. A local civic group invited a public official, who was an expert on conser- vation, to explain proposals for reducing pollution and for checking the alarming depletion of local water resources. The speaker un- wound with a detailed history of the government agency he repre- sented, and then he sketched its nationwide set-up. A half-hour of this and the audience was summoning up courage for a sprint to the nearest exit. Public meetings are plagued by speakers who drag in material extraneous to the business at hand. Get into the habit of thinking about your audience's expectations as you explore your subject.

INTEGRATE YOUR INITIAL SURVEYS

You are now ready to make some tentative decisions. Go over your preliminary inventory again, this time with your audience in mind. Select the points that look most promising as big headings for your speech. Under each, list the observations and notations that are directly related to it. You may not be able to include all the items from your preliminary inventory, but you may come back to some of them later on. Your new list is an organized guide to further exploration of your subject. Let's look at a specific example of how you can put your preliminary survey and analysis to work.

The Three Steps Illustrated

The experience of a student—we'll call him Arthur Lewis—provides us with an instructive example. You won't duplicate his experience in every detail when you work up your own preliminary survey and analysis, of course, but you will have a clearer idea of how to go about it.

Lewis took this subject for a class speech: "The values of mastering a foreign language." A number of things had led him to this choice—his own progress in mastering French; his pleasure in overcoming an early phobia toward foreign languages; and a story in *The New York Times* that reported an appalling deficiency in foreign languages among college students. As he proceeded, Lewis kept this purpose in the back of his mind: "I want to convince members of my speech class that they owe it to themselves to master at least one foreign language before they graduate."

■ STEP ONE: LEWIS' PRELIMINARY INVENTORY.   Lewis pondered his subject, broke it down in various ways, and came up with this list of leads:

> My summer abroad.
>
> The study of foreign languages as an aid to English (debatable).
>
> Being able to speak a foreign language helps to confer culture (belongs to the genteel tradition; probably not very convincing today).
>
> With isolationism breaking down, the ability to read and write in a foreign tongue helps us to relate ourselves to our new world.

Today there are student exchange programs that enable us to live and study abroad.

Leadership in your chosen vocation makes language facility of practical value.

Business is becoming increasingly international. Many large department stores hold night classes in French, German, Italian, etc. for buyers and sales personnel.

Knowing a foreign language will help you professionally by giving you access to professional literature from abroad. Many professional meetings are held in foreign countries.

Government service is badly in need of specialists in almost all lines of work who can speak the language of the country.

You may want to enter graduate school someday, and you may have to show ability in one or more foreign languages.

Your pleasure in traveling abroad on vacations will be doubled if you can speak a language besides your own.

Opportunities for language study at our college.

Language phobia? How I overcame mine.

New techniques and aids in learning a foreign language.

Which language or languages should you study? Some of the variables that will affect your decision.

Government subsidies to colleges and students who undertake a concentrated program of language study.

■ STEP TWO: LEWIS' ANALYSIS OF HIS AUDIENCE IN ITS SETTING. Through earlier speeches and class discussion, Lewis had already sized up the other eighteen members of his class. They were preponderantly freshmen and sophomores, people who still had plenty of time to make course decisions. About a third of the class were women, and he noted that their speeches ran to "cultural" subjects; most of the men seemed to favor more "practical" topics. He had a hunch that a few of his classmates would fall right in with his purpose; that some had already had a skirmish with a foreign-language course that left them reluctant to tackle another; that about half the class hadn't thought much about the matter.

Not satisfied with guesses, Lewis put together a little question-naire and asked each member to fill it out. The answers sharpened his analysis. He learned that (1) only three people talked or read a foreign language with any fluency; (2) a scattering of the class members had taken a high-school or college language course but had no strong desire to go on; (3) most of the class had no plans to elect a foreign-language course; and (4) several insisted that they lacked aptitude.

■ STEP THREE: INTEGRATING HIS AUDIENCE ANALYSIS WITH HIS PRELIMINARY INVENTORY.   Now that he had worked up an audi-ence profile, Lewis was ready to make some tentative decisions on which items in his preliminary inventory would best serve his pur-pose. Now he had to pick and choose. He decided to concentrate on (1) the lifelong personal satisfactions that knowing a foreign language would bring; (2) the practical benefits; and (3) some novel and interesting ways to learn a new language.

Looking over his inventory, Lewis crossed out some of the items (though he decided that he might be able to mention a few of them in passing), and rephrased others. He settled on three big headings, under which he grouped other items from his inventory.

> Fluency in a foreign language is a passport to travel and living abroad.
>> Two personal experiences from my summer abroad.
>> Interview some students who have lived abroad.
>> Consult brochures on student exchange programs re language requirements and suggestions.
>
> In today's world, your business and professional future may hinge on your ability to write and speak another tongue.
>> New job opportunities are opening as business becomes increasingly international.

Your chances for government service are greatly increased if you can speak the language of another country.

New devices and techniques make learning a language pleasant and speedy.

How Professor Andrews teaches his language courses in French. (Check with him on the results of his three-year experiment.)

The language "lab."

Records and tapes that have helped me.

My experience in learning French at the "language table" in McCullen Hall.

Opportunities for language study at our college.

Lewis now felt satisfied that his preliminary explorations had opened the way to directed inquiry. He had no intention of freezing his analysis or settling for the information he had on hand. He needed to know more, and he was quite willing to scrap or revise his analysis if further probing turned up something better.

Extending the Investigation

Your own preliminary analysis will put you on a trail that you can follow as far as you need to go. Along the way, you will encounter new ideas, points of view, facts, examples, illustrations, and all the other things that will enrich your perceptions, thinking, and speaking. You won't use everything, but in subtle ways "everything" will show through as you talk. Here, then, are some suggestions for pushing deeper into your subject.

INTERROGATION AND OBSERVATION

■ TALK OVER YOUR IDEAS WITH SOMEONE WHOM YOU CAN COUNT ON TO LISTEN AND GIVE THOUGHTFUL REACTIONS. As the writer

Robert Penn Warren aptly remarks, "Very often it is in conversation during the germinal stage of a project that I stumble on my meanings, or they stumble on me. . . ." If possible, arrange interviews with people who have special knowledge of your subject.

■ USE PAPER-AND-PENCIL DEVICES FOR COLLECTING INFORMATION. When you want to survey specific attitudes and practices, try your hand at working out simple questionnaires and opinion polls. Since most of us lack the time and the special knowledge needed to prepare and use these devices scientifically, be realistic about the results. Be aware of their limitations and make those limitations clear to your listeners.

■ TAKE A FIELD TRIP AND SEE FOR YOURSELF. This may mean that all you have to do is inspect a project so that you can talk about it with more familiarity; or it may mean some sleuthing. Virginia Watson kept hearing the charge that college students who drove cars were a menace to the citizens of Moresfield. She set out to test the charge. She went directly to the proper municipal offices and checked over the records of accidents during the past academic year. She interviewed a judge in traffic court. She talked to several traffic patrolmen. Her report was acclaimed as a masterful example of careful and productive field work. And incidentally, she learned that it was better to base her beliefs on research and critical thinking than on loose talk.

PUBLISHED SOURCES

For many subjects, the only place you can find the information you need is in the library. Logically, then, you will need a working knowledge of the basic tools and resources that you will find there.

■ REFERENCE BOOKS. First off, learn to use *Guide to Reference Books* by Constance M. Winchell. Although this guide is primarily for librarians, you will find it invaluable and easy to use. We can

"Public Library? How do you find a word in the dictionary if you don't know how to spell it?"

list here only a few of the types of standard reference work listed in the Winchell *Guide*.

Encyclopedias are surveys of knowledge organized on a topical basis. Outstanding are the *Encyclopaedia Britannica, The Encyclopedia Americana,* the *New International Encyclopaedia,* and their supplements. You will also find encyclopedias that cover special fields, such as the *Encyclopaedia of the Social Sciences.*

Then you will find many collections of short biographies of prominent people based on time periods, geographical areas, and occupations. Outstanding collections of national and international figures are the *Dictionary of American Biography,* the *Dictionary of National Biography* (English), *Who's Who in America, World Biography,* and *Current Biography* (international). *Biography Index* is a guide to current biographical materials.

When you want factual data about the contemporary world, look in the Winchell *Guide* for the yearbook that is most likely to contain them. You will find that *The World Almanac* is a compendium of facts for each year. *The American Yearbook* is an annual record of events in politics, economics, business, social conditions, science, and humanities. *The Statesman's Yearbook* supplies information on governments of the world, on population, religion, education, crime, finance, industry, and so forth. The *Statistical Abstract of the United States* is a source book of facts covering social, political, industrial, and economic subjects. *Facts on File* is a weekly world-news digest. And there are many others.

Two well-known dictionaries are Webster's *New International Dictionary of the English Language* and *Funk & Wagnall's New Standard Dictionary.* The *Oxford English Dictionary* and *A Dictionary of American English* are invaluable for information on the history and usage of words.

■ BIBLIOGRAPHIES.   A bibliography is a list of works on a particular subject. By looking in the *Bibliographic Index* you can locate lists of works on a great variety of subjects. *The Reference Shelf* series supplies bibliographies on timely, controversial questions that have been debated in schools and colleges.

■ BOOKS.   The card catalog is an alphabetically arranged index to all the resources of your library, primarily to books. The cards are usually filed in three ways—according to author, title of book, and subject of book. The speediest way to find an item is to look for it under the author's name or the title. But subject headings, in addition to supplying a third place to look for a particular item, often provide a list of additional works on your subject. If you can't find your book in the card catalog, and if it was published in English during the twentieth century, look for information about it in *The United States Catalog* or its supplement, *Cumulative Book Index.* Look in the *Book Review Digest* to locate reviews of a book, and to find short summaries of these reviews.

■ PERIODICALS.   *The Reader's Guide to Periodical Literature* is indispensable in exploring subjects for speeches. It will pay you to study carefully its system of abbreviated entries. Use *Poole's Index to Periodical Literature* for articles published in the nineteenth century. Scholarly articles in the humanities and sciences are listed in *The International Index to Periodicals.*

■ INDEXES TO SPECIAL FIELDS.   These indexes list all types of publications in a special field—books, articles, pamphlets, bulletins, and so forth. Examples are *Educational Index, Industrial Arts In-*

dex, and *Public Affairs Information Service.* Look in Winchell for a guide to the special field you have in mind.

■ UNITED STATES PUBLIC DOCUMENTS. The *Monthly Catalog* is a current bibliography of government publications and tells you how to order them. *The Congressional Record* contains congressional debates, speeches, extended remarks of congressmen, and Presidents' messages.

■ NEWSPAPERS. *The New York Times Index,* published since 1913, is a chronological and alphabetical index to that paper's news items and other features. Actually, this index serves as a master key to current affairs reported in other newspapers as well.

Recording Your Material

Human memory is fickle. A good set of notes will save you from little and big errors, and will spare you a return trip to the library to recover information you looked up before. Writing a thing down helps you get it right. A good investigator checks on himself as well as on his sources of information.

There are four kinds of notes you will want to make. Put a symbol on each card or slip of paper to show what type of note it is.

1. *Verbatim notes* contain somebody else's words and data exactly as he expressed them.

2. *Paraphrased notes* embody somebody else's ideas and data in your own words.

3. *Summary notes* are digests of a book, article, speech, interview, or conversation.

4. *Personal "idea" notes* are a record of your original thoughts and observations on a particular subject.

Each card or slip, in addition to the note itself, should carry a subject heading, designation of the type of note it is, the writer's name, a full and accurate statement of the source from which it is taken, and the page number. Sometimes information such as the library call number, the writer's identity and special qualifications, and any appraisal you care to make of the work proves valuable too. Below is a sample note card containing the minimum, essential information.

Here are some useful rules for note-taking:

1. Put notes for only one subject on each card, slip, or sheet.

2. Check and double-check your note against the original source. *Get it right* before you go on.

3. Never distort by lifting material out of context. Be faithful to the writer's or speaker's intended meaning.

4. Write legibly and follow a consistent style.

5. Before you file a note, be sure that you have indicated what type of note it is and have included all other necessary information about it and your source.

HEADING {

Career opportunities for college   **Ver**   ←*Abbreviation*
graduates in the federal service   *of the word*
                                                                    Verbatim,
NOTE {

The Federal Service Entrance Examination (FSEE)   *used by this*
is open to all college seniors and recent graduates   *writer to*
regardless of their major field of study in college.   *designate*
Those who pass the FSEE are then considered for a   *the type of*
wide variety of positions throughout the civil service. *note it is.*
The FSEE is also used to recruit potential "managers,"
and those who wish to be considered for "junior-
management internships" may qualify by passing additional tests. Although the FSEE is now the main entrance
to the federal career service for college students,
college training is also required for a great many
professional positions, such as engineer, chemist,
physicist, accountant, auditor, cartographer, dietician,
geologist, intelligence specialist, mathematician, and
meteorologist. Whatever a student's major in college,
chances are he will find a career opening in the
federal service.

**AUTHORS
AND SOURCE** {

Marian D. Irish and James W. Prothro, The Politics
of American Democracy. Englewood Cliffs, New Jersey:
Prentice-Hall, Inc., 1959, p.492.

Points to Keep in Mind

Follow a clear-cut plan when you are exploring a subject. Efficiency will save you time and yield better results.

1. Begin by making a preliminary survey of your subject, the audience, and the setting of your speech.

2. Go over your survey and select the key questions and main ideas that suggest lines of development for your speech.

3. Use these key questions and main ideas to guide you in an extended investigation and analysis of your subject.

4. Learn to be efficient, resourceful, and accurate when you go digging for material.

5. Be systematic and precise when you are taking notes.

Exercises

1. Prepare an extemporaneous talk. Turn in to your instructor the following items:

  a. Worksheets containing your preliminary survey of the subject.
  b. A list of all your sources of information.
  c. A few sample note-cards.

2. Schedule a series of reports on specific reference material in your library. Have one speaker report on *The United States Catolog,* a second on the *Oxford English Dictionary,* a third on the *Encyclopaedia of Social Sciences,* and so on. Report on the purpose of the reference item, its history, its scope and limits, its location in the library. Explain how to use it efficiently.

3. Organize the class into teams of two or three investigators. Have each team interview a librarian who is in charge of one department of your school's library—the circulation department, the reference room, the reserve room, the documents department, the archives, the order department, the periodical department. Each team should seek infor-

mation that is pertinent to an understanding of the materials and functions of the one department, and then hold a short discussion on its findings before the rest of the class.

4. Choose a topic on which you can make a first-hand investigation. Survey campus opinion, arrange interviews, make a personal check on facilities for the dining halls, and so on. Check and double-check your methods, data, and results. Make a report based on your investigation.

5. Inform yourself on a speaker's habits and methods of preparation. Interview an outstanding clergyman, businessman, public official, or instructor. Or you may wish to read up on a speaker's work habits in biographies or in special studies such as those contained in *A History and Criticism of American Public Address,* edited, respectively, by W. N. Brigance and Marie Hochmuth.

CHAPTER SEVEN

Outlining
Your
Speech

Well-organized speech helps everyone. Listeners like a speaker who gets off to a good start, heads straight to his destination, and makes the trip on schedule. Moreover, the speaker himself gains confidence when he knows where he is going and how to get there.

Unorganized speech is the hardest kind to de-

liver and the hardest kind to follow. Without a plan, the speaker wanders aimlessly, and his anxiety mounts as listeners show signs of impatience. But if he has an outline in his head or in his hands, these hazards are reduced. Even if he does make a few detours along the way, the outline will put him back on the track before he loses his audience forever.

Elements of an Outline

When you explored your subject, you turned up facts and ideas, testimony and statistics, examples and stories—the raw materials of speech. The next step is to compress all these materials into separate statements or points and to assemble them into an outline. Think of an outline as an interlocking network of main points and sub-points with your statement of specific purpose as its control center.

Suppose your statement of specific purpose is: "My purpose is to show that the quarter system is better for our university than the semester system." One segment of your outline might look like this:

I. The quarter system meets the special needs of certain schools of our university.
   A. It has advantages for students in Engineering and Journalism.
      1. Many of these students spend one term each year picking up practical experience in industry.
      2. Under the semester system they couldn't graduate in four years.

"I want you to know it was a real surprise when Ed McConnell told me at the last minute I was to speak tonight. Tell plumber to fix downstairs bathtub —I hastily grabbed some notes from my desk—ask Doctor about Aunt Martha . . ."

      B. Most of the professional schools have many courses that
         lend themselves to concentrated treatment within a
         twelve-week term.
    II. The student body likes the quarter system.

Note that Roman numerals designate the main points, capital
letters the first series of sub-points, and Arabic numbers the second
series of sub-points. If you have a third series, use lower-case letters.
For a fourth series of sub-points, use Arabic numbers within paren-
theses. Each new series of sub-points is indented.

With these mechanics in mind, we can take a closer look at the
principles that underlie all outlining.

Principles of Outlining

■ 1. Phrase each point clearly and concisely.   You want
each point to etch itself on your mind—and on your audience's
mind too. Long, involved sentences blunt points. This is cumber-
some: "Our antiquated system for levying and collecting real estate
and personal property taxes was devised in the last century when
most people had their money tied up in land, homes, and personal
belongings instead of intangible forms of investment." Here is a
concise restatement: "Our real estate and personal property taxes
belong to the horse-and-buggy days."

■ 2. Limit each point to one distinct idea or fact.   No
point should overlap or duplicate another. Take this example:

    I. Choose your camp site carefully.
      A. Keep the factor of water in mind.
        1. Be sure you have a source of drinking water.
        2. Pitch your tent in an area that is high and dry.
        3. A swamp makes a poor camp site.

Note that point 3 overlaps point 2. Point 2 had already established
the need for a dry camp site. Re-examine all points to insure that

they are really distinct and self-contained. Test your points by looking behind the words for meaning. If two points say the same thing,
drop one of them.

■ 3. ASSEMBLE YOUR POINTS IN PROPER RELATIONSHIPS.   Each
point in an outline must either (a) *directly* support or explain the
statement of specific purpose or (b) *directly* support or explain another point in the outline.

Items that have the same weight, value, or importance are called
coordinate points. They have equal status in your outline. Thus
main points are coordinate because they directly support your statement of specific purpose. Your first series of sub-points, A, B, and C,
are coordinate because they join in supporting a main point. If you
give equal status to items that are unequal in importance, your outline will be defective. Notice what has happened here:

WHY THE "BIG THREE" AUTOMOBILE MANUFACTURERS DECIDED TO ENTER THE SMALL-CAR MARKET

   I. Each year Americans buy more small cars.
  II. Tourists purchase cars abroad and bring them home.
 III. Small American cars such as the Rambler and the Lark
     have caught on.
 IV. Dealers have put pressure on the "Big Three."

As you see, points I, III, and IV belong to the same class of reasons
and are therefore coordinate. Point II, however, is *subordinate* to
point I because Americans who buy small cars include those who
go abroad to purchase them.

Unless a point is clearly self-supporting or self-explanatory, use
subordinate points to give it the necessary support. For example:

  I. The ability to speak and write a foreign language is an asset
    in the department store business.
    A. The large stores need people who buy and sell for them
      in foreign markets.
      1. Carson, Pirie, Scott and Company now offers courses
        in French and Italian to their representatives.

Here point A supports point I, and point 1 states a factual case to support point A. Include all reasons and data in the first draft of your outline and then be somewhat more selective in revised versions.

Make sure that each sub-point *directly* supports the point to which it is *immediately* subordinate. The example below violates this rule.

> I. There are compelling educational reasons for attending a good woman's college.
>   A. Students are freed from many social distractions in co-educational schools.
>   B. Its curriculum usually has a strong emphasis on cultural subjects.
>   C. Eighty-five per cent of the students from womens' colleges marry within five months of graduation.

Whatever the merits of sub-point C, it does not comprise a "compelling educational" reason in the sense of point I, and is therefore neither coordinate with A and B nor subordinate to point I. If point C is included in the outline at all, it must be made subordinate to some other main point, such as "A woman's college does not isolate its graduates from normal human experiences."

Patterns
of Organization

All speeches follow either a topical pattern or a logical pattern of organization. One pattern or the other may be followed strictly, or else the two may be combined to suit special purposes. In later chapters you will find outlines that combine these two patterns in various ways.

THE TOPICAL PATTERN

The topical pattern is based on a relationship of *parts to the whole*. In describing the styles of houses on your street (the whole), one possible breakdown could be—Georgian houses, Cape Cod houses, and ranch-style houses (the parts). If you had chosen some other factor to serve as the whole, such as the size, age, history, or market value of the houses, you would have a quite different set of parts. Your statement of the specific purpose should make explicit the whole you expect to divide into parts.

Be sure your list of parts is accurate and consistent. If you were discussing popular models of automobiles (the whole), your outline would be hopelessly confused by this breakdown, which throws together name and body style: Chevrolet, convertibles, four-door sedans, Ford, hardtops, and Plymouth.

The topical pattern of outlining is ideally suited to descriptive, narrative, and expository speeches. See pages 91-92 for an example of a complete topical outline.

THE LOGICAL PATTERN

This pattern of organization, which is quite different from the topical, is used in making a tight, logical case in behalf of some proposition. You ask your listeners to believe or act in a certain way on the strength of the reasons and evidence that you offer.

In a logical outline, the proposition serves as your control center. It may be a formal statement such as this: "Resolved: That the library stacks should be opened to all undergraduates." Or it may be an informal remark, such as: "Let's have dinner at six o'clock." The main points of your outline are the reasons that you are offering in support of your proposition. Your sub-points are statements of the premises that support the main point to which they are immediately subordinate.

The logical outline, then, is made up of one or more chains of reasoning that connect the central proposition with the facts, opinions, and the basic assumptions upon which it ultimately rests. Here is an example of a chain of reasoning:

> I. Most traffic accidents occur in the early evening hours, because,

A. Traffic is heavier than at any other time, because,
 1. Most people return home from work at the same hour.
 2. More and more they are relying on automobiles for transportation to and from work, because,
   a. Rail transportation has been reduced by twenty per cent.
   b. Bus lines have not been extended to take up the slack.
   c. Many suburbs are inaccessible except by car.
B. The driver's efficiency drops off at this time of day, because. . . .

The words "because," "for," or "since" are often written into logical outlines to show linkage among points in a chain of reasoning.

Divisions of the Outline

An organized speech has a beginning, a body, and an ending. You can spot these divisions most clearly in public speech, but you will find them in informal talk too. Don't think of them as formal and rigid. Rather, think of them as functions that the speaker must somehow perform. These divisions are closely knit, and it's hard to tell sometimes where one leaves off and the other begins. In outlining, these parts are usually referred to as Introduction, Discussion or Body, and Conclusion.

The Introduction

The introduction to your speech is an invitation to listening. It creates good relationships between you and your audience and paves the way for your subject. The length, ingenuity, and degree of formality of your introduction will vary with circumstances. Here are three general approaches that you can adapt to your needs.

KINDS OF INTRODUCTION

■ 1. QUICK DISCLOSURE OF THE SUBJECT AT HAND.   Sometimes you need to come to the point quickly, with just enough comment to connect your speech with what has been said before and to show where you are going. This is typical of conversation: "I'll go along with you. We do need a better campus newspaper. But I think we can get it without pouring more money into it. What we need is a better staff."

Notice the concise introduction that Helen Gahagan Douglas once made in a speech in the United States House of Representatives:

> Mr. Speaker, last Monday I was by unanimous consent granted official leave to go shopping for America's housewife because it is quite as important for members of this body to know what is going on in the grocery stores of America as in our munitions plants.
>
> I now wish to report my findings, and have brought with me in this market basket the results of my study.

■ 2. THE MOTIVATED INTRODUCTION.   Sometimes you will have to use your introduction as a means of enlisting your listeners' attention, especially if you suspect that they may be passive, disinterested, or downright hostile. A student talking on "Let the Handicapped Help You!" aroused interest at once with this opening.

> The world calls you and me normal people. We can see, hear, talk, walk, and learn. I know you're humane. You prove it every time I talk to you. If I stood before you today as a handicapped person, you'd be doubly courteous. That would do credit to your heart if not to your understanding of a handicapped person's psychology.
>
> Suppose you were an employer. Suppose a man or woman whom the world calls deaf and dumb applied to you for a job. And suppose this applicant was qualified to do the job. Would

you hire him on the strength of his credentials? Or would you get skittish and give him the gentle brush-off?

"Sure I'd give him the job," you say. Maybe you would. If so, you'd belong to the class of exceptionally enlightened employers. The blunt fact is that the handicapped person has a tough time landing a job no matter how well qualified he is. I know, because my father belongs to that group of people the world calls deaf and dumb.

Let's see if I can convey to you some of the frustrations of the handicapped person in our so-called normal world. More importantly, I'd like to suggest that we deprive ourselves when we deprive the handicapped person of legitimate job opportunities.

Motivated introductions make use of personal experiences, stories, challenging statements and questions, pat quotations, paradoxes, and other approaches. Whatever you decide to use, though, should be relevant, in good taste, and handled imaginatively.

■ 3. THE EXPLANATORY INTRODUCTION. If you are planning to explore a complex or technical subject in your speech, you will be wise to use an explanatory introduction in which you define terms, provide background, and offer a preview of the points you expect to take up. Here is an example of a businesslike explanatory introduction made by a man appearing before the planning commission of his city.

Gentlemen, my name is Roger Weldon. I am a businessman here, and I live at 1245 Kinsley Avenue. I am president of the Glendale Property Association, and I appear at the request of its members. This is a non-profit organization, whose members live and own property in the southeast section of our city, known as the Glendale area.

The Glendale Property Association is interested in all matters that affect the property values and the residential character of our neighborhood. Accordingly, we are concerned about the increasing traffic load on the streets of our area. Years ago the city dedicated a strip of land running through the heart of our neighborhood for the extension of Lake Road, now a dead-end road. Whether or not the road is ever extended, the possibility exists—and constitutes a threat to the property values and character of our area. I am here to request that the city authorities relinquish all rights to this strip of land now dedicated to the extension of Lake Road.

First, I wish to locate on a map the strip of land in question. Next, I wish to outline in detail why we think it should be vacated. Finally, I wish to indicate the legal steps that need to be taken if you approve our petition.

OUTLINING THE INTRODUCTION

Outline your introduction just as you do the rest of your speech. Here is a working outline for the introduction presented above:

I. I appear at the request of the Glendale Property Association.
   A. We are organized to protect homeowners in our area.
   B. We request that a strip of land dedicated to the extension of Lake Road be vacated.
II. I propose to discuss our petition under three headings.
   A. The description of the strip of land in question.
   B. The reasons why we ask the city to vacate the strip.
   C. The legal steps that need to be taken to vacate it.

The Discussion

This division of your outline is the body of your speech. It contains all the main points and sub-points by which you explain or support your topic or thesis.

■ 1. How MANY MAIN POINTS AND SUB-POINTS DO I NEED? This is a little like asking, "How many legs does a table need?" It depends on the size and shape of the table, how strong the legs are, and where they are placed. Some tables stand well on one leg, some on two, and some need four or more. If you tell a person he shouldn't drink the contents of a bottle because it contains poison, that one reason is likely to be enough.

In a short talk, it usually is wise to limit yourself to between one and five main points. One thing is certain: If you try to cover nineteen main points in a five-minute talk, you will be in a hopeless position. Either limit your purpose and therefore the number of your main points, or re-examine your analysis of the subject and combine some of your main points into a few bigger points.

The same answer holds for the sub-points. There's no good reason for spinning them out beyond your own needs or those of your audience. If your outline gets beyond two or three degrees of subordination, try recasting it into a simpler form.

■ 2. IN WHAT ORDER SHOULD I ARRANGE MY MAIN POINTS AND THEIR SUB-POINTS?   The answer to this question lies in your subject or in the special needs of the audience and occasion.

The points in a topical outline may be arranged in one of several different ways. You would probably discuss large labor organizations since the Civil War in the order of their appearance on the American scene. Here you would be following a *time sequence.* If you compared the mountain ranges of the United States, region by region from east to west, you would be using a *space sequence.* A speech explaining the physical needs of a school district might take up these needs in an *order of priority*—classrooms, laboratories, a lunch room, and a gymnasium. Points in a speech analyzing the composition of *The New York Times'* Sunday edition might be arranged according to the *interests of the audience* in various sections of the newspaper. Speeches of instruction often move from the *familiar to the unfamiliar* or from the *simple to the complex.* Once you have chosen a method of ordering the items of your speech, stick with it consistently throughout any given series of coordinate points.

Customarily, logical outlines open with arguments that establish a *need for change* or a *cause for action.* There are times, however, when it is wise to depart from this formula in order to accommodate your speech to the psychology of your audience. If you know that your audience has a keen interest in one of your arguments, capitalize on that interest. Open with that argument. Then again, if you feel that all your arguments will sustain interest but that one is especially strong, you probably would use it as a clincher or climax. Should your audience be divided on a controversial issue, open with the point that is likely to win agreement, in the hope that your other points will be given a more favorable hearing.

Whether your outline is topical or logical, your sequence should enable you to make an easy and natural transition from one point to the next.

■ 3. SHOULD I USE COMPLETE SENTENCES OR KEY PHRASES? It's usually better to use complete sentences for main points and major sub-points, particularly in the discussion or body. Complete sentences force one to think through all the points clearly and to express them with precision. If you want an outline to refer to while you are speaking, then reduce your formal outline from complete sentences to key phrases.

The Conclusion

A good conclusion ends smartly and strongly. Use the conclusion as a capstone for your speech, not as a dumping ground for left-over items. Think out your conclusion beforehand and make it part of your outline.

TYPES OF CONCLUSION

Three types of conclusion will cover most of your needs.

■ 1. SUMMARY. Often the best way to close is simply to re-state clearly and forcefully the main ideas or points of your talk. It's as if you were to say, "Now before you go, let's be certain we understand each other." Or you may wish to highlight the central idea of your speech without reviewing your analysis of it. Note how

William Trufant Foster restates in a somewhat more arresting way the essential message of his speech, "Should Students Study?"

> The undergraduate who is eager to excel in his life-work and who is brave enough to face the facts will take down that sign from the walls of his room, "Do not let your studies interfere with your college education," and replace it with this one: "Do not let your college life interfere with your life's ambition." The boy without ambition will take for his motto, "Let well enough alone," oblivious to the fact that boys who are content to "let well enough alone" never do "well enough." [1]

■ 2. EPITOME.   A somewhat more dramatic type of conclusion is one in which you enclose the essence of your speech in a capsule —a story, a single striking statement, an example, an illustration, a quotation, a maxim, or a proverb. The purpose of the epitome conclusion is to impress and to stir your audience emotionally. When the battle of France was raging in May, 1940, Winston Churchill ended his first speech as Prime Minister with this epitome conclusion:

> Today is Trinity Sunday. Centuries ago words were written to be a call and a spur to the faithful servants of Truth and Justice: "Arm yourselves, and be ye men of valor, and be in readiness for the conflict; for it is better for us to perish in battle than to look upon the outrage of our nation and our altar. As the Will of God is in Heaven, even so let it be."

■ 3. PLEA FOR ACCEPTANCE OR ACTION.   If you have made a good case for your proposition, you have won the right to ask your audience to share your beliefs and act upon them. You do your cause an injustice if you fail to enlist the vital interests and emotions of your listeners.

In his first inaugural address, Woodrow Wilson had already paved the way for this final, moving plea for public support:

---

[1] Lew Sarett and William Trufant Foster, eds., *Modern Speeches on Basic Issues.* Boston: Houghton Mifflin Company, 1939, p. 75.

This is not a day of triumph; it is a day of dedication. Here muster, not the forces of party, but the forces of humanity. Men's hearts wait upon us; men's lives hang in the balance; men's hopes call upon us to say what we will do. Who shall live up to the great trust? Who dares fail to try? I summon all honest men, all patriotic, all forward-looking men, to my side. God helping me, I will not fail them, if they will but counsel and sustain me!

Though with less eloquence than Wilson's, the following conclusion is more specific in indicating the action to be taken:

Start building your library now. Buy good books and then make them your own. Your purchase slip gives you title to a book, but it doesn't confer real ownership. The marks of ownership are the questions and notations you scribble in the margins, the underlining of important ideas, the digests you write at the ends of chapters, and the reactions you list on the blank pages. Never mark a book until you have established title to it. Once the title is clear, own the book. Owning a book calls for an active mind and a sharp pencil.

If you have been an effective advocate throughout your speech, you won't have to resort to stunts or high-pressure tactics to get action. Your audience will be ready to vote, sign up, buy, give, and even sacrifice.

OUTLINING THE CONCLUSION

Make your conclusion a part of your outline. The conclusion of a speech in behalf of the Red Cross, for example, might look like this:

I. Support the Red Cross throughout the year.
  A. Help keep its blood-bank stocked.
  B. Contribute as much money as you can.
  C. Give time to hospitals and emergency relief.
II. The Red Cross may one day be your life-line.

Specimen Outlines

Up to this point we have been examining small sections of outlines as examples. Here are two full-length, sample outlines for short speeches. One exemplifies the topical pattern, the other the logical pattern.

SAMPLE TOPICAL OUTLINE

Title: The Anonymous Doctor
Subject: The role of the pathologist
Specific Purpose: My object is to inform my audience on the principal responsibilities of a pathologist in a modern hospital.

Introduction

I. A pathologist is a doctor's doctor.
   A. He works directly with internists and surgeons.
      1. His job is to analyze and interpret diseased tissue.
      2. Every accredited American hospital has at least one pathologist.
   B. Since he does not treat patients, the public at large knows little about his work.
II. We owe it to ourselves to learn more about his role.
   A. As a patient, this knowledge will add to your confidence in hospital procedures.
   B. Knowing about his work may suggest professional opportunities to you—as a doctor, technician, nurse, or hospital administrator.

Discussion

I. The pathologist is an indispensable partner to other doctors.
   A. His diagnostic reports may save both the patient and the surgeon.
      1. He warns the surgeon against operations that have been planned if analysis shows them to be unnecessary.
      2. Or he calls attention to an urgent need for an operation.
   B. Often the surgeon calls upon the pathologist to look over his shoulder while he operates.

      1. As a tissue specialist, he may make on-the-spot interpretations of unexpected discoveries.

      2. The surgeon may suspend an operation that is in progress until the pathologist makes a quick microscopic analysis of a piece of tissue.

    C. The pathologist prescribes for pre-operative and post-operative care of the patient.

II. The pathologist presides over hospital laboratory work.

    A. Each day brings its routine of laboratory analysis.

      1. Every organ removed in the operating room must be inspected.

      2. Every sample of blood extracted must go under the microscope.

    B. Much of the "lab" work is done by technicians, but the pathologist has final responsibility.

III. The pathologist is a standard-maker.

    A. As a research man he contributes to medical knowledge.

    B. He is a watchdog for the profession.

      1. He reports to the "tissue committee" all healthy tissue removed in an operation.

      2. He serves as a member of the "tissue committee."

        a. This committee reviews and adjudicates doubtful procedures.

        b. It may call on a surgeon to explain his reasons for the procedure in question.

Conclusion

  I. The pathologist is the patient's anonymous doctor.

  II. He serves both you and the medical profession.

SAMPLE LOGICAL OUTLINE

Subject: A mock political convention

Specific Purpose: I wish to persuade the Student Governing Board to sponsor a mock political convention during the spring term of the next presidential election year.

Introduction

I. A mock political convention simulates a national political convention.
   A. It follows procedures common to the political conventions of the major parties.
   B. It drafts and enacts a political platform.
   C. It brings to campus prominent political speakers from both major parties.
   D. It nominates candidates for the offices of President and Vice-President of the United States.
II. Since this proposal involves the whole school, the Student Governing Board is the logical group to get the ball rolling.

Discussion

I. This project would add to our political education, because,
   A. It would supplement our academic studies, for,
      1. It would strengthen our interest in the history of political campaigns and conventions.
      2. We would apply information about political procedure that we learn in political science.
   B. It would stimulate interest in contemporary political issues, because,
      1. We would have to read widely in current sources of information.
      2. It would encourage informal discussion among students.
      3. We would have a chance to hear and meet prominent political figures in person.
II. A mock political convention would contribute to the personal development of students, because,
   A. Many students would have opportunities for leadership in areas of their special interests, for,
      1. Money has to be raised and budgeted by students.
      2. There would be publicity and public relations assignments for many people.
      3. Technical arrangements would require students who have knowledge of electronics and lighting.

        4. Staging the convention would bring students of theater and music into the act.

        5. All who have political ambitions would gain experience in the art of politics.

    B. Students generally would learn a great deal about group behavior, for,

        1. They would learn what it means to work together in order to get things done.

        2. They would gain experience in cooperative descision-making with partisans on controversial issues.

III. The convention would instill meaningful school spirit, because,

    A. Students would get to know each other better, for,

        1. Each house and dormitory would be organized to act as a state or territorial delegation.

        2. Campaign activities are great mixers.

    B. It would promote good student-faculty-administration relationships, for,

        1. Faculty members would be called in as advisers.

        2. Students and administrative officers would need to work closely on arrangements.

IV. A mock political convention is a feasible project, because,

    A. Other colleges and universities have been successful at it.

    B. We have adequate building facilities.

    C. We can handle the financial side of it, for,

        1. There is an accumulated surplus of $1000 in our student activities budget.

        2. We can sell advertising space in convention programs.

        3. We can charge a door admission for all outsiders.

Conclusion

  I. We should and can stage a mock political convention, because,

    A. It confers valuable educational benefits.

    B. It will contribute to campus unity.

    C. It is a feasible project.

 II. I ask that the Student Governing Board endorse this proposal and forward it to the administrative officers for their consideration.

Points to Keep in Mind

1. A tightly developed outline is your best guarantee of a well-organized speech.

2. The items in your outline should conform to the rules governing phrasing, distinctness, and relationship among points.

3. Base all outlines on a topical pattern or logical pattern, or on a combination of the two.

4. Divide every outline into Introduction, Discussion, and Conclusion. Each division serves a function that is natural and necessary to speech.

Exercises

1. Each student writes the outline for a speech on the blackboard. Or better still, each outline is typed on a stencil, duplicated, and distributed to the class. Spend a class period or two analyzing one another's outlines and making suggestions for improvement.

2. Deliver a talk based on a carefully developed outline. Ask the class to jot down your main points and sub-points as they come through while you are speaking. If your prepared outline fails to agree with your listeners' records, either you need to improve your organization or make it come through better *when you talk.*

3. Focus on introductions and conclusions. Plan and deliver an interesting introduction to a ten- or fifteen-minute speech; you need not go beyond the introduction. Revise and strengthen the conclusion of some speech you have already given. Refresh your listeners' memory on the whole speech, then deliver your revised conclusion.

4. Analyze and outline a short printed speech. Many speeches have ill-designed and rickety structures. But make an honest and diligent effort to find the main points, to see if they follow in sensible order, and to determine whether the whole outline holds up. Make a thoroughgoing critique of the organization.

CHAPTER EIGHT

The Personal Equation in Speech

Speech is an intensely personal act. One person speaks; others react. You will master all the basic principles of speech much more easily if you first master yourself.

We deal with two closely related problems in

this chapter: How to make a good personal adjustment in speech; and how to establish good personal relations with your audience. These are two sides of the same coin. Understanding the personal equation in speech contributes to poise and maturity in human relations.

You Can't Escape

You as a person inevitably influence everything you say. You must call on your personal resources when you speak, and your listeners inevitably form impressions of you. You can't escape. Nor should you wish to. Your speech gives you some of your best opportunities for personal identification and fulfillment.

You have already discovered that it is easier to talk with some people than with others. You know, too, that tension mounts when the occasion is important to you, or more public than you are accustomed to, or more complex and demanding. These tensions may be energizing factors that spur you on to greater effort. Or they may impose serious handicaps. In either case, your speech will be better if you are in full control of yourself.

The means to good personal adjustment in speech are two: First, discover what personal qualities will serve you best; and second, learn how to bring your best personal resources to bear when tension threatens to take over.

Many corporations employ public-relations experts to enlist the goodwill of the audience in which they are interested. But, as a speaker, you have to do this job for yourself. Your audience sees you as you are. And remember that you represent the cause you are pleading as well as yourself. Rightly or wrongly, attitudes toward *you* rub off on your subject.

Here again, there are two things you can do: First, discover the personal qualities audiences react to most favorably; and second, learn how to enlist these qualities in establishing good personal relations with your listeners.

Personal Qualities That Contribute to Good Speech

The personal equation in speech varies from speaker to speaker and from audience to audience. And fortunately so, for differences in personality give freshness and variety to human relations. It is hardly necessary to point out that success in speech is achieved by persons of very different temperament, personality, and capacity; and that peoples of different cultures, backgrounds, and motivations react differently to speakers. But do *not* jump to the conclusion that this variety and complexity in human relations means that any kind of behavior is acceptable. Far from it! Granting individual differences, there are certain personal qualities that will help any speaker do a better job. Students of speech have been aware of these qualities for centuries, and there is a remarkable consensus in their findings despite differences in time, place, and circumstances.

The most rewarding personal resources in speech are a compound of intellectual, emotional, moral, and social qualities. Taken together, they may describe a person of considerably more stature than many of us are likely to achieve. But this is not a fair test! If it is true that any speaker will be *more effective* to the degree he possesses these qualities, then we have established a goal worthy of our best efforts.

$$
\underbrace{\begin{Bmatrix} \text{Insight} \\ \text{Judgment} \\ \text{Imagination} \end{Bmatrix}}_{\substack{\textit{Intellectual} \\ \textit{Qualities}}} + \underbrace{\begin{Bmatrix} \text{Stability} \\ \text{Control} \\ \text{Strength} \end{Bmatrix}}_{\substack{\textit{Emotional} \\ \textit{Qualities}}} + \underbrace{\begin{Bmatrix} \text{Integrity} \\ \text{Sincerity} \\ \text{Courage} \end{Bmatrix}}_{\substack{\textit{Moral} \\ \textit{Qualities}}} + \underbrace{\begin{Bmatrix} \text{Warmth} \\ \text{Tolerance} \\ \text{Sympathy} \end{Bmatrix}}_{\substack{\textit{Social} \\ \textit{Qualities}}} = \begin{array}{l} \text{Good personal ad-} \\ \text{justment and good} \\ \text{personal relations} \\ \text{in speech} \end{array}
$$

Most of the qualities in this equation are familiar enough in your day-to-day life. But how do they affect your speech? And how can you use them to best advantage? First, let's identify them briefly, and then see how they can be made to work for you.

■ INTELLECTUAL QUALITIES.   A speaker with clear insight, good judgment, and imaginative power is well equipped intellectually. He understands his subject and how it is related to his listeners, the occasion, and himself—he has clear insight. He thinks straight and evaluates men and ideas carefully—he has good judgment.

And he is creative in coming up with new ideas—he has imaginative power and vision.

▪ EMOTIONAL QUALITIES. Even well-prepared speakers with their best intellectual powers at work may fail to do themselves justice if they lack emotional stability, control, and strength. We have all experienced frustration in speaking because we were nervous, ill-tempered, or apathetic. Emotionally stable people are objective in their reactions to potentially disturbing situations. Their emotions are disciplined. And yet they have the strength and the emotional energy enabling them to fight for important causes in which they believe deeply.

▪ MORAL QUALITIES. The moral component in your personal behavior can make or break you as a speaker. Let your listeners doubt your integrity, sincerity, or moral courage, and you will soon be without an audience. Integrity is a matter of choice—it is within the power of all of us. Sincerity means genuineness—freedom from affectation, smugness, and little conceits. It also means forthrightness and good intentions. Moral courage is the will to hold fast to your deepest convictions, even when they are unpopular. It does not call for churlishness or stubbornness, but it does call for self-respect and firmness when firmness is required.

▪ SOCIAL QUALITIES. The social qualities—warmth, tolerance, and sympathy—are closely related to your feelings and attitudes toward other people. Warmth and friendliness are relaxing, outgoing qualities that make speaking easier for you. And your listeners are likely to respond with the same attitudes. Tolerance of differences in others gets you closer to people, breaks down barriers, and wins respect and a fair hearing. Sympathy is the power of entering into the feelings of another—appreciation and understanding of the attitudes and points of view of other people, whether or not you agree with them. This is the way to close rapport between speakers and listeners.

How to Improve
Your Personal Adjustment
in Speech

We have no magic for you here. Self-improvement springs from experience, and it often is a pretty slow process. But we have seen students improve their speech immensely by acquiring better understanding of their personal resources and by learning to use them with greater sensitivity and assurance.

■ 1. SELF-APPRAISAL.   This is the first step. What kind of a person are you? What are your personal assets and liabilities as a speaker? What are your intellectual, emotional, moral, and social qualifications? How well do *you* measure up to the personal standards we have set?

We are not referring to the reflection you see when you look in a mirror. This is less important than you think. What we have in mind is what you discover when you honestly and objectively assess your strengths and weaknesses as an individual, particularly in your relations with other people. Make this appraisal a continuing process throughout your course in speech.

■ 2. COMPARE YOURSELF WITH OTHERS.   Observe the personal behavior of others when they speak. Why do you respond favorably to one speaker and not to another? What are the special strengths and weaknesses of these speakers in personal adjustment and human relations? How do these strengths and weaknesses compare with your own? Which of the speakers you have heard show the personal qualities you would most like to possess?

Cicero, in his *De Oratore,* tells the story of the young Roman, Sulpicius, who made great strides as a speaker by deliberately modeling himself after Crassus, one of the distinguished orators' of his time. Cicero cautions the student to select the best model and "to strive with all possible care to achieve the most excellent qualities of the model he has approved," without imitating mannerisms in "pose or gait" or other eccentric habits.[1]

You can often pick up valuable pointers by studying the personal qualities and adjustments of other speakers. No one wants you to make yourself a carbon copy of another speaker, however successful he may be. But to emulate the best qualities of good speakers is a way of profiting by their experience.

■ 3. ADOPT POSITIVE ATTITUDES.   Chronic self-derogation is self-defeating. Be realistic in self-appraisal, but always work with a positive image of yourself—an image of yourself at your best.

One of the surest ways to build up tension is to dwell on all the disasters that may befall you in the speech you are planning: "I might drop my notes." "Maybe she'll hang up on me." "I'd rather drop the course than give that speech." "He wouldn't possibly consider me for the job." "I just know I'll forget my lines." "I'll probably make a fool of myself."

You can't turn confidence on and off like a water faucet, but you can direct your mind to thoughts that build confidence.

■ 4. PLAN A ROLE FOR YOURSELF.   In preparing for a speech or conference, planning the disposition of your personal resources is as important as planning your case. Ask yourself these questions: What mien or bearing should I assume? What mental attitudes should I adopt toward the people and ideas involved? What emotional tone will best serve the occasion?

If you make firm decisions on these matters beforehand, you will avoid mental and emotional drifting when you begin to speak. But what is more important, you will narrow the areas in which tensions are most likely to develop.

■ 5. RELAX PHYSICALLY.   One good way to relieve emotional tension is to relax physically. This relatively simple expedient is one

---
[1] Cicero's *De Oratore*. II. XXII.

of the better ways of restoring the poise and ease essential to good personal adjustment. We will have more to say about this in Chapter 14.

■ 6. PROFIT BY EXPERIENCE.   In spite of your best efforts, you may sometimes come away from a conversation, conference, or speech with the sick feeling that you have handled yourself very poorly indeed. The best therapy for this feeling is to make an objective analysis of what went wrong, devise a careful prescription for improvement, and resolve to do better next time.

Every speech you give really consists of three speeches—the one you give in anticipation, the one you give to your audience, and the one you give to yourself on the way home. This third one is often the best of the lot, for then the pressure is off and you can profit by your mistakes while they are fresh in your mind. If you make these "third speeches" standard practice, you are likely to do better with the one that counts.

How to Improve Personal Relations with Your Audience

As you gain in experience, you will find that the personal adjustments that make life easier for you as a speaker are also well received by your hearers. In other words, the same personal qualities that help you make a good adjustment as a speaker also recommend you to your audience. If your listeners see you as a well-adjusted person—intellectually, emotionally, morally, and socially qualified—you have gone a long way toward winning their confidence. How can you capitalize on these qualifications in gaining personal acceptance?

We have four suggestions. The first is basic and fundamental. The others are special applications that will serve you in many situations.

■ 1. REVEAL YOUR BEST SELF.   Every time you speak, you make certain choices—in *what* you say and *how* you say it. Most of the visible and audible symbols you offer your listeners are within your power to control.

The list of controllable factors is endless, but here are a few of them: The subjects you choose to discuss, the emotions you display, the interpretations you make, the stories you tell, the evidence you present, your attitudes toward yourself and others, your movements and gestures, your vocal inflections, your choice of words, pronunciation, diction, and so on. Out of this welter of clues, the listener traces out his opinion of you as a person.

> . . . When an individual makes a voluntary selection of words to use in any human situation, he describes himself. To be sure, a person may recite, "Two plus two equal four" without giving himself away. But if he talks of anything more intimate than that—anything about which he has a free choice of what to say and how to say it—we do not have to listen long before we can guess what we can reasonably expect of him as a human personality.
>
> That words reveal personalities is not accidental. Language serves the purpose of giving public form to otherwise private thoughts. Words, in short, get people out into the open. They may think they are talking about something quite other than themselves—about a stranger who cuts across their lawn; or about an editorial in the morning paper; or about an educational experiment, a minister's sermon, a housing project, a strike, a radio program. But it is *they* who are doing the talking, who choose the words and the tone of voice, and who, with those words and that tone of voice, recite their own philosophy, their own attitude toward human beings and human arrangements.[2]

You *do* reveal yourself—your personal qualities—through the visible and audible symbols *you choose* to use. Unless your listeners

---

[2] Bonaro W. Overstreet, *Freedom's People.* New York and London: Harper & Brothers, 1945, pp. 60-61.

know you well, they have no other way of judging you. And you may be absolutely certain that they will size you up, whether or not you make any conscious effort to influence their judgment. We all make evaluations of other people. Sometimes we are right and sometimes we are wrong. But right or wrong, it will pay any speaker who cares about the outcome of his speech to do all he can to merit the respect and confidence of his hearers.

■ 2. Adapt to your reputation.   People have a tendency to form an opinion of a speaker before they ever hear him. They draw on a great many clues—press reports, public-relations releases, personal associations, conversations with people who know him, introductory remarks by the chairman, and so forth. This initial impression may work for or against you as a speaker.

James Brown speaks to a group on "Let the People's Voice Prevail." His argument is a solid one, yet his listeners greet it with raucous laughter. Such is the price of Brown's reputation as the Machiavelli of Siwash. But reputations work the other way too. Helen Green is known as a thoroughly democratic person. So when she defends the right of a social organization to be as exclusive as it pleases, she receives a fair hearing even though most of her listeners disagree with her position. John Jones has flown fifty missions in a Sabre-Jet and has been decorated for bravery. Even though he has a quaver in his voice, none of his listeners will question his courage.

You may discover that your reputation has followed you into your speech class. You will either have to live up to it or else live it down.

■ 3. Make a good first impression.   First impressions have a way of growing into lasting impressions. You meet a person for the first time and you make a quick appraisal of him. Once this judgment is made, you are likely to stick with it unless later evidence forces you to revise it. A speaker who makes a poor opening has to work hard to overcome this disadvantage. And one who makes a

"I want you to know how much I appreciate your asking me here tonight. I was home with a bad cold, watching the snow slosh against the windows, when your genial chairman called and . . ."

strong impression at the start can draw on this strength throughout the conference or speech.

■ 4. Give information about yourself. A speaker usually provides a certain amount of information about himself during his speech—either inadvertently or for a specific purpose. That specific purpose is often to establish himself as someone who knows what he is talking about.

You have heard speakers use remarks like these: "I have always been a friend of the farmers; I should like to take this opportunity to make my voting record on farm aid a matter of public record." "I have three sons in service and I know how vital this matter is to you." "I spent two years of my professional life in the Orient and I have seen these things for myself." "I wrote the labor platform and I have kept my promises to the working men and women of America." "You can't tell me anything about dormitory food; I've been eating it for four years."

We all issue such guarantees—both in conversation and in public speech. The very fact that we do is proof of how important this matter of personal status is both to speakers and listeners. We know that in one way or another we must establish ourselves as worthy of our listeners' attention if we hope to get a fair hearing. But remember that careful listeners will check your credentials, and a false guarantee is sure to be detected.

Points to Keep in Mind

1. The personal equation in speech is made up of intellectual, emotional, moral, and social qualities that contribute to good personal adjustment and good personal relations.

2. You can improve your own personal adjustment in speech by (a) self-appraisal, (b) comparing yourself with other speakers, (c) adopting positive attitudes, (d) planning a role for yourself, (e) relaxing physically, and (f) profiting by experience.

3. You can improve personal relations with your audience by (a) making choices that reveal your best self, (b) adapting to your reputation, (c) making a good first impression, and (d) giving information about yourself.

Exercises

1. Write an analysis and appraisal of your own personal qualifications in making a satisfactory adjustment in speech. What are your strengths and weaknesses? What special problems do you face? What steps can you take to meet these problems?

2. Write an analysis and appraisal of some speaker you admire—a speaker whose personal qualifications enable him to make effective adjustments in speech. Make a list of his special strengths—the personal qualities you admire and the ways he manages his personal resources. Conclude your paper with a list of specific suggestions for your own speaking.

3. Use the analysis in Exercise 2 as the basis for a class speech. Characterize the speaker you are discussing and explain what you believe to be the personal resources that contribute to his strength. Be specific. Give examples drawn from the speech or speeches you have heard him deliver.

4. Bring to class a published speech that exemplifies the methods a speaker uses to establish his competence on his chosen subject. You

may have to read the speech more than once to discover all the methods he uses. Read the speech to the class; then tell what methods you think the speaker has used to establish his competence.

5. Prepare a short talk in which your primary aim is to establish your competence to speak on a particular subject. Try to win your listeners' confidence without parading your qualifications. If you are describing an event, and if you were present when it occurred, say so. If you are talking about another person, tell your audience how well you know him. The important thing is to establish your right to talk about your subject, but to do so unobtrusively.

CHAPTER NINE

Listening
to
Speech

We listen to many sounds from many sources, but none has greater potential than the spoken word—the sound that admits us to the thinking and feeling of our fellow men. The ultimate rewards of all speaking are realized

through listening. We want people to listen to what we
have to say, and we want to get something out of what
others say. In this chapter we shall examine the nature
of listening and the ways in which each of us can contribute to good listening.

What Is Good Listening?

The fact that people are within hearing range of your voice does not necessarily mean that they are listening to you. They may close their ears to you, wander away, or switch the dial on their radio or television set. You may even have a captive audience—such as the fellow members of your speech class—but you can't force them to listen to you. And the minute listening stops, communication ceases—even though your voice goes on and on.

Kinds of Listening

As you gain experience as a speaker, you will discover that your audiences listen in different ways. True, any listening may be better than none at all, but there are certain kinds of listening that get the best results.

VOLUNTARY VS. INVOLUNTARY LISTENING

Some sounds we listen to by choice; others we hear whether we want to or not. Involuntary listeners seldom make a good audience. You may win an initial hearing from listeners simply by talking loudly enough for them to hear. They listen at first without really choosing to listen. But unless you succeed very quickly in capturing their interest and in making them *want* to listen, chances are they will tune you out.

"And I feel I can state without fear of contradiction . . ."

CASUAL VS. PURPOSEFUL LISTENING

A casual listener is one who gives offhand, careless, or irregular attention to what you say. He is likely to drift off unless you provide him with some good purpose for hearing you out. And remember that a purposeful listener may soon become a casual listener if you fail to recognize his purpose and help him carry it out. Casual listening is a very short step from no listening at all.

DISCIPLINED VS. MOTIVATED LISTENING

Fortunately for dull speakers, some people force themselves to listen out of courtesy, or habit, or in the hope that they may get something worth while if they work hard enough at it. And sometimes these self-disciplined listeners reap a fine harvest, because poor speakers may be able men. But much more comes through to listeners when they listen because they want to, and when they find pleasure in doing so. Motivated listening takes place when the promise of reward is great enough to command the listener's attention without his having to exercise great self-discipline.

CRITICAL VS. UNCRITICAL LISTENING

The critical listener follows the speaker's ideas carefully and thoughtfully and tries to evaluate them objectively. He is alert and keeps all his mental faculties at work. A critical audience is the best kind of audience for a speaker who knows what he is talking about and who is willing to enter his ideas in a free, competitive market where they must stand or fall on their own merits. Speakers with less confidence may be better off with less discerning listeners. In fact, some speakers even try to create an atmosphere that invites uncritical acceptance of their ideas. The motives of such speakers may be either good or bad, but the listener who yields to their efforts does so at his own risk. Uncritical acceptance may imply indifference or poor critical acumen.

COOPERATIVE VS. HOSTILE LISTENING

The cooperative listener hopes for the best from the speaker and gives him friendly attention; the hostile listener dislikes the speaker or his ideas, and makes it as rough for him as he can.

The Responsibility for Listening

A quick review of the kinds of listening will show that people are more likely to give close attention to a speaker when they *want* to hear what he has to say—when they believe he has a message of value to them. This simple fact provides a very practical criterion for determining who is responsible for good listening. If a person has some information you want very badly, you will listen when he speaks and gladly assume the responsibility for doing so. On the other hand, if the speaker is very anxious to get something across in which you are not especially interested, the burden of commanding your attention rests on him. In other words, the primary responsibility for good listening lies with the party to communication—the speaker or the listener—who stands to reap the greater gain.

Fortunately, there are many situations in which the speaker and his audience have a mutual interest in the outcome—where *both* stand to gain. Here the responsibility for good listening is shared. The speaker does his best to maintain interest and the listener does his best to follow what is being said. Mutual interest and shared responsibility are desirable goals in all communication.

Principles of Good Listening

What are the principles of good listening? Perhaps the best way of getting at these principles is to examine several situations that invite good communication.

As you read the following examples, imagine yourself first as the speaker and then as the listener.

1. The day before a final examination, the professor summarizes for his class what he regards as the highlights of the course.

2. A successful writer of mystery stories explains to a group of hopeful writers how to plot a marketable "whodunit."

3. A judge gives final instructions to conscientious jurymen who are about to bring in a verdict in a case where a man's life hinges on their decision.

4. A technician reports to other technicians the phenomenal results of an experiment that has made old methods obsolete and that will determine future procedure.

5. Alert, intelligent parents attend a popular lecture given by a professor who has favorably altered the course of their sons' or daughters' lives.

6. Men in the club car of a train pull their chairs closer as one man says, "I just heard a good one."

7. A builder explains to his carpenters a new construction method he expects to use in several homes under contract.

8. A doctor explains to a cardiac patient the adjustments he must make in order to prolong his years of usefulness.

9. Following a disastrous flood that has stripped the topsoil from miles of farm land, an engineer suggests to the owners methods of restoring fertility and of preventing another flood.

10. In a strike-threatened factory, the manager calls in a respected foreman and asks him to explain and interpret the causes of the workers' grievances as he understands them.

11. A month before an important election, the candidate of a major party speaks for the first time in your home town.

Three principles of good listening are implicit in these examples: (1) The more rewarding the outcome promises to be, the higher the quality of the listening will be. (2) Listening is best when both speaker and audience have a stake in the communication. (3) The person who stands to make the greater gain from the communication has the primary responsibility for promoting good listening.

Review our eleven examples with these three principles in mind. Answer these questions in each case: What opportunities for a useful or pleasurable experience are there? What does the listener stand to gain? What does the speaker stand to gain? Who is likely to have the greater interest? What might the speaker and listeners do to improve communication? The following pages will help you answer this last question.

What Can the Speaker Do to Achieve Good Listening?

No one is going to listen for long unless he starts out with a good reason for listening, or unless the speaker is skillful enough to provide him with such a reason. This means that the speaker must know his audience and must accommodate his remarks to it. In short, analyzing the audience and adapting to it are the speaker's best approach to good listening.

ANALYZE THE AUDIENCE

Your speech class will be your audience for most of the speaking you do in this course. You will face the same people day after day. And if you don't already know them pretty well, you soon will. But don't jump to the conclusion that your audience will always be the same just because it is made up of the same people each time you get up to speak. You may talk to them one day on "the hazards of blind dates" and the next on "the values of crop rotation." Chances are the quality of listening will be very different on these two occasions. What seems to be the same audience will react quite differently to different subjects and occasions.

Outside your speech class—now and in the years ahead—you will encounter an almost infinite variety of audiences. No two audiences are exactly alike. And the characteristics of the particular audience you happen to be addressing will guide you in adapting your speech to your listeners. Audiences differ in five important characteristics: *composition, information, attitude, participation,* and *homogeneity.*

Composition refers to the membership of your audience. How large is it—one, two, or a hundred people? What age? What sex? What is the educational level, religion, occupation, economic status, political outlook? In any given situation, you will be interested in those factors that appear to affect the receptivity of your listeners. The economic status of your audience, for example, need not even enter into your thinking if you are discussing "What we know about the moon." But it would be critically important if you were proposing a hike in corporation income taxes. The political attitudes of your listeners would obviously be important if you were campaigning for public office, but would be of little significance if you were describing the plight of our migratory waterfowl.

How much *information* do your listeners have about your subject, about you, and about the occasion? Let's say you are a member of a research team assigned to investigate a specific problem. You are all experts on the subject, know each other well, and meet together frequently and informally. You are talking to your colleagues, as you have many times in the past, to report and evaluate your findings. Compare your behavior in that situation with what it would be if you were addressing a group of people who knew little or nothing about you or your subject or each other. Clearly, your listeners (or potential listeners) may be informed, uninformed, or misinformed. It will help you as a speaker to know the informational background of your audience.

What is the *attitude* of your audience? How do your listeners regard you as a person? How do they feel toward one another? What interest do they have in what you plan to talk about? And what is their attitude toward your purpose and your stand on this subject? The attitude of your listeners may range from deep respect for you, strong group cohesiveness, keen interest in your subject, and complete acceptance of your ideas, to open hostility, rejection, disinterest, and complete disagreement.

How much opportunity does your audience have for *participation* in the proceedings? Audience participation may be overt or covert, but participate it must if there is to be any kind of listening at all. If the physical setting makes it difficult or impossible for your audience to see or hear you, there will be little or no participation—and little or no communication. Most of the remedies for this barrier to communication are within the power of the speaker to control. But audience participation may go well beyond silent responses. It may reveal itself in the form of applause, expressions of disapproval, or questions, replies, and remarks which place a member of the audience at least temporarily in the role of speaker. This kind of overt behavior may seem disruptive at the moment, but it may also lead to a dramatic improvement in the quality of listening.

Is your audience composed of people who are essentially alike or of people who have almost nothing in common? An audience of like composition, information, and attitude, and with equal opportunities for participation, is known as a *homogeneous* group. Such an audience may or may not be a good audience, but at least its members are likely to respond in a fairly similar way to what you say.

A *mixed* audience presents special problems, however. Should you try to appeal to what appears to be the majority? Or should you give special attention to a minority? Or should you diversify your approach in an attempt to hold the entire group? The answers depend mostly on your purpose and the occasion. But it's wise to make some decisions at the outset and set some goals for yourself. Otherwise you may find yourself appealing to no one at all.

ADAPT TO THE AUDIENCE

Almost everything you say and do as a speaker can be adapted to your audience—your choice of subject, your purpose, the structure and materials of your speech, your language and style, your manner of speaking, and sometimes even the time and place of your

speech. These, and many other choices, are usually yours to make. But how, you may ask, can you know what the best choice will be in each case? We already know that the best listening takes place when your audience thinks it is going to get something of value out of what you have to say. Your job, then, is to make your audience want to listen. This is where your analysis of the audience comes into play. The better you know your audience and the circumstances under which you are going to talk to them, the easier it is to command their interest and attention. The basic purpose of audience adaptation is motivated listening. There are, of course, other obvious accommodations—speaking loud enough to be heard, using language that can be understood, providing necessary information, and so forth—but the subtleties of audience adaptation are involved in this business of making your audience feel that they have an important stake in the proceedings.

We all act in response to needs, wants, desires, drives, urges, or whatever name you choose to call them by. And we listen in response to the same basic motivations, because listening is a kind of action. True, we respond to different motives in different situations, and certain motives operate more strongly in some of us than in others. That is why knowing your listeners helps you to enlist their interest. But a working knowledge of the more basic motives that affect human behavior—listening included—is part of the equipment of every effective speaker.

Other things being equal, audiences are more likely to listen if their *security, status, ambitions, affections,* and *pleasures* are related or appear to be related to the speaker's purpose.

■ SECURITY.   Some of the most powerful motives are those that spring from our desire to preserve and perpetuate ourselves. These involve both physical and psychic security—health, comfort, and freedom from danger, care, and fear. Most people identify their happiness and well-being with security. Anything that threatens their security is a matter for concern, and anything that promises them greater security is a matter of interest. By capitalizing on these con-

cerns and interests, effective speakers command the attention of their listeners.

■ STATUS.   Many of our real and fancied needs spring from our desire for social approval. What others think of us is often more important to us than we care to admit. We strive for a reputation that will give us satisfaction, compete with others for social recognition, and conform to custom in order not to lose caste. Even the nonconformist is lonesome if his aberrant behavior goes unnoticed. Many of the beliefs we profess and many of the things we want have their greatest value to us as status symbols. A pat on the back, an approving comment, or any token of recognition sincerely given will help you enlist the interest of the people to whom you speak.

■ AMBITIONS.   Most people have goals, objectives, and values that they seek as a means to self-realization and personal growth. These goals represent what we want to be and what we want to accomplish with our lives. They can be low and crass, but they can also be high and worthy. The desire to realize one's potentialities, to make something out of oneself, continues to be a strong drive in our culture. Our hopes, dreams, and ambitions may be dulled by cynicism or frustration, but the skillful speaker can energize them into powerful motives for listening.

■ AFFECTIONS.   Strong emotional attachments control our behavior in many situations. We develop these emotional bonds with people, institutions, traditions, ideals, and even with some of our material possessions. These affections explain many of our loyalties and many of our defensive and protective attitudes. They are usually rooted in long associations, familiar conditions and circumstances, and often are surrounded by nostalgic memories. Wherever the speaker's message impinges on the strong affective ties of his listeners, he will soon discover that he has to work with these ties or work around them. Our affections seldom yield to a frontal attack.

■ PLEASURE. The desire for pleasure—relaxation, release, escape—is a primary reason for listening in many situations. We often
listen to be entertained and we are held by speakers whose recommendations give promise of pleasurable rewards.

You have probably noticed, though, that motives never exist in
pure form—they are always modified and affected by countless influences. Most of the things you want for yourself are things that
you also want for others—for your family, your friends, your church,
your school, or your town, state, or country. These group-centered
motives are often even stronger than self-centered motives. A father
will risk his life to save his child, people will make sacrifices to build
a new church or synagogue, and fanatical loyalties grow up around
group symbols.

To add to the complication, motives are usually *mixed*—compounded of several of the motivations we have discussed. And these
mixed motives often contain competing elements that pull in different directions. The expression, "I have mixed feelings about that,"
is usually an indication that conflicting motives are at work.

In many cases, the motives for listening are already present in
your audience. Your job is to recognize the interests at work and to
make the most of them. If these interests do not exist, your job is to
discover the motives that can best be enlisted in your cause and to
involve them in the development of your subject. In either case, you
face a task that must be handled subtly and adroitly. Any obvious or
overly contrived attempt to capitalize on the motives of your listeners
is likely to alienate them rather than win favorable attention.

Ask yourself this question: Why should this audience want to
listen to me discuss this subject? If there is no good answer, you
had better look for another audience or another subject. If you find
the answer, you have found the motives that will serve you best.

Always remember, though, that adapting your speech to your
listeners is not the same as capitulating to them. The customer is
not always right, and you may need to tell him so point-blank at

times. A speaker who sacrifices his integrity for the sake of expediency betrays both himself and his listeners.

What Can the Audience Do to Achieve Good Listening?

The final decision on all listening is necessarily made by the listener. We can resist the best efforts of any speaker if we choose to do so. We face two questions as potential listeners: *When* should we listen? And what are the *best ways* to listen if we decide to listen at all?

WHEN SHOULD YOU LISTEN?

Almost every waking minute of every day someone is demanding that you lend him an ear. You should, and usually will, give your attention to the speakers who seem to have the most to offer. Apart from observing common courtesies, you are under no obligation to listen to every speaker in search of an audience. Choose wisely, for much of the wisdom and pleasure of life is transmitted through the spoken word. And remember that in many cases good listening is much more important to you than it is to the speaker. You may have more to gain than he has.

You will be exposed to many speeches in your course in speech. You will be the listener today and the speaker tomorrow. If you want the attention of your classmates when you speak, they have a right to expect the same of you. Not all good speakers are good listeners and not all good listeners are good speakers. Use your speech class as a means of improving both your speaking and listening skills.

HOW SHOULD YOU LISTEN?

There are two answers to this question: First, listen in ways that will encourage the speaker to give you his best. Second, listen in ways that will enable you to profit by the best the speaker gives you. Both efforts contribute to the same result—the best communication possible, no matter how effective or ineffective the speaker may be.

An attentive audience is an incentive to any speaker. Under most circumstances, if a speaker is worth listening to at all, it will pay you to give him a fair hearing. This does not mean that you have to make serious compromises with your own values and convictions; nor does it mean that you have to put up with incompetence. If and when your best listening efforts fail to bring rewards, then is the time to tune the speaker out.

In listening to a speaker for the first time, try to size him up as a person and assess his ideas carefully. Guard against being taken in by a superficially attractive manner. But don't be too niggardly with your listening energies, or else you will deny yourself the counsel of able men and women who do not happen to be very prepossessing.

Critical listening also demands skill in analysis—the ability to perceive a speaker's purpose, his main points, and how he develops them. Here is the first test of critical listening: Do you know *what* has been said? Then ask yourself this question: Does it *make sense?* This second step involves judgment, interpretation, and evaluation. Every word of advice that we give to you as a speaker in this book will help you as a listener as well. If you know what makes good speech, you will be a far more intelligent consumer of speech.

Points to Keep in Mind

1. The best kind of listening is *voluntary, purposeful, motivated, critical,* and *cooperative.*

2. The best listening is achieved when (a) the speech holds promise of a rewarding outcome, (b) when both speaker and listener have a stake in the communication, and (c) when the person who stands to make the greater gain assumes active responsibility for good listening.

3. The speaker can help to achieve good listening by analyzing his audience and adapting to it in ways that motivate listening.

4. The listener can promote good communication by giving the speaker thoughtful attention.

Exercises

1. Plan a group discussion on a question that has evoked great public interest: a trial, a strike, a prison riot, a crime, a legislative proposal. Find out all you can about the event beforehand. But in the discussion concentrate on the *people* who were involved in it. Try to see through their eyes what happened. Try to find out all you can about the backgrounds and conditioning that motivated them. Your purpose here is not to evaluate their motives but to understand them.

2. Bring to class two or three "human-interest" news items—stories about people who caught the public eye for a moment because they did something unusually kind, amusing, stupid, or bizarre. Tell or read the stories and analyze *why* the behavior of these people attracted attention. Can you find any clues to the motives that led the people to act as they did?

3. Select two speeches directed to a nation-wide audience by a public official. Have all members of the class analyze them. What did the speaker try to accomplish? What motives did he appeal to? Did he appeal to them directly or obliquely? Did he choose the right appeals for his purpose? Organize a class discussion based on the analyses.

4. Each member of the class presents a five-minute speech designed to explain how something is done that involves a fairly complex process or method. You are trying to teach the class how to master the process. When you have finished, question members of the class to test how well they grasp and understand what you have said.

5. Think of an audience that you know well. Prepare a speech for this audience that will impose heavy demands on you if you are to capture its interest and win it over to your point of view. Deliver your talk to the class; but before you speak, ask the class members to "become" the audience you have in mind. Describe your hypothetical

listeners in detail. Let members of the class ask you further questions so that they will have a clear idea of the audience you are aiming at. After you have given your talk, have the class members discuss how well they think you have succeeded.

CHAPTER TEN

The
Content
of Speech

Allll speech is made up of facts, opinions, and the interpretations of facts and opinions. They may grow out of ordinary human experience or out of special fields such as economics, science, religion, and art. Obviously a course in

126

speech cannot teach you the mysteries of sociology or law. But it can show you how to talk sense on any topic from these or other areas of knowledge. Above all, talking sense demands the ability to make accurate, reliable, and convincing statements.

Facts

Facts are distinct items that we can verify. Facts are objective (they are based on reality), and, like sound money, they are negotiable. Facts are not created. They simply exist. They may be discovered by anyone who cares to look for them and who knows how and where to look. Facts are impersonal. We cannot talk them into or out of existence. Facts are not determined by majority agreement. Whole families have been wiped out because they mistook toadstools for mushrooms.

Most of us like to think that we "face the facts." We hear people exclaim with a ring of pride, "I have the facts" or "Let's look at the record!" Since most of us want to talk facts, it is fair to ask: How do we decide what are the facts and what are not? How do we know who has the facts? Here are some ways of checking up on alleged facts.

■ Is the alleged fact consistent with human nature and experience?   It is hard to believe that a small child fatally injured a grown man by striking him with his fist, or that a drug addict was completely cured by a five-day jail sentence. Whenever you offer a factual claim that seems to defy human nature and normal experience, be sure to double-check it before you use it; and if you do use it, be prepared to give an explanation that will make your claim believable. Remember, though, that what strikes us at first as being inconsistent with human nature and experience may only reflect the limitations of our own experience.

■ Is the alleged fact consistent with established facts? This is a good test for checking up on speakers who tend to make loose or exaggerated claims. If the listeners are in possession of certain established facts, they will reject alleged facts that seem to be inconsistent with what they know to be true. If we know that student X submitted an original theme to his instructor and that student Y copied portions of this theme without the knowledge or consent of X, then the charge that X was in collusion with Y cannot be sustained. Or if Brown was in Canada at the time of the State Fair, we cannot accept the claim that he attended the Fair. When such inconsistencies are pointed out, a speaker must qualify his claim, admit his mistake, or explain away the seeming inconsistency. Otherwise he will lose the respect of his listeners.

■ ARE ALL THE SPEAKER'S FACTS CONSISTENT?   Never be guilty of inconsistencies within your own remarks. A real estate promoter is trying to induce people who live in a crowded city to buy building lots in Suburbia. In one breath he claims that Suburbia possesses all the advantages of "spacious country living"; in the next breath he boasts that Suburbia is so attractive that its population has jumped from three thousand to ten thousand in three years. The wary listener, knowing the town limits of Suburbia, concludes that spacious country living and a sky-rocketing population just don't go together. The two claims are incompatible. If inconsistencies turn up in your remarks, your listeners have the right to conclude that you may be right on one claim and wrong on the other, or that you may be wrong on both; but you cannot be right on both.

■ IS THE PERSON WHO IS REPORTING THE ALLEGED FACT MENTALLY AND MORALLY QUALIFIED?   Without being wantonly suspicious or cynical, remember that prejudice, exaggeration, rumor, inaccuracy, poor memory, and downright falsification are among the facts of life. Be on guard against people who are given to loose talk or who have a motive for distorting facts. One of our most common human failings is the tendency to report only those facts that support our vital interests or that prove to be the least damaging to those interests.

■ CAN THE ALLEGED FACT BE VERIFIED?   Whether you are a listener or a speaker, verify any alleged fact that seems questionable before you adopt it. One way is to make direct observations of your own. Look, listen, or make inquiries. Which class gift do the seniors favor—a book fund or a new stage curtain? Poll the class to see what the majority wants. Has there been a trend in the last five years toward greater or smaller enrollments for our courses in logic? Check the records in the registrar's office for the answer. Did the death of Ann Rutledge drive Abraham Lincoln to the verge of suicide? Consult the authorities. Legend to the contrary, scholars such as J. G. Randall have sifted the evidence and have concluded that the impact of Ann's death upon Lincoln has been greatly exaggerated, if not fabricated.

There are three ways, then, to verify an alleged fact: make direct observations yourself, check the records, and consult the authorities.

Opinions

An opinion is some person's judgment of a matter that we are asked to accept because he is represented to us as an authority. If an opinion contains factual claims or an interpretation based on facts, we must test it just as we test facts and interpretations themselves. But here we shall talk only about strictly personal judgments that are offered without factual support or interpretation—opinions that we are asked to accept solely because the person who makes them is presumed to be an authority.

Here are some tests that you may apply to personal opinions.

▪ Is THE OPINION OFFERED BY AN EXPERT? Obviously, we have more confidence in an expert's opinion than in a layman's. But remember that an expert in one field may know little or nothing about some other field and that a layman in one subject may be an expert in another. We may accept a layman's testimony on *matters of fact,* if it stands up to the tests of facts, but we must treat his *opinions* with extreme caution in fields where expertness is required.

For example, the opinion of a distinguished atomic physicist on the amount of energy likely to be released by an atomic explosion carries great weight. But his opinion on our moral right to bomb a city might be less useful than a clergyman's or philosopher's, or no more valuable than your own. You may accept the opinion of an automobile mechanic on the condition of your car without asking his advice on the care of your teeth.

■ How does your audience feel about the expert you are citing? If you offer the opinion of an expert in support of a point, your listeners must agree that he is really an expert. If he is unknown to them, or if his qualifications are doubtful, be prepared to establish his competence. Show that his training, position, and experience qualify him to speak with authority.

■ Is the opinion being offered as a substitute for facts? Most of us prefer facts to opinions—when we can get them and if we can understand them. But sometimes we must get along without them. The facts may be so technical or complicated that we simply can't grasp them. For example, a building contractor asks you for a quick decision on the kind and amount of wall insulation to use in the house he is building for you. You race to the library and desperately try to evaluate technical reports on experiments with rock wool, aluminum foil, and other insulating materials. Finally you throw in the sponge, call up a qualified engineer, describe the structure and materials of the house, and ask for his recommendation.

Always get the facts and interpret them for yourself whenever you can. But whenever it is difficult or impossible to get the facts or to understand them, make use of expert opinion. This is what you do when you accept a physician's diagnosis.

■ Is the opinion being used to confirm factual evidence? For instance, you might state the facts on athletic facilities for women at your college, draw a conclusion about the need for additional space and equipment, then cite the opinions of members of the athletic staff and of administrative officers to confirm your conclusion. Or you might begin with an expert's opinion, and then explain the factual basis for it. Either way, you strengthen your own conclusion by citing expert opinion, and your listeners have a chance to inspect the factual basis of the opinion.

■ Do THE EXPERTS AGREE?   Expert opinions are stronger and more reliable if you can show that the experts agree. If they do not agree on the important points, your listeners are likely to reserve their own opinions.

Interpretations of Fact and Opinion

Interpretations are the meanings we give to facts and opinions and the conclusions we draw from them. We make use of interpretations every day. We decide to take the dog for a walk and discover he has disappeared. When and where was he last seen? He was around an hour or so ago. Maybe another member of the family has taken him out. His leash is gone. That must be the answer. We pick up the evening paper and read about a threatened steel strike. An editorial suggests that the government is prepared to take over the plants. Is this a wise move? Can you blame the workers for asking for a wage increase with prices the way they are? On the other hand, can you expect management to absorb the wage increases without raising steel prices? You recall an article in a journal you glanced at a few days ago and pick it up to see what it has to say on inflation.

So on it goes. All these interpretations are based on inferences. We think or reason our way to conclusions from facts, or what we take to be facts, and opinions. In order to draw sound conclusions of our own and weigh the conclusions offered by others, we need to be able to identify several types of inference and to test their validity.

GENERALIZATION

A generalization is a conclusion that we reach on something common to a whole group of things after we have examined a good sample of the group. Speech abounds with generalizations. In fact, our daily life would be completely disorganized unless we generalized from our experiences and then acted according to our generalizations. When you eat in a restaurant, you act on dozens of tacit generalizations—that public buildings are safe, that restaurants do not put poison in their food, that public eating places are reasonably sanitary, and so forth. Here are just a few generalizations that came up in a single conversation: Country living is more healthful and wholesome than city living; the University Theatre produces the best plays in this area; football players are subsidized; labor leaders lack a social conscience; the food in England is terrible.

These examples show how often we use generalizations, and they suggest the danger of making hasty generalizations. Some of our examples appear to be false generalizations, and every one of them is open to exceptions. How can you draw generalizations that are safe and useful? Here are some tests.

■ HAVE YOU EXAMINED ENOUGH SAMPLES?   Our confidence is quickly undermined when we hear a speaker draw sweeping, general conclusions that have little or no basis in fact. You are sitting in on a bull session with four or five other students. Each remarks that he is taller than his parents. So you all agree that the present generation of college students is taller than their parents. Obviously, this generalization is not based on enough samples. All sound generalizations depend on an adequate survey of the field.

■ ARE THE SAMPLES EXAMINED TYPICAL OF THE WHOLE GROUP? Often we have to generalize without having the time or the opportunity to examine very many samples. So we must be careful to base our conclusion for the whole group on typical cases. Avoid basing generalizations on exceptional or bizarre examples. Suppose you declare that foreign-made motion pictures are superior to American-made films. This conclusion is unwarranted and unfair if most of the American movies you see are class-B pictures, and if the only foreign films you know about are carefully selected for export to the United States.

▪ HAVE YOU ACCOUNTED FOR THE EXCEPTIONS? In our enthusiasm, or in our desire to make a point, we sometimes overlook the exceptions to a generalization. Suppose we assert that summer vacations are now a standard practice among all Americans. No doubt you can think of many exceptions, and you would be quite right to insist that the generalization be scaled down to fit the facts. We might say that summer vacations are a standard practice among Americans *except for* farmers and other groups who have to work through the summer; or we might say that *many* or *most* Americans enjoy a summer vacation. Better still, if the statistics were available, we might supply the *exact percentage* of Americans who take summer vacations. Almost every generalization needs to be qualified in terms of quantity, time, place, or special circumstances.

ANALOGY

An analogy is an inference based on a comparison of two items. If you can show that the two items resemble each other in all significant respects, you may infer that they resemble each other in an attribute known to belong to one but not known to belong to the other. Here are some familiar analogies: "Jane looks wonderful in that hat; I think I'll buy one." "Since the honor system works in X college, I submit it will work in Y college."

Apply the following tests to analogies before you accept them as valid:

▪ ARE THE CASES ALIKE IN ALL ESSENTIAL RESPECTS? This is the key test. The success of the honor system in X college (and this must first be established) is no guarantee that it will succeed in Y college if Y college has different traditions, is much larger and more impersonal, and has a different kind of student body and curriculum. Jane's appearance in her new hat (she may look wonderful with or without any hat) says nothing about how another person will look in the same hat.

■ HAVE SIGNIFICANT DIFFERENCES IN THE CASES BEEN AC-COUNTED FOR? If you discover such differences, you must either show that they do not affect your conclusion, or else qualify your conclusion. Suppose both X and Y are liberal arts colleges, endorse the same values and codes, enroll the same number of students, draw students from the same kinds of homes, and so forth. However, one is a school for men, the other for women. You will have to show that this difference fails to impair your conclusion—that Y college too should adopt the honor system.

CAUSAL RELATIONS

In establishing a causal relationship, we try to show the probable cause for some known event or condition, or we try to predict the effect of some event, condition, or proposal. We speak of the first of these two methods of interpretation as reasoning from a *known* effect to an *alleged* cause. The following questions will help you test this method.

■ DID THE ALLEGED CAUSE ACTUALLY CONTRIBUTE TO THE KNOWN EFFECT? This is the first and most elementary test. Often the actual cause is obscure and lies below the surface. Did the men really strike because of poor working conditions? They knew that improvements had been made and that others had already been contracted for. Don't jump to hasty conclusions. Analyze the problem and scrutinize all possible causes. People often draw hasty and therefore ill-founded conclusions. You are hardly convinced when someone tells you that the pain in your side is caused by your appendix when you know it was removed years ago. The wrong cause is offered to explain an effect. When you hear comments such as these, you know this test is being applied: "No, it can't be the fan belt; I just had a new one put in." "Surely it's not lack of water; why, I watered the plant every day!"

▪ Is the alleged cause the whole cause of the known effect? Don't try to explain an effect by a cause that is only *partially* responsible for it. Sometimes we hear a man's poverty charged to his laziness when, in fact, poor health and lack of opportunity may have contributed to it. Whenever a known effect seems "too big" to be explained by the "little" cause assigned to it, treat the explanation with caution.

▪ Is the alleged cause too general and vague to explain the known effect? If the known effect is too "little" for the "big" cause assigned to it, look for a more specific cause. To say that Frankie's misbehavior at school is caused by a wave of juvenile delinquency sweeping the nation fails to tell us much about Frankie's problems. This alleged cause, even if it is remotely true, is too big, and too far removed from Frankie's immediate difficulties to help us straighten him out.

Now let's reverse the process. We have a *known cause* and we want to predict what effect it will have. This is what we usually do whenever we explain, defend, or attack a proposed course of action (offered as a known cause). For example, perhaps someone urged you to attend college because a college education would broaden your outlook, enable you to meet interesting people, or increase your earning power (alleged effects). A plea to lower our tariff schedules might be urged in the interest of "trade not aid," world economic stability, and world peace (alleged effects); the same plea might be challenged on the grounds that it would lower wage rates for American laborers, dislocate industry, and lead to inferior products.

Apply these tests to interpretations based on cause-to-effect reasoning:

▪ Is the known cause sufficient to produce the alleged effect? Will insulating my house reduce my heating costs by two hundred dollars a year? Will eating Wheaties make me a champion? This is a good test to apply to many of the claims of enthusiastic promoters and salesmen. Never mistake a half-truth for a whole truth.

■ WILL THE KNOWN CAUSE PRODUCE EFFECTS OTHER THAN THOSE ALLEGED? Even if insulating my house will save me money in the long run, its immediate effect may be to throw me into bankruptcy. Certain proposals for federal aid to education may mean better educational facilities as claimed, but they may also mean increased federal control of education. Try to discover *all* possible effects, good or bad, before you commit yourself.

■ ARE THE ALLEGED EFFECTS TOO VAGUE TO BE CONVINCING? "Turn the rascals out and return to good times" is a familiar political theme. Because the times are always a little upset in our imperfect world, this slogan appeals to disgruntled and undiscriminating voters. But before you accept as probable outcomes the general claims that are made for or against a proposition, reduce them to specific items. In politics, this would mean reviewing a candidate's position on definite issues.

CORRELATIVE RELATIONS

Correlative relations are simply implied relations between two or more items. You take the presence or absence of one as an *indication* of the presence or absence of the other. You take the familiar red and white barber pole as a sign of a barber shop. You interpret dark clouds to mean wind or rain. An open front door is taken to mean that someone is home. Rainy weather on election day is sometimes taken as a sign that the rural vote will be light.

As with other methods of interpretation, we must test the reliability of the correlative relations that we hear and use.

■ IS THE KNOWN ITEM A CERTAIN SIGN OF THE ALLEGED ITEM? How close, how sure, how constant is the relationship attributed to the two items? We can answer these questions only after making close and repeated observations. If we're looking for a barber shop,

"I didn't catch the title of Mr. Colby's speech, but I think it's probably something about Christmas."

we may head for the red and white pole with confidence. Less convincing are these inferences: "If he's so smart, why isn't he rich?" "The food must be good here; the prices are high enough." Unless you have made enough observations to support a firm correlative relationship, qualify your conclusions, present them tentatively, and act on them with caution.

■ Is the relationship between the two items real or accidental? Many superstitions and old wives' tales collapse under this test. Try it on these: Misfortune will stalk you if a black cat crosses your path. Potatoes should be planted during a certain phase of the moon. A horseshoe nailed above the door brings good luck.

Racial bigotry and prejudice thrive on accidental relationships. No race or creed is exempt from undesirable members, and thoughtful people are not easily duped by accidental associations. Yet it is tragically true that many people who are usually cautious seize upon the frailest kind of relationship when their prejudices are threatened.

■ Have special factors entered in to alter normal relations? Black clouds probably mean rain *if* the wind is in the northeast. The party would have been well attended *if* the invitations had gone out on time. The deal was practically in the bag *until* his wife stepped in. Unforeseen conditions often upset what we would normally expect. The older we grow, the more we realize that few signs are absolutely reliable. So we should try to anticipate

138

as best we can the factors that might upset relationships between signs and that might destroy the conclusions we are tempted to draw or to accept uncritically.

Points to Keep in Mind

Facts, opinions, and interpretations of facts and opinions are the raw materials of speech.

1. Before you accept an alleged fact, find out if it agrees with nature and experience, if it agrees with other facts, and if it comes from a reliable source.

2. If you can't find or understand the facts you need, turn to the opinions of authorities. Be sure your "authorities" are really experts on the subject.

3. Keep close watch on generalizations. Be sure that they are properly qualified and are based on a sufficient number of typical cases or items.

4. When you draw an analogy, see to it that the cases are essentially alike and that important differences are explained.

5. In reasoning from a known effect to an alleged cause, make sure that the "cause" actually did produce the effect.

6. In reasoning from a known cause to a probable effect, make sure that the effect is really likely and that it will not carry along with it undesirable effects.

7. Be cautious about accepting a conclusion based on correlative relationships. First find out if the presence of one factor indicates the presence or absence of a second one. And be sure there's no third factor that will upset things.

Exercises

1. Prepare a short talk in which you offer at least three alleged facts and their sources. Go to some length to inform your audience why

you have confidence in your sources. Maintain an attitude of inquiry. When you have completed your speech, remain facing the group until everyone has had the privilege of questioning you about the sources. Respect the efforts of your questioners to assess further the reliability of your sources. This exercise should encourage critical thinking on the part of all, including yourself.

2. Begin to keep a list of statements alleging facts that raise some doubt in your mind. You will find such statements readily in conversation, public speeches, or printed material. You will come up with a long, heterogeneous list, including statements made by your best friends and other members of the class.

Apply the five tests of facts offered in this chapter and present your analysis of the statements to the class. Avoid giving names that might embarrass anyone. Call on other members of the class to assess your analysis of the statements. Remember, this class hour is not spent with the object of reaching any conclusions except on the factual acceptability of the statements themselves.

3. Use as the basis of this talk a news story, an editorial, a magazine article, or an advertisement to which you take exception because of (a) the alleged facts or the omission of facts; (b) the opinions offered in behalf of the contention or claim; or (c) the interpretations made of alleged facts and opinions. In your speech, you will report the claim or contention that is made, tell what support is offered in its behalf, and enter your objections on one or more of the grounds suggested above.

4. Choose as your subject for a talk some problem about which you have limited knowledge and no settled opinion. It may be a problem in politics, sociology, international relations, medicine, architecture, literature, agriculture—any field. You have neither the time at the moment nor the background to undertake a thorough-going study of the problem, but you do want guidance from people who offer credentials for writing and speaking about it. Look up some articles and speeches presented by people who seem to write and speak as authorities on the matter. Then find out all you can on the qualifications of these people. What tentative conclusions are you prepared to draw about the subject based on the several opinions and their sources? Report your findings and conclusions to the class.

5. Prepare and present a talk in which you develop your subject *primarily* by means of *one* of the four methods of interpretation: generalization, analogy, causal relations, or correlative relations. Most of us use all these methods in our daily speech, but this time you are to concentrate on one method. Make your inferences as tight and invulnerable as you can. After you have spoken, ask the class to (a) identify the method of interpretation you employed, and (b) apply the appropriate tests of inference listed in this chapter.

6. Analyze the printed text of a recent speech. Identify statements of alleged fact, opinion, and interpretation of fact and opinion. Which predominate? After testing these statements, are you prepared to accept or reject the speaker's conclusions? Did you detect any significant fallacies? Present a written or oral report of your findings.

7. For this exercise, select the printed text of a speech by which the speaker won your confidence because of his respect for facts, his discriminating use of opinions, and his sound interpretations of facts and opinions. Offer it to the class as a model of straight thinking. Briefly review the speech as a whole for the class, point out its merits, and read portions of the speech to illustrate and enforce your conclusions about it.

CHAPTER ELEVEN

Developing
Your
Ideas

F acts, opinions, and interpretations may speak
for themselves. More commonly, they need to
be amplified. It is a *fact* that thousands of families on "the wrong side of the tracks" live in
crowded, poorly ventilated, substandard hous-

ing; but this fact becomes far more meaningful if you can tell a vivid, first-hand story of the plight of one of these families.

Ideas gain power through clarity, warmth, color, and human interest.

Development by Definition

Define important terms that may be unfamiliar to your listeners or that may be misunderstood. No one should take liberties with well-established meanings, but when a term has several possible meanings, make clear the one you are using.

A definition establishes boundary lines. It places a term in a general class or category, and then shows how the term differs from other members of the class. If you can offer an example or two that further pinpoints your meaning, so much the better.

Suppose you wanted to define the word *manslaughter*. You might say, "Manslaughter means killing another human being without malice. If someone kills a person in self-defense or through reckless driving, he may be charged with manslaughter but not murder." Here you place manslaughter within a category of actions called killing. Immediately you draw distinctions, pointing out that manslaughter is limited to the killing of human beings, not other forms of life. And you add that it must be done without malice, which distinguishes it from murder. Finally, you offer two examples of killing under circumstances that warrant the charge of manslaughter.

Often we need to define our terms with great precision. Other times we wish only to highlight an already familiar term by throwing out a few points of reference that will help your listeners catch the special sense and importance you attach to it. Notice the somewhat satirical vein in which Robert M. Hutchins, formerly president of the University of Chicago, sets forth his conception of a university. Notice too how he first classifies his term, then separates it from other "communities."

> A University is a community of scholars. It is not a kindergarten; it is not a club; it is not a reform school; it is not a political party; it is not an agency of propaganda. A University is a community of scholars.[1]

---

[1] *Vital Speeches*, May 20, 1935, p. 547.

Development by Example

An example is a *specific case in point* that supports or explains a general statement. "Give me an example," your listeners say. There are *real* examples and *hypothetical* examples. A *real* example is an actual case that can be documented. A *hypothetical* example is one you create for the occasion.

In the following excerpt from a speech by William G. Carleton, note the six real examples that he uses to support his general point.

> The truth is that the people of Britain and France realize that the age of imperialism is over, and they have been steadily yielding to the anti-imperialist revolutions. . . . The British yielded gracefully when they withdrew from India and Burma, which had constituted the very heart of the old British Empire. Since World War II, the French have withdrawn from Lebanon, Syria, Tunisia and Morocco. . . .[2]

In this instance, the listeners were familiar with the examples, and the speaker had only to name them to make his point.

Some examples, however, need to be developed in detail before they become convincing. Observe how Frederick Mayer uses a single example to give impact to his point.

> I can think of one of my students as a freshman. She was a replica of Middle-Town, a product of what Sinclair Lewis described in *Babbitt*. She called Plato—Pluto. Her spelling was atrocious. Her first test was chaos roughly organized. Her taste in music was influenced by Elvis Presley. Three years later she is reading Kafka, Thomas Mann, and Gide. She has just written a superb essay on Albert Camus. . . . She is a different person today—alive, vibrant, idealistic. This shows what education can do.[3]

---

[2] *Vital Speeches,* January 15, 1959, p. 211.
[3] *Ibid.,* April 15, 1959, p. 414.

Sometimes an entire speech is developed through a single master-example. One student, arguing that it is possible for a small town to have a lively cultural life, based her entire speech on the example of a small town in Colorado. She recounted in detail how the residents stimulated community interest in literature, theater, and painting, and the resourceful means they used to bring an occasional artist and writer with national standing to their town.

In the following quotation from an address by Oscar E. Ewing, on "What Health Insurance Would Mean To You," all the examples are hypothetical. Not one actual case is cited. All are introduced by "suppose" or "if."

> Good evening. I want to talk to you tonight, not about the nation's health, but about your own health. Suppose that tomorrow morning, you should become suddenly ill—seriously ill. Suppose you found that you needed an operation, with special medical care, and all kinds of x-rays and drugs. Suppose you had to stop working for some months while you went through your operation and your convalescence. Suppose the doctor's bill, the hospital bill, the bills for special laboratory services and medicines, added up to hundreds of dollars—maybe even thousands. Would you be able to afford it? . . .
>
> If you have been lying in a hospital bed after an operation, worrying about where the money to pay the bills would come from, you know what I mean. If you have had to go to a loan company and borrow money to pay a hospital bill, you know what I mean. If you had ever received a note from your child's school, telling you that your little boy or your little girl needs adenoids or tonsils out, and wondered how you'd pay for it, you know what I mean. . . .[4]

Hypothetical examples are not always used this effectively, though. Most people prefer real examples because they are authentic. If you make up too many examples, the listener is apt to con-

---

[4] *Vital Speeches,* May 15, 1952, p. 478.

clude that real examples do not exist or that you do not have any at hand. When used skillfully, hypothetical examples vividly dramatize reality and call up real examples in your listeners' minds.

Development by Statistics

An example is *one* case in point. Statistics are a shorthand method of summarizing a large number of examples.

BE ACCURATE IN HANDLING STATISTICS

■ KNOW THE MEANING OF THE UNIT YOU USE. Statistics can be misleading unless you define your terms carefully. Suppose a university reports an enrollment of 5,000 students. Does that mean full-time students, or are part-time students included? If a student is registered in two different divisions, is he counted once or twice? In other words, the unit "student" must be defined before the statistics can be interpreted reliably.

■ BASE YOUR STATISTICS ON A FAIR SAMPLE. Offhand, it might seem that the records of a college health service should accurately reveal the incidence of common diseases among students. But if you investigate, you might find that commuting students seldom use the health service, and that even resident students go to their family physicians when they are seriously sick. As a result, the health-service records alone do not give you an accurate picture. Statistics must be based on a sufficient number of representative cases if they are to be reliable.

■ ESTABLISH THE STABILITY OF THE UNIT IN MAKING STATISTICAL COMPARISONS. Statistics compiled at one time and place may seem to be based on the same unit as those compiled at another time or place. A comparison of 1890 statistics on cancer with those compiled 70 years later might make it appear that the incidence of cancer is increasing. Actually it may mean merely that we now identify cancer more accurately. A fund-raiser for a political campaign pointed out that the cost of Lincoln's campaign for the presidency in 1860 was $100,000. Today a half-hour of TV time for political campaigning on a national network costs this much. Granted, the cost of political campaigning has skyrocketed, but the comparison is misleading because the dollar has depreciated in value.

■ BE SURE THAT YOUR STATISTICS MEASURE WHAT THEY SAY THEY MEASURE.   If you are reporting on the real income of wage-earners, statistics that give their income in dollars might be deceptive, since "real income" means dollars translated into things the worker buys. If women have fewer automobile accidents than men, can you conclude without question that women are better drivers? Or could it mean that women drive fewer miles than men, and that they drive in places and at times when accidents are less likely to happen?

USE STATISTICS SPARINGLY AND SKILLFULLY

A blanket of statistics may smother your listeners, particularly if the statistics are highly complex. Translate statistics into concrete items that your audience can grasp. In the statement below, C. Langdon White reduces to human terms complicated data on the land-population ratio.

> Taking the world as a whole, there is only one acre of arable land available to each person and even in the United States only three acres per head. If the world population continues to increase at the present rate—that is, unchanged in 600 years— there will be only one square yard of land surface per capita. This "standing room" figure takes into account more than arable land; it includes all land—polar wastes, deserts, jungles, mountain tops, as well as available living space.[5]

[5] *Vital Speeches*, May 15, 1959, p. 462.

Use round figures when you can compare them strikingly to make your point. For example, in the year 1800 there were 900,000,-000 people in the world; in 1959, the figure had grown to approximately 2,760,000,000; and the best estimates are that by 2050 the population of the world will be between 9,000,000,000 and 13,-000,000,000. It may be more efficient and effective to convert figures into percentages. For example, to say that 20 per cent of the students are commuters may be more effective than giving the actual number.

Use statistics dramatically if you can do so without distorting them. The following "stix" story (so-called because it is designed to make statistics stick!) is an example:

> The first printing of the Revised Standard Version of the Holy Bible was 970,000 copies. These Bibles—each 1½ inches thick—stacked in one pile would tower 24 miles into the stratosphere—higher than 100 Empire State Buildings.[6]

Development by Illustration

Although the word "illustration" is popularly used to cover many methods of developing ideas, we used it here to mean an extended comparison between two things drawn from quite different fields. An idea that is unfamiliar or doubtful is more likely to be accepted when it is compared with something your listener knows or feels confident about.

In one of his fireside chats, Franklin D. Roosevelt sought to interpret the nature of the New Deal at a time when it really was new, and to counter charges that it was revolutionary. He used an illustration to assure the people that the New Deal was wholly consistent with the American political tradition.

> While I am away from Washington this summer, a long-needed renovation of and addition to our White House office building is to be started. The architects have planned a few new

---

[6] Bernard Kalb, in *The Saturday Review*, December 20, 1952, p. 8.

rooms built into the present all too small one-story structure. We are going to include in this addition and in the renovation modern electric wiring and modern plumbing and modern means of keeping the offices cool in hot Washington summers. But the structural lines of the old Executive office building will remain. The artistic lines of the White House buildings were the creation of master builders when our Republic was young. The simplicity and the strength of the structure remain in the face of every modern test. But within this magnificent pattern, the necessities of modern government business require reorganization and rebuilding.

If I were to listen to the arguments of some prophets of calamity who are talking these days, I should hesitate to make these alterations. I should fear that while I am away for a few weeks the architects might build some strange new Gothic tower or a factory building or perhaps a replica of the Kremlin or of the Potsdam palace. But I have no such fears. The architects and builders are men of common sense and of artistic American tastes. They know that the principles of harmony and of necessity itself require that the building of the new structure shall blend with the essential lines of the old. It is this combination of the old and the new that marks orderly peaceful progress, not only in building buildings but in building government itself.[7]

The value of an illustration lies in its suggestive power. It should never be offered or taken as a literal or complete demonstration of a point.

Development by Stories

We recount anecdotes and tell stories for pleasure, and we use them to cinch points. Some of these stories we draw from personal experiences, literature, or history; others we create to point up some true-to-life situation. A well-

---

[7] Fireside chat, "Reviewing the Achievements of the Seventy-Third Congress," June 28, 1934.

told story is one of the most effective means of kindling interest and dramatizing ideas. In a speech called "Awake the Dawn," Bishop Gerald Kennedy uses several well-placed stories to highlight ideas and strengthen points. Here is one example:

> The late Bishop Francis J. McConnell was once president of DePauw University. He always liked to be on the land, and after retirement he lived on a farm in Ohio. When he was at DePauw he had a small acreage where he raised chickens. He said that everything went all right except in the middle of the night the rooster would start to crow and wake everybody up. He could not understand this behavior so he stayed up one night to find out the trouble. He said that along about two o'clock in the morning, the interurban train coming out from Indianapolis would swing around a curve, and the headlight would shine into the chicken house. The rooster, thinking it was the sun, would begin to crow. And the bishop said, "It is not only roosters that mistake headlights for dawns." Indeed it is not! If men can sometimes bring the darkness, so sometimes in their pride and in their limited knowledge they can promise dawns which never come, and bring disillusionment.[8]

The value of a story, of course, may be more apparent than real. Be on guard against stories that oversimplify and that substitute a pleasant, facile explanation for rigor and accuracy. And unless you speak merely to entertain, your story must bear sharply on the point. You may have heard listeners remark, "I became so interested in his story that I missed the point he was trying to make."

Development by Quotations

Quotations may be drawn from anything in the vast reservoir of human expression—from history, literature, biography, technical reports, newspapers,

---

[8] A. Craig Baird, ed., *Representative American Speeches: 1956-1957.* New York: The H. W. Wilson Company, 1957, p. 185.

speeches, conversations. Apt statements by somebody else may lend weight to your own views, or may simply be more impressive, beautiful, or amusing than anything you can devise. A quotation loses its value though if it is laboriously dragged in or is too long. Make it clear that you are quoting and from whom you have taken your material.

Dr. J. Martin Klotsche uses many short quotations in his speech "On Being an Educated Person." Through these borrowed statements he sets forth with great economy a variety of views on education. Here is a small sample:

> A former distinguished professor of the faculty of the University of Wisconsin once defined an educated person as one "who tries to understand the whole of knowledge as well as one man can." Mark van Doren held that the purpose of education is to see that "each man becomes more than he is," while William Whewell thought of education as the means "to connect a man's mind with the general mind of the human race." [9]

Development by Maxims, Proverbs, and Slogans

A maxim is a general statement of principle, advice, or counsel on human conduct and affairs expressed in tight, epigrammatic form. To be effective, a maxim must suggest its idea with memorable deftness. Here are a few examples:

> An Englishman is the unfittest person on earth to argue another Englishman into slavery. (*Edmund Burke*)

> Men may be sorely touched and deeply grieved in their privileges as well as in their purses. (*Edmund Burke*)

> Error of opinion may be tolerated where reason is left free to combat it. (*Thomas Jefferson*)

[9] *Vital Speeches*, August 1, 1957, p. 635.

It is better to work on institutions by the sun than by the wind. (*Ralph W. Emerson*)

Only a people who can achieve the moral mastery of themselves can hope to win the moral leadership of others. (*Adlai Stevenson*)

Self-criticism is the secret weapon of democracy, and candor and confession are good for the political soul. (*Adlai Stevenson*)

A *proverb,* as distinguished from a maxim, is a short, pithy saying that expresses a widely accepted truth based on common sense and practical experience. Proverbs are part of the folk-wisdom of a people. Benjamin Franklin's counsels, offered as the words of Poor Richard, are examples:

He that falls in love with himself will have no rivals.
'Tis hard for an empty bag to stand upright.
If you'd have it done, go; if not, send.

A word of warning: Use proverbs and maxims sparingly. Your speech will sound stuffy if you use too many, particularly if your advice is premature or unwelcome.

A *slogan* is a short, catchy statement used as a rallying point by a person, group, or party. Some slogans have undeniable social value, such as "The life you save may be your own" or "Help fight cancer with a check-up and a check." But slogans that boost products and services are often half-truths designed to beguile the unwary. However valid, a slogan soon becomes trite and loses its appeal.

Development by Repetition

When you are reading a book or a magazine, you can flip back through the pages to refresh your memory on a point. You do about the same thing for your listeners when you repeat in new ways what you have said before.

By coming back to an idea again and again, you give it a chance to sink in; you underline and clarify it.

Theodore Roosevelt was a master of the art of *meaningful* repetition. On April 14, 1906, he spoke on "The Man with the Muck-Rake," in which he recalled the man in Bunyan's *Pilgrim's Progress* "who could look no way but downward, with the muck-rake in his hand; who was offered a celestial crown for his muck-rake, but who would neither look up or regard the crown he was offered, but continued to rake to himself the filth of the floor." From this allegory, Roosevelt drew his theme: that dishonest men in public and private life should be exposed, but indiscriminate muck-raking dulls the public conscience and benefits the scoundrels. In various ways, Roosevelt restates this theme, repeating it over and over again, dinning it into public consciousness.

Avoid needless repetition, of course. And when you do repeat a point, find new ways of putting it.

Development by Visual and Auditory Aids

Visual and auditory aids include charts, maps, graphs, diagrams, outlines, pictures, cartoons, posters, lantern slides, moving pictures, models, tape-recorders, and objects used in demonstrations. These aids are particularly useful in teaching and in other types of informative speaking. In fact, a great deal of our conversation takes place in sight of the objects we

"Right here is where the boss made me his private secretary."

are talking about. Television has an advantage over radio not only because the speakers can be seen as well as heard, but because they can use visual aids to supplement the spoken word.

Here are suggestions for your use of aids:

■ 1. LET THE AIDS SUPPLEMENT YOUR WORDS. Ask yourself, "Will visual and auditory aids help me achieve my purpose?" If so, use them. Fortunately, many ingenious devices are available. If you cannot find just what you want, home-made devices are well worth the time and effort spent in getting them together.

But don't drag in visual and auditory aids for their own sake. If your listeners conclude that you are simply parading a set of gimmicks, you will lose their respect as well as their interest. The best advice is this: Don't overload your speech with aids and never use them as mere "fill-in."

■ 2. MAKE SURE THAT YOUR AUDIENCE CAN SEE YOUR VISUAL AIDS WITHOUT STRAINING THEIR EYES. "That should be obvious," you say. True. But many speakers still hold up a chart the size of a postage stamp and expect their audience to study it. If for some reason you can't arrange for maps, charts, diagrams, graphs, or pictures that are large enough to display, then have them duplicated and passed out to your audience.

■ 3. KEEP YOUR AIDS SIMPLE AND EASY TO GRASP. The story is told of an "inventor" who created a wonderful machine that would do the work of five men; but it took six men to operate it. Some visual aids are just about as useful. If it takes more time and ingenuity for you to explain a chart than it would to explain the point you are trying to make, everyone will be happier if you skip the chart. The point of your exhibit must emerge quickly and easily, or else be lost.

■ 4. SYNCHRONIZE YOUR AIDS WITH YOUR REMARKS. To be effective, visual aids must become visible at exactly the moment they are needed. We have all seen lecturers who competed for attention with their own devices. They make the mistake of handing out charts, pictures, graphs, and the like before such aids are needed. As a result, the audience's attention is distracted from the speaker's words.

■ 5. HAVE YOUR AIDS IN WORKING ORDER.   Have you ever suffered along with a speaker who tried to use electrical gadgets that would not operate, lantern slides that were unnumbered or mixed up or upside down, maps that fell down, or demonstration kits that lacked an essential component? The strange thing is that some people seem not to learn very much from their own lack of preparation. Check up on things beforehand.

Points to Keep in Mind

Present your facts, opinions, and interpretations so that they will come through to your listeners with clarity and impact.

1. Define all unfamiliar or ambiguous terms of any importance.

2. Should your listeners need a "for instance," be prepared to provide them with real or convincing hypothetical examples.

3. When you introduce statistics, be sure they are reliable and readily understandable.

4. An illustration will help your audience translate the unfamiliar into the familiar.

5. A human-interest story dramatizes a point.

6. A quotation is useful if it lends authority to your ideas or if it expresses a point more effectively than you can state it.

7. Well-chosen maxims, proverbs, and slogans serve to drive your points home.

8. Repeating your main ideas in new ways helps to clarify and instill them in your listeners' minds.

9. Use visual and auditory aids to supplement your speech whenever they are needed.

Exercises

1. Choose a term about whose meaning your audience is likely to be a bit fuzzy. Define the term. Then go on to clarify it further with an example or two, an illustration, a story, or a visual aid. For instance, take your listeners into a corner grocery, figuratively speaking, and show them how the law of supply and demand (an abstraction) actually works. Terms such as cubism, thermodynamics, agronomy, socialism, semantics, neurosis, and group dynamics make good subjects for this talk.

2. We call this exercise the "Master-Example Speech." Spend from half to two-thirds of your time developing a single example that makes the point of your speech. Don't just cite an example and then let it go at that. Be skillful in working out a full speech based on this single example.

3. Choose a subject that calls for a statistical development. Limit yourself to an aspect of some general problem such as membership in campus religious organizations today as compared with ten years ago, tuition charges, popular interest in TV programs, automobile sales, depletion of natural resources. Be mindful of all instructions for the preparation and use of statistics. A visual aid may help you present them.

4. Choose a subject that can be best developed by means of one or more auditory or visual aids. If you talk on voting machines, bring in a miniature model. Use some prints to make points about modern art. When analyzing jazz, interlace your remarks with some recorded excerpts. Work up some interesting posters to display statistical data. Plan some blackboard sketches for a talk on an architectural subject. Put into use the advice this chapter has presented on visual aids.

5. Make a place, event, institution, or process come alive through skillful description and explanation. Make your listeners see vividly

the Bingham Copper Mine, a session of the UN, the inside of a prison, or the stages in getting a cartoon from the drafting board into a newspaper.

6. There are three steps in this exercise: (a) open your talk with an example, story, or illustration that discloses your purpose; (b) develop each main point with one method listed in this chapter; (c) conclude with a maxim, proverb, slogan, or quotation.

CHAPTER TWELVE

Language
and
Style

Language is a pattern of words. Everyone has a speaking style, a characteristic way of patterning his words. But not every style is born free and equal. Many people lack verbal mobility because they are shackled by their lan-

160

guage habits. Wisdom and skill in using language open new worlds of thought, action, and human association.

In this chapter we invite you to make an appraisal of your own oral style, and we shall suggest ways that may help you use language more effectively.

Make Yourself Understood

Clarity is the first require-ment of good style. Your listeners must grasp what is being stated or asked before they can respond intelligently. Then they can take the next step—accept it, disagree with it, or disregard it, as they choose. Irwin Edman once said of Bertrand Russell, "He has the gift or the achievement of a style unfailingly lucid so that even when one disagrees with him, one knows exactly what it is with which one is disagreeing."

To establish clear lines of communication, (1) treat words as symbols, not "things"; (2) anchor your words to valid facts and thoughts; (3) practice good usage and strengthen your vocabulary; and (4) avoid saying things the hard way.

TREAT WORDS AS SYMBOLS

Words are merely sound waves that vibrate membranes of our ears, or black marks that are reflected by light waves to our eyes. Words are symbols that we endow with meaning. We should not confuse the symbol with the "thing" nor should we act toward the symbol as if meaning were inherent in it.

Words vary in the stability of the meaning we assign them. Tech-nical words used by specialists tend to be more restricted in their meaning and therefore more stable than words used in ordinary parlance. With time, most words acquire a greater range and variety of meaning. As Charles C. Fries, a distinguished language scholar, points out, The Oxford Dictionary records and illustrates from our literature 14,070 separate meanings for the 500 most commonly used words in the English language.[1]

All kinds of misunderstanding may arise when a speaker uses a word, or when a listener responds to it, as if it held exactly the same meaning for everyone. To say that a person is or is not a Christian is open to as many interpretations as there are denomina-

---

[1] Quoted by Irving J. Lee, *How to Talk With People*. New York: Harper & Brothers, 1952, p. 15.

tions and sects. "You call yourself a liberal," someone exclaims, "but you're anti-labor." Comes the angry retort, "You bet I'm a liberal, and I'm telling you that labor is the most reactionary group in the country." As the conversation warms up, we become hot champions of our labels rather than cool-headed investigators of the meaning they carry for the other fellow.

Come to an early understanding with your listeners on ambiguous terms. Be particularly careful when you use words that are abstract, that are unfamiliar, or that arouse emotions, such as the "common man," "socialism," "big business," "radical," "reactionary," "love," "existentialism," and a host of others you can think of. Avoid trouble by saying at the outset, "Now when I talk about academic freedom, I mean limited and specific things. I have in mind these priv-ileges . . . , these responsibilities . . . , for these people. . . ."

Since you can't always anticipate what words will spawn mis-understanding, be alert to signals of confusion, perplexity, or hos-tility from your listeners. Then pause to find out if they are reacting adversely to your language as such, or to what you are really talking about. You can often find out by asking, "Do I make myself clear?" Or, "I notice you seem to disagree. I wonder why?" Or, "Let me put it another way and see if we understand each other."

Of course you may discover that your listeners are perfectly clear about what you mean but that they just don't agree with you. Then you must either accept these differences or work them out by re-course to facts and reasoning. But be sure that you differ on a *real* issue, not simply on what the words mean.

ANCHOR YOUR WORDS TO REALITY

Communication becomes an illusion whenever a speaker and his listeners cut loose from their moorings and drift off together in a cloudland of words.

Verbomania is a virulent disease to which many people have low resistance. Our world of talk is infested with empty words, plati-tudes, and clichés. They pass from individual to individual, from group to group, until, through social osmosis, they get into our

"I CAN'T make a speech like THIS, Dudley—it's just one clearcut statement after another."

nervous systems; we respond to them as a dog does to a whistle.

The epidemic of verbomania once inspired A. Parker Nevin to write "A Speech for Any Occasion," a minor classic of satire on speechmaking. Job E. Hedges, who also could toss words around, said of it, "You can call it 'The Crisis,' 'Justice,' 'Solution,' 'Destiny,' or anything you want. It covers the whole range of human thought and is unanswerable." Here it is:

Mr. Chairman, Ladies and Gentlemen:

It is indeed a great and undeserved privilege to address such an audience as I see before me. At no previous time in the history of human civilization have greater problems confronted and challenged the ingenuity of man's intellect than now. Let us look around us. What do we see on the horizon? What forces are at work? Whither are we drifting? Under what mist of clouds does the future stand obscured? My friends, casting aside the raiment of all human speech, the crucial test for the solution of all these intricate problems to which I have just alluded is the sheer and forceful application of those immutable laws which down the corridor of Time have always guided the hand of man, groping, as it were, for some faint beacon light for his hopes and aspirations. Without these great vital principles, we are but puppets responding to whim and fancy, failing entirely to grasp the hidden meaning of it all. We must re-address ourselves to these questions which press for answer and solution. The issues cannot be avoided. There they stand. It is upon you—and you—and yet even upon me that the yoke of responsibility falls.

What, then, is our duty? Shall we continue to drift? No! With all the emphasis of my being I hurl back the message *No!* Drifting must stop. We must press onward and upward toward the ultimate good to which all must aspire. But I cannot conclude my remarks, dear friends, without briefly touching upon a subject which I know is steeped in your very consciousness. I refer to that spirit which gleams from the eyes of a newborn babe, that animates the toiling masses, that sways all the hosts of humanity past and present. Without this energizing principle all commerce, trade and industry are hushed and will perish from this earth as surely as the crimson sunset follows the golden sunshine. Mark you, I do not seek to unduly alarm or distress the mothers, fathers, sons and daughters gathered before me in this vast assemblage, but I would indeed be recreant to a high resolve which I made as a youth if I did not at this time and in this place, and with the full realizing sense of responsibility which I assume, publicly declare and affirm my dedication and my consecration to the eternal principles and receipts of simple, ordinary, commonplace *JUSTICE.*

For what, in the last analysis, is justice? Whence does it come from? Where does it go? Is it tangible? It is not. Is it ponderable? It is not. Justice is none of these, and yet, on the other hand, in a sense it is all of these things combined. While I cannot tell you what justice is, this much I can tell you: That without the encircling arms of justice, without her shield, without her guardianship, the ship of state will sail through unchartered seas, narrowly avoiding rocks and shoals, headed inevitably to the harbor of calamity.

Justice! Justice! Justice! To thee we pay homage. To thee we dedicate our laurels of hope. Before thee we kneel in adoration, mindful of thy great power, mute before thy inscrutable destiny! [2]

---

[2] Robert H. Davis, "Bob Davis Recalls," *New York Sun,* March 22, 1927. Reprinted by permission

Remember, you were warned in advance to be on your guard. But ask yourself if you have ever applauded a "speech for any occasion." The writer once read Nevin's speech to a class of twenty adults, then asked them to summarize the message and evaluate the talk. No two could agree on what it was all about, but most of the class thought it was a fine speech. Only one person acknowledged that he hadn't the foggiest notion of what the speaker was driving at. None recognized the speech as satire. You see, all had been listening to speeches for any and all occasions most of their lives.

You may delude some of your listeners by tossing unanchored words about. And you may also delude yourself. It is poor praise to be complimented for your ability to sling the King's English. It's high praise to be assured that you talked sense, and to know that your listeners carried away a clear idea of what you wanted to get across.

As a listener, you have a choice: You may surrender to the spell of language or you may hold off until critical inspection satisfies you that the speaker's ideas and words are firmly anchored to reality. Critical listening is the best defense against gaseous speaking, and how you react as a listener is likely to influence how you yourself behave as a speaker.

PRACTICE GOOD USAGE
AND STRENGTHEN YOUR VOCABULARY

When you talk extemporaneously, you are privileged to take more liberties with language than when you write. By means of vocal inflection, change of pace, and emphasis, you are able to give force and clarity to a sentence that would not pass muster in writing. This liberty, however, does not give you license to disregard the accepted rules of good usage and syntax. Mangled sentences such as "I crossed in an airplane the distance of the continent that took my grandfather a week to ten days in eight hours" imposes a considerable strain on listeners who must reconstruct the sentence to extract the meaning.

There are no bad language habits that cannot be corrected. Familiarity with the basic ground rules as set forth in grammars, books on good usage, and dictionaries is a requirement that nobody can ignore without victimizing himself and his listeners. Supplement your study with practice sessions in which you experiment with various ways of expressing an idea until it emerges with clarity and economy.

To transmit our meanings accurately, we must have an adequate vocabulary. We can recognize and identify many more words in our reading and listening than we use in our writing and speaking. To develop an effective working vocabulary, you will need (1) to keep adding words to your recognition vocabulary from your reading and listening; and (2) to recruit new words for speaking from your recognition vocabulary. Some people resort to word lists compiled by somebody else. A better way is to build your own, for then you can draw on the synonyms and highly expressive words that already are part of your recognition vocabulary.

Learn the meaning of new words and check your understanding of familiar ones. Pronounce them out loud and fix their spelling in your mind. Often the origin and derivation of a word will help to establish it in your vocabulary. Put each word into sentences and practice using it in private. Finally, assimilate each word by introducing it into your conversation and speeches. If you make a habit of following this procedure, you will be on your way toward building a larger speaking vocabulary.

Many people, even college students, use barbarisms like *irregardless* and *irrevelant*—words that have no status in any lexicon. Betrayed by superficial resemblances between words, they reach out at random and grab whatever comes to mind. "My opponent flaunts public opinion," the politician charges. He means "flouts." "This building is inexhaustible," declares a travel guide; he means "indestructible." "Our education takes up a great part of our formidable years," says a student, who means "formative." "You excelled the speed limit," insists the traffic cop, meaning "exceeded." A speaker who confuses "noisy" and "noisome" describes an attractive residential neighborhood as noisome because it falls within the traffic pattern of a metropolitan airport.

Our language is filled with words that have almost, but not quite, the same meaning: amiable and amicable; comprehensive and comprehensible; impassive and impassible (impassable means something different from either); bellicose and belligerent; glance and glimpse; intrude and obtrude; minute and moment; rigid and rigorous. Verbal acuity enables you to sense the distinctions between such words in various contexts. A good, standard dictionary is indispensable, and a useful adjunct is *A Dictionary of Contemporary Usage* by Bergen and Cornelia Evans. You will discover that the Evans' *Dictionary* makes word study not only informative but fascinating as well.

AVOID SAYING THINGS THE HARD WAY

A plumber once wrote to a government agency, saying he found that hydrochloric acid quickly opened drain pipes. Was this a good thing to use? A scientist at the agency replied that "the efficacy of hydrochloric acid is indisputable, but the corrosive residue is incompatible with metallic permanence." The plumber wrote back, thanking him for his assurance that hydrochloric acid was all right. Disturbed by this turn of affairs, the scientist showed the letter to his boss—another scientist—who then wrote to the plumber: "We cannot assume responsibility for the production of toxic and noxious residue with hydrochloric acid and suggest you use an alternative procedure." The plumber wrote back that he agreed— hydrochloric acid worked fine. Now greatly disturbed by these misunderstandings, the scientists took their problem to the top boss. He broke through the jargon and wrote to the plumber: "Don't use hydrochloric acid. It eats holes in the pipes."

The point is this: Be as economical as you can without impoverishing your thought. Choose the simple, direct way of expressing yourself; or at least, when there are several ways of saying the same thing, choose the simplest way. Simple speech is not to be confused with speech for the simpleton. Simple speech is unencumbered speech.

Use Vivid and Energetic Language

SPECIFIC LANGUAGE ETCHES IMPRESSIONS

Specific words and phrases focus attention and etch sharp mental images. Sentences made up of nonspecific language hint at vagueness and leave a blurred impression. Compare these examples:

> Somebody told me that a good many people in this general area are down with an ailment of some sort.

> Dr. Hewitt reports that there are 32 cases of bronchitis in Belleville.

CONCRETE WORDS RECREATE EXPERIENCE

Walt Whitman once said, "Language, be it remember'd, is not an abstract construction of the learned, or of dictionary-makers, but is something arising out of the work, needs, ties, joys, affections, tastes, of long generations of humanity, and has its bases broad and low, close to the ground."

Concrete words are linked in our minds with the things we hear, see, smell, touch, taste, and feel—so closely, in fact, that when we hear concrete words spoken our nervous system reproduces vicariously the sensory experience itself. When you hear somebody tell of a crackling fire, you can almost hear the crackle of a bonfire, camp-fire, or burning building.

Compare these two descriptions:

> In autumn the leaves display diversity in color.

> In October the leaves go wild with color—purple and green, red and gold, all running into each other.

The first statement is clear and precise, to be sure; the second is just as clear and just as precise but, in addition, it is "close to the ground." Its language stirs associations and stimulates us to feel the tangy air and see the riot of color.

GOOD FIGURES OF SPEECH DRAMATIZE RELATIONSHIPS

A figure of speech points up the resemblance between two seemingly dissimilar things. It helps us to understand something unfamiliar, abstract, or complex by comparing it with something familiar or simple. If the figure is particularly deft, we are surprised by a resemblance we have never perceived before. A figure that is pertinent and fresh may also give us aesthetic pleasure or amusement.

The two basic figures of speech are the *simile* and the *metaphor*. The simile is a short statement in which the comparison is spelled out. Words such as *like, as,* and *as if* usually provide clues to a simile. For example: "She plays the piano as if she were wearing boxing gloves." "Talking is like playing on the harp; there is as much in laying the hands on the strings to stop their vibrations as in twanging them to bring out their music" (Oliver Wendell Holmes). Lincoln likened the thinness of Douglas' arguments on popular sovereignty to soup made from boiling the shadow of a starved chicken.

The simile calls attention to the fact that a comparison is being drawn. The metaphor merely *implies* a comparison. For example, a secretary of state, trying to show that the objectives of "X" country remain the same despite appearances to the contrary, once declared that "The switch is simply from hob-nail boots to carpet slippers." The implication is that only the tactics of the country have changed, not its objectives. Some years ago, Winston Churchill brought home a complex problem in international relations with a metaphor: "From Stettin in the Baltic to Trieste in the Adriatic, an iron curtain has descended across the continent."

Our everyday talk abounds with similes, metaphors, and variations on these basic forms. Many of the figures we use are no longer novel and no longer catch our ear, but we go on using them out of habit and because they possess universal applicability. We say a person is a tower of strength, straight as a ramrod, a bundle of energy, has nerves of steel, is dirty as a pig. But these and hundreds of other familiar figures of speech are overworked and tired. If we rely only on the old expressions, discriminating listeners will conclude that our speech is trite and our minds dull. Fresh, vivid figures inject life and color into our speech.

Don't strain in your efforts to be original, however. Poorly devised and mixed-up figures make a speaker look ridiculous. A young teacher, groping for a figure to convey his impressions of what teaching was like, ended up this way: "You carry all thirty of the students on your back, and just when you're ready to throw up the towel, you strike gold." *Block that metaphor*—unless low comedy is your business.

PERSONAL FORMS ARE NATURAL TO SPEECH

We all like dialogue. We are familiar with its patterns, and we enjoy its intimacy and movement. Real and hypothetical illustrations used in informal and formal talk can often be couched in the form of dialogue. Notice how R. W. Jepson makes you a party to this dialogue. He is talking on "Potted Thinking: The Necessity of Going Deeper Than the Headlines."

> Have you ever come across the man who buttonholes you and poses you with a question and insists on your answering, "Yes" or "No"? He will say to you: "Now then, are you a Free Trader, or aren't you?" And you might reply: "Well, the removal of all restrictions and barriers on international trade would be an ideal thing to my mind. But as things are—" Then he will burst in and say: "Come along now, I asked you a plain question. Give me a plain answer." Once again you will probably stammer out a few "buts." Then he will tell you you are hedging. "Either you are, or you aren't," he will say.

"Which is it? 'Yes' or 'No'?" You know the kind of person: the real whole-hogger.[3]

In public speaking, rhetorical questions help bring the listener in as an active partner in communication. Observe how Franklin D. Roosevelt created the sense of dialogue between himself and his listeners even though he didn't really expect them to answer back:

> But the simplest way for you to judge recovery lies in the plain facts of your own individual situation. Are you better off than you were last year? Are your debts less burdensome? Is your bank account more secure? Are your working conditions better? Is your faith in your own individual future more grounded?

Use personal pronouns in formal talks much as you do in everyday speech. Remember, you are talking with people, not to mannequins. The personal pronouns "I," "you," and "we" are natural, simple expressions of sincere speech. They help establish rapport. Impersonal substitutes for real persons are stilted and affected. It's less wooden and more direct to say "I think that . . ." than it is to say "In the estimation of this speaker, it is not an unjustifiable assumption to say. . . ." Of course, the personal pronoun may be conspicuously overworked.

STURDY SENTENCES ADD STRENGTH TO SPEECH

Make your sentences stand on their legs and march. Flabby sentences start off with a limp and end in a crumpled heap. You know how they get under way: "And then there's another thing . . . And then there's something else . . . and incidentally, there's still this that I might mention. . . ." And here's how they end: ". . . and things like that," ". . . and so forth," or ". . . several other miscellaneous matters."

Avoid overloading your sentences with so many phrases and clauses that they jostle each other. Take this one, for example:

---

[3] *Vital Speeches,* December 15, 1937, pp. 135-136.

Now my friends, we all believe in the purposes of public education, the great bulwark of our free country, our greatest heritage, but we also must be realistic and inquire closely into the financial feasibility of expanding our school plant at this moment when we contemplate an augmentation of salaries for the instructional staff, whose members are charged with shaping our childrens' futures.

Now note how these sentences step along:

We all want the best in plant, equipment, and staff for our public schools. We agree on this. But let's ask, "Can we afford to build a new gymnasium this year and at the same time improve salaries for teachers?"

Sturdy sentences feature nouns and verbs. Excessive use of clamorous words like *very, great, colossal, stupendous,* and *terrific* drowns out the essential ones.

Clinch your main ideas with climaxes. Before leaving an important point to go on to the next, drive home the sense and significance of what you have just said. For example, one speaker capped a key point on the threat of communism by saying, "The greatest danger communism presents to America is not by arms but by invitation." A series of strong, climactic sentences is particularly suited for the conclusion of speeches of advocacy and evocation.

Use Language with Propriety

SUIT YOUR LANGUAGE TO THE OCCASION

Ordinary speech is colloquial. We don't "study out" our words when we are bargaining over the counter, asking someone to pass the butter, or swapping the news of the day. But we all know there are times when our handy, everyday words are inadequate.

Some occasions demand that we sort out our words and compose speech with distinction.

Compare the snatch of conversation below with a short passage suitable to a formal speech on the same subject. First the conversation:

> A university is not out to please customers. It's more of a busybody than a business. Its job is to poke around, sniff out facts, air them—no matter whether people like 'em or not. It ought to puncture prejudices and platitudes. Let the bigots howl. A university is a people's hairshirt.

Now the formal speech:

> A university that does not lead is a university only in name. A true university diligently pursues facts amid appearances. It is a critic of what is, and a standard-bearer for what ought to be. Often it must speak as a solitary voice, championing truth against the clamor of outraged opinion and prejudice.

The language in the first passage is colloquial and suggests the informality of a living room or office conversation. Most of the words in the second passage are colloquial too, and the sentences are simple. But it is evident that the style has been refined and elevated for the public platform. It is not a question of which style is better—the formal or informal. Each is suited to its setting. In general, audiences expect the language of public speech to have tone and distinction that lifts it above the level of casual, off-the-cuff conversation.

AVOID WORDS THAT VIOLATE GOOD TASTE

Some words are plainly taboo. Public disapproval of such words is spelled out, for example, in radio and television codes. These are not the decrees of self-appointed censors; they are reflections of our social mores. It is risky to skirt the boundaries of good taste, and it is suicidal to flout public standards.

Slang should be used cautiously and sparingly. When it is picturesque and earthy, it spices conversation and public address. But slang quickly loses its freshness and appeal. It is seldom appropriate for formal occasions, and a slangy tone debases style on any occasion.

Points to Keep in Mind

1. Clarity is the first requirement of a good speaking style:
   a. Treat words as symbols that may have different meanings for different people.
   b. Anchor your words to reality.
   c. Practice good language usage and strengthen your vocabulary.
   d. Be direct and unpretentious in your style. Avoid saying things the hard way.
2. Use vivid and energetic language.
   a. Specific words and phrases etch impressions on your listeners' minds.
   b. Concrete words recreate experience.
   c. Good figurative speech dramatizes relationships.
   d. Make your speech direct and personal through the use of dialogue, rhetorical questions, and personal pronouns.
   e. Speak in short, crisp, sturdy sentences.
3. Suit the degree of formality or informality of your language to the audience and the occasion.

Exercises

1. Choose a concept that is unfamiliar to your listeners or about which they have imprecise ideas. Examples are: humanism, existentialism, nationalism, the poetic attitude, the American way of life, psycho-

somatic medicine. Make your concept the subject of a report. Develop your talk with specificity and concreteness.

2. Take a stand on a controversial issue. Be as precise as you can in outlining your position. As you speak, keep checking on the reactions of your audience. Respond to signs of disagreement or misunderstanding by putting your thoughts in other words. If the signs keep coming, don't hesitate to stop and clear up possible misunderstandings. Determine if the disagreement is verbal or substantive. The object here is not "smooth talk" but to experiment in reaching a meeting of minds on what is being said.

3. Prepare a two-minute descriptive talk on a topic such as one of these: a sunset, an airplane ride through a thunderstorm, a horse race, landing a salmon, the Golden Gate Bridge, the New York skyline, Niagara Falls, a quaint village, an impressive monument or painting, Main Street on Saturday night, sailing a boat, a locker room between halves. Through vivid language recreate the scene or event for your listeners.

4. Rework a speech you have given before. Clarify and brighten your language and style in ways that will win a new interest for your subject.

5. Select a short speech that has appeared in print—one that falls short of the standards of good speech style. Revise it. Read portions of the original speech and of your revision to the class.

6. Arrange a group discussion on a controversial question. Most of the class will take part in the discussion, but appoint four or five members as observers to take notes on the language behavior of the speakers. Have the observers look especially for these things:

   a. Instances of remarkably clear and precise statements of a point.
   b. Instances when the discussion bogged down because of cloudy or rambling "contributions."
   c. Language that blocked or sidetracked the discussion.
   d. Instances when members spotted and clarified misunderstandings; instances when misunderstanding went unchecked.
   e. Differences that sprang directly from opposing convictions rather than from confusions in language.

7. Take note of unfamiliar words in the sample speeches at the end of this book. Look up their meanings. Underline the familiar words that are not now part of your speaking vocabulary. First use some of these words in sentences, and then make a point of introducing some of them into your next speech.

CHAPTER THIRTEEN

Voice, Articulation, and Pronunciation

A good speaking voice is expressive, well projected, and pleasant. Expressiveness calls for vocal flexibility to convey meaning and register feeling. Projection is achieved largely through control of force. A pleasant voice has a warm,

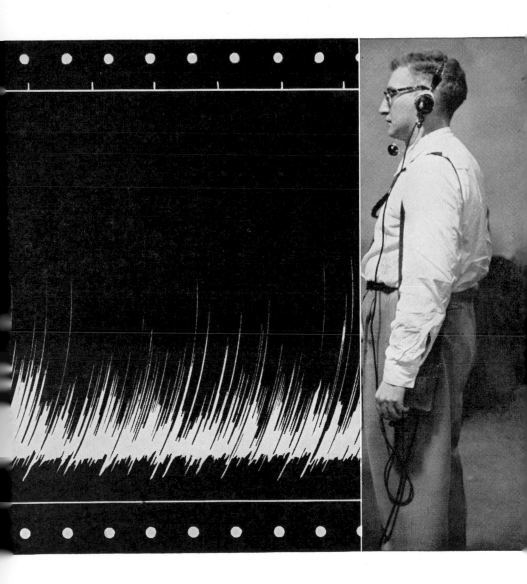

sympathetic quality; it is unobtrusive, effortless, and free from disagreeable qualities. Good articulation shapes voice into clear and recognizable sounds; good pronunciation complies with prevailing standards. These aspects of your vocal process merit analysis.

Why You Speak
As You Do

The way you speak is largely determined by organic, environmental, and personality influences.

ORGANIC FACTORS

If you are healthy and robust, you are more likely to have a strong, vibrant voice than if you are frail and weak. A small larynx with short vocal cords produces a higher-pitched voice than a large larynx with long vocal cords. A receding chin or poorly aligned teeth may cause a lisp. Chronic hoarseness is frequently caused by malformation of the larynx. Adenoids impair nasal resonance. A hearing deficiency may result in blurred speech or vocal monotony.

If your trouble springs from organic problems, arrange for a medical examination before you undertake voice training.

ENVIRONMENTAL FACTORS

A child's environment furnishes models for his own speech. By trial and error, he perfects the form of speech that meets with surest acceptance. We talk very much like the people with whom we communicated while our speech habits were being formed.

Geographic environment influences the rate of our speech, tonal patterns, our articulation and pronunciation. Even an untrained ear can detect differences between speech that is indigenous to the Deep South and speech that is indigenous to parts of New England. Skilled linguists can detect dialectal differences within relatively small geographical areas.

Home and community environment may affect our speech for good or bad. A child who is reared in a discordant home atmosphere may speak in a voice that reflects tension. A child surrounded by people who speak English with a foreign accent may learn to speak English with the same accent.

Speech patterns determined by environment are learned, and therefore they can be unlearned. New and more desirable habits can be substituted through directed exercises.

PERSONALITY FACTORS

Your voice is a mirror of your personality. A person who talks loudly and with exaggerated heartiness, or who gushes over trivialities, is probably insecure in his relations with others, is over-compensating for his timidity, and is overanxious to please. We recognize a whining, complaining voice as belonging to a person who feels mistreated, abused, and discriminated against. And we can spot the flat, impersonal tone and the monotonous lack of inflection of the inhibited person who tries to shield himself from the intrusion of outsiders.

If you recognize that your voice lacks confidence, warmth, vibrancy, or expressiveness because of poor personal adjustment, you have taken the first step toward improvement. Your speech course offers a favorable environment to re-evaluate yourself as a person and to re-direct your vocal habits.

Effective Use of the Voice

The source of energy for the voice is the breath stream, which sets into vibration the vocal folds (also called cords or bands) that are housed in the larynx. Since speech occurs as the breath is exhaled, exhalation needs to be controlled, steady, and adequate. Inhalation needs to be quick enough not to interrupt continuity, silent, and accomplished without tension in the neck and throat. The vocal folds, then, are our vibrator. Vibrations are built up or resonated principally by the pharynx, mouth, and nasal cavities—all located above the larynx.

With this equipment we produce sounds of varying degrees of loudness, at different pitches, with qualities of different kinds, and of varying durations. Breathing (the source of energy) is particularly important in loudness and duration; phonation (the vibration of the vocal bands) is the most important factor in pitch, and a determining factor in vocal quality; and the resonators are of great importance in bringing out qualities of tone.

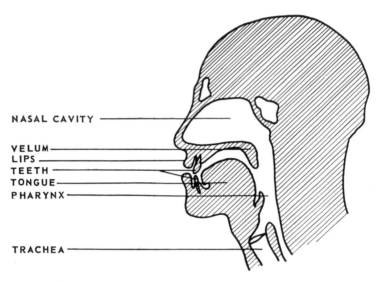

NASAL CAVITY

VELUM
LIPS
TEETH
TONGUE
PHARYNX

TRACHEA

Cross-sectional view of the head with resonating chambers and articulators. *Drawing by Donald K. Cadley.*

The human voice, like other sounds, has four physical characteristics—force, pitch, quality, and time. Properly controlled, these four elements contribute to effective use of the voice.

FORCE

Talk loudly enough to be heard easily, and quietly enough to be heard without annoyance. With attention and practice you can bring force under control. If people are not hearing you, it may be that you need, not more volume, but more projection.

Varying the force of your voice to convey meaning and feeling is a much more subtle matter. *Stress*—making a word, sentence, or point "stand out".—is an important part of it. Added loudness serves to underline what you say. And so does reduced loudness. Any notable departure from your normal level of loudness serves to draw attention. This means that you can use variations in loudness to mark anything that you want to emphasize. Such variations also help to reduce monotony in speaking.

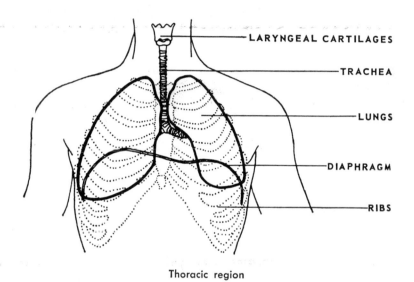

Thoracic region

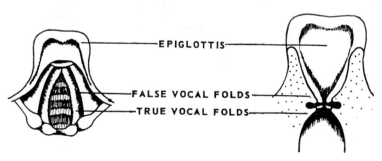

Left, superior view of the vocal folds; right, cross-sectional view of the vocal folds. *Drawings by Donald K. Cadley.*

PITCH

Is your habitual pitch level the best pitch level for you? In what ways can you use variations in pitch sensitively and meaningfully?

Each person uses one pitch level more frequently than any other. This is the level on which he most often begins speaking and to which he returns after shifting up or down the scale. It is his *habitual* pitch level.

For each voice there is one pitch level or a small band of pitch levels at which the voice operates most easily and most effectively. This is called the *optimum* pitch level. To achieve best results, try to make your habitual pitch level the same as your optimum pitch level.

Many people begin speech training with a notion that they would like to "lower their voices," because they admire low-pitched voices. Whether this is a realistic purpose depends on the capacity of a particular person's vocal mechanism. If you owned a fine violin, people would think you foolish if you tried to make it sound like a cello. The two instruments operate in the same fashion, just as two voices do. But the cello has larger and longer strings and a larger and differently shaped resonating cavity. The violin's most beautiful tones are considerably higher than the best tones of the cello. A young man who attempts to force his pitch down to the level used by a public speaker or actor whom he admires may be sacrificing tonal beauty in the process. Even though his father's voice is a bass-baritone, his may be a tenor. On the other hand, some people continue to talk at a childish or early-adolescent pitch level long after their matured vocal mechanism has become suited to a lower pitch.

Listen to yourself and see if you detect a harsh, "gravelly" quality, especially when your voice moves down the scale, as at the ends of sentences. If you do, it may mean that you are forcing the pitch of your voice uncomfortably low. On the other hand, do your high pitch levels, as when you accent a word, sound thin and sharp, as if the voice were strained? If so, your habitual pitch level may be too high.

An expressive voice moves up and down the musical scale continuously in an infinite variety of patterns. This variation in pitch, which we call *melody,* is one of the most important factors in conveying emotions and meanings. Consider this sentence: "You are not going out of the house today." Say it with a continuous downward inflection, and it has the authority and finality of an order. Use a rising inflection, and it becomes a simple question. Leap to a high pitch on the word *not,* and it takes on a threatening tone. Use a gliding inflection upward and then downward on the word *you,* and it become contemptuous. For greatest effectiveness, melody should be combined with variations in force and rate, but melody itself permits more subtlety of expression than does either force or rate.

Monotony in melody is of several types. The true monotone, who literally does not vary from a single pitch level, is comparatively rare. A more common offender is the speaker who shifts back and forth among three or four notes in a repeated pitch pattern that is quite unrelated to the meaning of what he is saying. Such a personality seems colorless and dull. The person who ends every sentence on a rising inflection seems indecisive and lacking in self-confidence. A speaker who repeatedly uses heavy downward inflections seems dogmatic and aggressive. True melody demands the use of changes in pitch to supplement and emphasize the intellectual and emotional content of speech.

QUALITY

Vocal quality is the most sensitive indicator of emotion in speaking, and it is the least subject to direct control by the speaker. The *quality* of a sound is determined by the relations between the overtones and the fundamental tone (the basic pitch).[1] And these

---

[1] Do not confuse *pitch* and *quality*. Sound the identical pitch on the piano and the violin and note the differences in the sound. These are differences in *quality*.

relations are determined by the vibrating mechanism and the resonators. The muscles involved in voice production respond to the
emotion of the speaker. This response is pretty much involuntary
—it is largely beyond the speaker's control, except as he is able to
control his emotions.

This means that it is very hard to disguise or simulate emotion,
because vocal quality always gives clues to your real feelings. A
mechanical approach to varying your vocal quality produces artificial effects. Sincerity of emotional expression stems from sincere
involvement in the emotion itself.

TIME

We have all heard speakers who rattled along at a rate far
too fast to be understood, and others who spoke so slowly you could
almost take a nap between words and phrases. These extremes are
both undesirable, and yet there is no one ideal rate of speaking.
What is good for one speaker in one environment, in one situation,
for one subject, is not necessarily good when any one of these factors is altered. How, then, can you hit on a good rate of speaking?

■ THE SPEAKER'S TEMPERAMENT AND PERSONALITY.   The speaking rate of a slow-moving person will naturally vary from that of an
excitable, high-strung person. Follow your individual pattern, so
long as it does not hamper intelligibility, annoy your listeners, or
seem inappropriate to what you are saying.

■ THE SPEAKER'S ENVIRONMENT.   As we have seen, we form
our speech habits, including our rate of speaking, on the basis of
models provided to us early in life. In some sections of the United
States, people speak more rapidly than in other sections. Your speaking rate should be largely determined by what your listeners are
used to.

■ THE SITUATION.   Use a slower rate in addressing a large audience than in intimate conversation.

■ THE CONTENT OF THE SPEECH.   Complex ideas, statistics, or problems that the audience has not previously considered take longer to grasp than more simple or more familiar statements. In expressing some emotions, such as joy and excitement, we usually speak more rapidly than when we are expressing grief and reverence.

Duration is the time spent in pronouncing a single word or phrase. *Pause* is the space of silence between words or phrases. The two combine to determine the over-all rate of speech.

Pauses are the punctuation marks in speech. Use them:

> **1.** To separate ideas and to set them apart as units of thought. "He rose awkwardly, / looked about furtively, / cleared his throat, / shifted his weight once or twice, / and finally began to speak.
>
> **2.** To point up an important idea that you are about to express. "The most dangerous force operating today to undermine our political structure is / apathy of the electorate."
>
> **3.** To give yourself time to organize your thoughts. But don't use too many pauses for this purpose, or prolong them excessively. Be especially careful to avoid the vocalized pause "er."

Pauses provide you with a natural opportunity to inhale. If you find that you are interrupting phrases by gasping for breath, practice deeper breathing and give more attention to spacing your inhalations so that they come at logical stopping places. If you find that you are talking on and on without pausing for breath, your audience will grow anxious over whether or not you will make it to the end. Practice phrasing your thoughts to allow for more frequent pauses, and avoid trying to talk on the last molecule of air you can squeeze from your lungs.

Articulation

Articulation means the adjustments and movements of the organs involved in producing speech sounds and in joining these sounds to form words and phrases. As we use it here, the term has about the same meaning as enunciation. The sounds of spoken English include *vowels, diphthongs,* and *consonants.*

Four actions are essential in producing *vowel sounds:* The vocal folds vibrate, producing voice; the opening into the nasal passage is closed or reduced; the tip of the tongue is held down behind the lower front teeth; and the mouth is opened to permit the sound to come out. How widely you open your mouth varies with different vowels, as do the shape of the lips and the position of the tongue.

A *diphthong* is a continuous blending of two vowel sounds to form one syllable. For example, say these two sounds rapidly, one after the other: the *ah* in father and the *oo* in hoot. The resulting sound is the diphthong *ow* as in cow.

Consonant sounds are formed by interrupting or restricting the breath stream. For example, say the word *up.* Notice that you produce the consonant *p* by closing your lips and stopping the breath stream. Then say the word *his.* Here the consonant *s* is produced by forcing air through a narrow aperture formed by tongue and teeth.

ARTICULATING VOWELS AND DIPHTHONGS

Whether or not your voice is pleasant may be determined by the way in which you produce vowels and diphthongs. Let your ear be your guide. Try for clear, mellow, resonant intonation. Avoid harsh, guttural, strident tones.

If you are careless about producing vowels and diphthongs, you

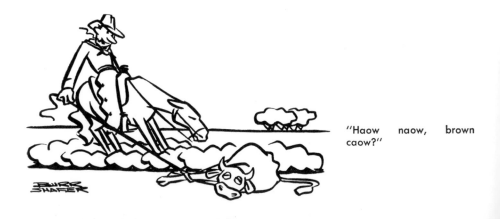

"Haow naow, brown caow?"

will also impair intelligibility. Poor production of these sounds will cause listeners to confuse your words and thus mistake your meaning. If you say *tar* when you mean *tower,* you can hardly expect your listeners to know what you are talking about.

ARTICULATING CONSONANTS

The consonants are most important in giving distinctness and clarity to speech. Poor enunciation results largely from a failure to produce consonants with precision. For most consonants, two organs—such as lip and teeth—actually come in contact. If this contact is not sharply made, the sound produced by releasing the contact is weak. Poor enunciation can usually be improved by more active, precise formulation of consonant sounds.

ASSIMILATION OF SOUNDS

We seldom give speech sounds their full value as we talk along. This is perfectly all right so long as we do not seriously impair our vocal quality and so long as we identify sounds clearly enough for listeners to understand us. Stilted speech that results from loving attention to each individual sound is either an affectation or a bad habit.

Speech sounds are affected by their neighbors. Omissions and glides and carry-overs from one sound to another are inevitable in free-flowing, easy speech. This sort of natural adjustment is called *assimilation.* Say this sentence: "Pat takes science." Notice that one *t* serves for both Pat and takes, and one *s* for both takes and science. More assimilation is admissible, of course, in conversation and informal speech than on occasions where considerable volume is required.

Pronunciation

Good pronunciation depends on (1) the speech sounds you choose in saying a word and (2) the syllable or syllables you choose to accent in a word. Sup-

pose you use the same vowel sound in *pour* and *poor*, or in *but* and
full; or suppose you use the final consonant sound of *rage* in *garage,*
or the initial consonant sound of *chill* in *charade,* or say *bus* exactly
like *buzz;* or suppose you accent the wrong syllable in *pretense,
cigarette, infamous.* These are examples of errors in pronunciation.
They are failures to conform to good usage in sound or accent, and
they may occur even though your articulation is perfect.

STANDARD PRONUNCIATION

If you have traveled widely through the United States, you
were probably impressed by the variety of pronunciation patterns
you heard. Even within one of our large cities, varying patterns of
pronunciation are noticeable. Pronunciations in the various sections
of the United States, and at different social levels within any one
section, differ in many particulars.

The greatest uniformity in pronunciation occurs among educated
speakers. Less uniformity exists at lower cultural levels. When a
given pronunciation becomes the predominant usage of educated
speakers over a large area, it is accepted as a *standard* pronunciation.
A pronunciation that is limited to less-educated speakers or to a very
small area is termed *substandard.*

DIALECTS OF THE UNITED STATES

By far the largest number of words in English have one
"correct" pronunciation—*i.e.,* one pronunciation that all cultivated
speakers of English prefer. There are, however, certain groups of
words that are pronounced with a slight difference in various large
geographical areas.

A *dialect* is any pattern of pronunciation that is commonly used
in one geographical area, but that differs somewhat from the usage
of other areas.

A *provincial dialect* is a pattern of pronunciation that is limited
to a narrow geographical region and that is not accepted by good
speakers over a large area.

A *standard dialect* is a pattern of pronunciation that is used by most good speakers in a large geographical area, but that differs somewhat from the predominant good speech of another large area.

In the United States there are *three standard dialects:* (1) *Standard Eastern,* which is used in eastern New England and New York City. (2) *Standard Southern,* which is used in the states that roughly made up the Confederacy. (3) *Standard General American,* which is used in the rest of the United States.

The General American dialect is spreading in usage, because it is the most common form of pronunciation in radio, television, and movies. The Eastern dialect most closely resembles standard British pronunciation, which is the model for stage diction.

Each of the three major dialects has a beauty of its own, and none is superior to another. All are standard and entirely correct. The criterion of good pronunciation is what is preferred by the majority of educated, careful speakers in a large geographical area. The best choice for an individual is the best speech of his own area.

USE OF THE DICTIONARY

You can improve your pronunciation if you get in the habit of using a good dictionary. Referring to a dictionary is futile, though, unless you know how to interpret what you find there.

Many people think that a dictionary's function is to *prescribe* pronunciation. But if you read the preface of several dictionaries, you will discover that the editors have attempted rather to *describe* the pronunciation used by most good speakers.

Other people think that when a dictionary lists more than one pronunciation for a word, the first is the "preferred" pronunciation. Actually, when several pronunciations of a word are used by large numbers of good speakers, the dictionary lists all of them. The order of listing is simply an attempt to indicate their relative popularity. It does not mean that any one pronunciation is superior to the others.

But how can you decide which pronunciation is "preferred"? When you have pronounced the word in each of the ways listed, choose the one that sounds most familiar to you. That pronunciation is likely to be the one most frequently used by good speakers in your dialect area. It is, therefore, the preferred pronunciation for your dialect.

In using a dictionary to improve your pronunciation, be sure you understand the symbols it uses. Mispronunciation of the key words cited by the dictionary to identify sounds will result in mispronunciation of the words you are checking. For example, if you check the pronunciation of *any* in Webster's *Collegiate Dictionary*, you will find it respelled as ĕn′ ĭ. The key word given for ĕ is *end*. Now suppose you happen to pronounce *end* as *ind*, a substandard pronunciation that is common in some areas. By transferring the vowel sound you use in *end* to *any*, you come up with the mispronunciation *iny*. Although the key-word system of indicating pronunciation is always open to this misunderstanding, an awareness of the problem and care in identifying the pronunciation of the key words will help you to avoid most mistakes.

Suggestions for Self-Improvement

■ 1. FIND OUT HOW OTHERS REACT TO YOUR SPEECH.   Ask for frank opinions. What is good and what is bad? Do you project your voice? Is your vocal quality pleasant, jarring or distracting? Do you speak distinctly? Is your pronunciation accurate? Sampling the reactions of others enables you to judge how well you are coming through to them.

■ 2. LEARN TO LISTEN OBJECTIVELY TO YOURSELF.   This is difficult but essential. Frequent recordings of your voice on a disc, tape, or wire recorder will help. If the result seems unflattering, don't jump to the conclusion that the recording is bad. It is more likely that you are getting the full impact of some "badness" in your voice for the first time.

▪ 3. LISTEN ANALYTICALLY.   Casual listening, however objective, won't help you spot problems that need attention. Analytical listening means the ability to isolate your individual characteristics of volume, quality, pitch, rate, and the elements of your articulation and pronunciation. You will need the ability to detect fine distinctions. This may require ear training.

▪ 4. DRAW UPON VISUAL, TACTUAL, AND KINESTHETIC IMPRESSIONS.   Some parts of your vocal mechanism are hidden from view, but you can observe the functioning of others with the aid of a mirror as you perform exercises. The sense of touch will help you identify and reshape your articulatory habits. For example, you can feel the point where your tongue tip touches to form a *t* or where your lower lip comes against your teeth in forming an *f*. Through kinesthetic impressions you can acquire the *feel* of a relaxed pharynx, the degree of tension in the tongue when a particular vowel sound is formed, or the relaxation of laryngeal muscles not needed in phonation.

▪ 5. PRACTICE.   A finer control over voice, articulation, and pronunciation is possible through daily work-outs. Start with the exercises at the end of this chapter and collect others to meet your needs. If your problem is relatively minor, it can usually be cleared up quickly. Should your problem be deep-seated, then patience, time, and work will be required to reform your speaking habits.

Points to Keep in Mind

1. A good speaking voice is expressive, well-projected, and pleasant. It should be accompanied by distinct articulation and accurate pronunciation.

2. Speech is shaped by organic, environmental, and personality influences.

3. Voice is produced through a sequence of breathing, phona-tion, and resonation. Like other sounds, the human voice has four characteristics—force, pitch, quality, and time.

4. Articulation means the adjustments and movements of the organs involved in producing speech sounds and in joining these sounds to form words and phrases.

5. Standards of pronunciation are determined by the pre-dominant usage of educated speakers within a large geographi-cal area.

Exercises

1. Stand erect before a full-length mirror. Support your weight on both feet, with the center of support toward the front of each foot. Imagine that one string is tied to the top of your head, and that another is tied to your breastbone; imagine that you are being held up by these two strings. Try to "grow upward" in the line of these imaginary strings. Be sure your shoulders and neck are relaxed; your body should be erect but not stiff. Now your lungs are free to fill with air. Remem-ber that slouching crowds the chest cavity and hampers breathing.

2. Place your left hand lightly on your breastbone, and your right hand across your abdomen between the navel and lower ribs. Take a quick, silent breath. Watch your two hands; the left one should re-main steady, for the breastbone should not move (nor should the shoulders rise); the right hand should be forced outward, since the abdominal wall is forced against it when the diaphragm pulls downward against the viscera. Watch the lower ribs also. Do you see the lower chest expanding? Now you have inhaled in an easy, natural manner for speech, "packing the breath against your belt."

Remaining erect and keeping the breastbone steady, *gradually* force the breath from your body by pulling inward with the abdominal muscles. Your left hand on the breastbone should remain steady; your right hand should pull inward as the abdominal muscles contract. As you exhale, say the vowel *ah*. Prolong it, keeping the tone smooth and steady.

3. Slowly repeat the question, "Who are you?" five times each on a separate breath. The first time, use a small inhalation and control the exhalation so that the words are loud enough to carry to a person five feet away. Next, imagine you are speaking to someone ten feet away; then twenty; then forty. Beware of tightening the throat or raising the pitch level as you increase your strength of tone. Make each successive question louder by taking a slightly deeper inhalation than the time before, and, on exhalation, by pulling inward more firmly with your abdominal muscles.

4. In the following selection, underline the words that need greater force to carry emphasis. Practice reading the poem as you marked it.

> Teach me to feel another's woe,
> To hide the fault I see;
> That mercy I to others show
> That mercy show to me.
> —*Pope*

5. Each of the following sentences has an obvious mood. Read each one aloud, using pauses and varying the rate of your speech to convey the particular mood.

> Life is a narrow vale between the cold and barren peaks of two eternities. (*Ingersoll*)
>
> I wish I knew what to do about it.
>
> Let me tell you the wonderful news!
>
> Will you tell me how to get to Vine Street?
>
> Why don't you look where you're going?
>
> I'm too tired to go another step.

6. Hold your head erect. Now let the neck muscles relax until your head drops forward on your chest. Be sure you don't pull it forward, but let it drop of its own weight. Rotate your head slowly toward the right shoulder, then to the back, to the left shoulder, and front again, letting it fall of its own weight, relaxed. Keeping your muscles relaxed, read the following sentences. Then read the three lines from Matthew Arnold and listen critically to your tone to detect any return of tension.

> Ah, how easy this is!

I will relax and relax and relax.

The sea is calm to-night.
The tide is full, the m⌐ ⌐n lies fair
Upon the straits—
     —*Matthew Arnold*

7. Using various melody patterns, discover how many different meanings and emotional shadings you can express with each of the following sentences:

I don't know why you want me to go to the movies with you.

How would you like to move to the moon?

I've always been polite to Tom.

I should change my attitude toward mathematics.

8. Read the following sentences. There should be no nasal sounds.

This is the house that Jack built.

She goes to school every day.

Who left a light gray hat by that chair?

Now read these sentences, giving full nasal resonance to the *m, n,* and *ng,* none to the other sounds.

Nobody expects him to come home.

Turn left at the next corner.

His name must be in the telephone book.

9. Practice reading the following selection aloud, paying particular attention to the way you produce the vowels and diphthongs:

If thou must love me, let it be for naught
Except for love's sake only. Do not say,
'I love her for her smile—her look—her way
Of speaking gently,—for a trick of thought
That falls in well with mine, and certes brought
    A sense of pleasant ease on such a day'—
    For these things in themselves, Beloved, may
Be changed, or change for thee—and love, so wrought,
May be unwrought so. Neither love me for
    Thine own dear pity's wiping my cheeks dry:

A creature might forget to weep, who bore
   Thy comfort long, and lose thy love thereby!
But love me for love's sake, that evermore
   Thou mayst love on, through love's eternity.
          —Elizabeth Barrett Browning

10. Practice reading the following selection aloud, paying particular attention to the way you articulate the consonants:

   Trust thou thy Love: if she be proud, is she not sweet?
   Trust thou thy Love: if she be mute, is she not pure?
   Lay thou thy soul full in her hands, low at her feet;
   Fail, Sun and Breath!—yet, for thy peace, She shall endure.
          —Ruskin

11. During the next five days, listen for the mispronunciations that other people make. List all that you hear.

CHAPTER FOURTEEN

Bodily
Action

Bodily action is the visible code of speech. As long as you are in sight of an audience, you are communicating with it, even though you aren't saying a word. Your eyes, facial expressions, the tone of your muscles, your posture—all reveal something about you whether you

want them to or not. And if words and actions say conflicting things, the audience will intuitively take their cues from your actions. A speaker's manner can make us feel unwanted even though he speaks words of welcome. Bodily actions carry meaning in their own right, and they can reinforce or defeat your words.

Some Common Misconceptions

CONFINING BODILY ACTION
TO GROSS MOVEMENT

Some people think that bodily action refers only to big movements of the entire body, or sweeping gestures made with arms and hands. They are suspicious of instruction in bodily action, for they have watched persons who behaved like acrobats rather than speakers intent on communicating ideas.

The fact is that you can gesture eloquently without making big movements. Your body has hundreds of muscles. All of them contract and relax, some voluntarily, some involuntarily. This contracting and relaxing *is* bodily action. An expressive face, a thrust of the jaw, a toss of the head, a shrug of the shoulders—these and dozens of other small movements constitute bodily action.

Don't jump to the conclusion that big movements are taboo. Far from it! Our only point is that bodily action includes more than the gross movements of arms, legs, or the body as a whole.

TREATING BODILY ACTION AS MECHANISTIC

Mechanical actions, like mechanical phrases, say very little to your audience—except that you have spent a lot of time practicing how to turn them out. Old-time elocutionists often went astray in this matter of bodily action. Some of them charted elaborate classifications of gestures, and worked out precise instructions for making each one. The result was a mechanical speaker with puppet-like movements that had little to do with his thought or mood. You still see this kind of speaker from time to time—he feels he must "make" gestures even when there is no good reason for them.

CONFUSING NATURAL WITH HABITUAL MOVEMENT

Sometimes people insist that good bodily action is whatever "comes naturally." This is like saying that natural behavior is the same as habitual behavior. The truth is that we often hold Nature responsible for what really is the product of habit. Through the years we acquire habitual patterns of behavior until at last the familiar seems the most natural thing in the world.

This confusion gets us into trouble when we excuse bad habits as being natural. Look around you, and you are likely to see people who have developed unfortunate habits of posture or gesturing that interfere with communication. New habits are needed no matter how natural the old ones seem. This calls for objective self-study followed by corrective exercises.

How Bodily Action
Works For or Against You

ACTION WINS AND HOLDS ATTENTION

A listener can rivet his attention to a fixed point for only a few seconds. You must constantly adapt your matter and manner to his shifting energies. You can catch his ear by keeping your ideas and language lively; you can catch his eye by matching your physical movements to your marching ideas.

An animated window display attracts more attention than a stationary one. Similarly, a "stationary" speaker excites less interest than one who is physically alive. A vital speaker stimulates listeners to "feel in" with him. Listeners respond to a lively speaker much as a fan in the bleachers responds to the backfield in action. When you stir your listeners to participate in communication, you win their active interest.

ACTION COMMUNICATES MEANING

Look about you. Out of earshot but within eyesight you see two people lounging on the lawn. One leans forward in a confidential manner. The other throws back his head and slaps his leg. Both seem to laugh uproariously. You see two other people standing on the sidewalk. Their bodies quiver like steel fishing rods. One gestures menacingly at the other. Without hearing a single word, you reach conclusions about each conversation, the moods of the participants, and their attitudes toward each other. Action is loaded with meaning.

■ PHYSICAL BEHAVIOR IS AN INDEX TO PERSONALITY.   We pick up our impressions from a speaker's total behavior, from many co-operating cues so faint and fleeting that we can seldom isolate them. For instance, our initial confidence—or lack of it—in a speaker's ability to do a good job depends upon "something" we sense in his general manner. Not that we actually sit back and muse, "Here's a fellow who walks energetically, has a bright eye, has an easy, comfortable manner, and for these and other reasons warrants my confidence." Still we sense these things without realizing it, and we respond favorably to him. In the same way, we respond unfavorably to a speaker whose facial muscles are taut, who shuffles about, and who darts furtive glances here and there as if seeking to escape. His anxiety transfers itself to his audience.

Certain patterns of physical behavior lead us to make snap judgments. Mincing movements suggest a prissy person. A scowling face and a jutting jaw send listeners off to a neutral corner for safety. The man who descends upon us, gives us a bone-crushing handshake, and flashes smiles on and off like a neon sign, puts us on guard and stimulates our sales resistance. Whenever you speak, your listener responds to your mannerisms as well as to your words. He is sizing you up. We may deplore snap judgments, but people go right on making them. The man who totters onto the platform like Casper Milquetoast may have nerves of steel and the courage of a lion, but unless his listeners have a chance to test these qualities on the spot, many of them will never revise their first impressions of him.

■ GESTURES AID IN DESCRIPTION, NARRATION, AND EXPOSITION. Gestures supplement words and fill in gaps. A traveler excitedly describes the volcanic eruption of Mt. Paricutín, in Mexico. His arms and hands begin to speak, suggesting clouds of billowing smoke and a flood of white-hot lava. His actions help you to create the scene in your own imagination. Or let's say you are lost and want to find Highway 42, westbound. You spot a farmer plowing a field and ask him for help. As the farmer talks, he points north and west to help you get your bearings; his arms cross to suggest an intersection; he moves hand and arm in a sweeping curve to indicate a bend in the road. Indeed, it is difficult to instruct—either formally or informally—without gestures that indicate location, space, size, shape, speed, force, and procedure.

■ GESTURES EXPRESS CONVICTION AND FEELING. We speak forcefully with our entire body when we are under the influence of strong convictions and feelings. Even someone who is usually shy and reserved becomes a person transformed. His face becomes mobile; there is a new set to his shoulders; and his arms and hands suddenly go to work without any conscious effort on his part. Unless a person's emotions get out of control, he is at his best when he speaks for a cause that means a great deal to him. His mind and body cooperate in an accent and rhythm of expression that the audience quickly detects and respects. Any one of his gestures—a shrug of the shoulders, a clenched fist, an expression of scorn—may be ambiguous in itself; but in the full context of the speaker's unmistakable attitudes and feelings, it will move the audience to give undivided attention, and to react correspondingly with laughter, vexation, or indignation.

ACTION RELIEVES TENSION

Some tension, though we may scarcely be aware of it, is normal even in our day-to-day speaking. Heightened tension is inevitable when you are on the spot, so to speak—whether in a conference, a public reading, or a public speech. From autobiographies and biographies of great speakers, we learn that before each speech they too built up tensions bordering on stage-fright, even after years and years of experience. Norman Thomas, himself a brilliant and seasoned speaker, describes this universal reaction:

> Some degree of nervous tension one must expect before an important speech. At least before certain speeches, especially in a debate or symposium, one shivers on the brink of speech as before diving into cold water. But once in, the speech, like the water, is bracing.[1]

As tensions mount, some speakers seem to freeze in their shoes, unable to think clearly and to find the right words. If this happens to you, take deliberate steps to break the cycle of tensions before you get stuck on dead center. Change your position. Move about. Make some gestures. Clearly these are only temporary expedients to use in emergency situations. No matter how awkward you feel in taking these steps at first, the important thing is to shake off your immobility and to loosen up. Physical activity is your best way to gain freedom and relaxation.

If you don't find some way to relieve these dammed-up tensions, they may spill over into random, nervous movements. In effect, these are the body's involuntary and uncontrolled attempts to relieve itself of strain. You have seen people move about the speaker's platform in a distracted manner, shifting their weight from one foot to the other, clenching and unclenching their hands, forcing a ring up and down a finger, stretching their necks to relieve the pressure of their collars. Actually this distraught behavior doesn't really relieve the tension; and once the speaker becomes aware of it, he responds to it as a further distraction. And so does his audience.

The way to break up random behavior is to focus sharply on what you are saying, then *induce* some purposeful activity that will enforce your statements. The gestures you make may not be the best, but they will help to re-direct your energies. With increased poise and self-control, your body will begin to speak purposefully without conscious direction.

---

[1] *Mr. Chairman, Ladies and Gentlemen* . . . New York: Hermitage House, 1955, pp. 80-81.

Characteristics of Good Bodily Action

■ 1. VITALITY.   Energized speech keeps the listener listening. A person who is alive from head to foot relays his vitality. A droopy, lethargic speaker suggests, in effect, "I'm sorry to take your time. I'll be through soon." A vital speaker mobilizes his audience.

■ 2. VARIETY.   Physical flexibility is the key to variety. Unrelieved action wearies an audience. Overworked gestures, no matter how well they are executed, are monotonous. Still worse are the unvaried and meaningless gestures, such as the perpetual motion of a bobbing head or chopping the air with an arm and hand. Tension or poor habits usually account for this monotony. Variety is achieved through self-appraisal, a keener appreciation of purposeful movement, and exercises that induce flexibility.

■ 3. COORDINATION.   Though varied, gestures may be awkward and disjointed. Any single gesture should mesh smoothly with all parts of a totally responding body. A speaker who bobs his head around but holds his shoulders stiff reminds his viewers of a poorly manipulated puppet. And if he thrusts out his arm and hand mechanically, he calls to mind a badly adjusted mechanism of wheels and springs. When all movements are well coordinated, no single gesture is conspicuous as a detached action.

■ 4. INTEGRATION.   Effective action springs from the meanings a speaker is trying to convey. He shrugs, smiles, scowls, points, draws himself up because he is responding to an inner impulse to do so. Action is integrated when it is keyed to a speaker's mind and emotions.

■ 5. TIMING.   A good gesture is timed to fit the word or phrase it is intended to enforce. An arm or hand gesture is ludicrous when it precedes the essential word or phrase it is supposed to emphasize, or when it comes as an after-beat. Poor timing is the result of uncoordinated activity, weak integration between action and meaning, or "canned" gestures.

■ 6. RESERVE. Expend energy freely in speaking, but don't squander it all at once. If you unwind with a terrific burst of gestures, you will soon dissipate your initial impact. Give your listeners the same feeling they have when they are driving a high-powered automobile—that there is plenty of power left if it's needed. Listeners grow uneasy when a speaker strains or wilts. End your speech as you begin it, with energy to spare.

■ 7. APPROPRIATENESS. Adapt your action to both the audience and the occasion. A pep rally calls for abundant action from a cheer leader. But exaggerated gestures at a dinner party or in a small group suggest that the speaker is either an exhibitionist or that he suffers from an over-heated mind.

How to Improve Your Bodily Action

■ 1. STUDY OTHER PEOPLE'S PHYSICAL BEHAVIOR. Observe the part bodily action plays in the speech that goes on around you—in lectures, movies, TV programs, and your classmates' talks. Sensitize yourself to the role of bodily action in communication. Note how bodily action works for or against the people you observe. How would you advise those with poor bodily action to improve?

■ 2. GET AN IMAGE OF YOUR OWN CHARACTERISTIC PHYSICAL BEHAVIOR IN SPEECH. This may not be easy. You can get some visual glimpses from candid camera shots, or, better yet, from home movies. But the image we're talking about also includes a feeling for what you're doing when you're doing it.

"What's the matter—can't you stand a little constructive criticism?"

Welcome your classmates' descriptions of your physical behavior. Try to see yourself objectively through their eyes. Then run a check on their descriptions by talking before a full-length mirror. If you see an unrelieved dead-pan expression or an unbroken frown, remember this is what your audience has to look at each time you speak.

■ 3. FORM A CLEAR IDEA OF HOW TO CORRECT YOUR PROBLEMS. Once you have pinpointed your problems, let your instructor and classmates help you find procedures for correcting them. Short workout programs in class are particularly helpful. Experiment on the spot with the suggestions that are made and get your classmates' reactions to the results. If you don't get the hang of a suggestion, invite someone else to demonstrate it for you.

■ 4. WORK UP A SPECIFIC PLAN AND PRACTICE PRIVATELY. Follow through on helpful suggestions made in class. A posture problem has to be worked at every day, not just when you speak before a group. Devise special exercises for work-outs at home to deal with persistent problems. If your bodily action is inhibited, stiff, and awkward, use pantomime exercises in which you imagine yourself as a tennis player on the courts or a swimmer in a pool. Or read aloud excerpts from dramatic literature that stir up muscular responses in you. Now and then, practice these exercises before a full-length mirror to check on results. After a time you will acquire the new sense of physical freedom that you need in reading and speaking.

■ 5. CHOOSE SUBJECTS FOR YOUR CLASS SPEECHES THAT CALL FOR PHYSICAL ACTION.   Demonstration talks are especially helpful, talks in which you show how to build a piece of furniture, assemble an apparatus, or execute dance steps. Or recall some exciting event you have witnessed; then re-create the event with actions as well as words. Speeches on subjects about which you have especially strong convictions induce action.

Some Special Problems
That Plague Public Speakers

■ How SHOULD I WALK TO AND FROM THE PLATFORM?   The important thing is to make the trip without calling unfavorable attention to yourself. A hesitant manner suggests timidity, and a hurried, nervous walk marks you as overanxious. Shuffling feet suggest indifference. A stilted, strutting, or lilting entry leads to speculation about your personality, and makes listeners more interested in proving their hunches than in listening to what you have to say.

Simply pick up your feet and walk to your place in a firm easy manner that tells your audience you have business with them. Once you have finished speaking, make your exit in the same easy, unhurried manner.

■ WHERE AND HOW SHOULD I STAND?   Stand where it will be easiest for you to establish the best contact with all your listeners. Normally, this will be at the front and toward the center of the group. Stand as close to your audience as you can without seeming to press in on them or crowd them. Avoid turning your back on any of them. If your listeners are scattered, don't hesitate to ask them to move together. This will reduce the strain on you and will give you better contact with them.

Good posture improves appearance and contributes to bodily action. Stand upright but not stiffly. Avoid both the slouch of a bum and the strut of a drill sergeant. And don't drape yourself over the lectern, lean carelessly against the wall, or dangle one leg in midair. The Napoleonic stance, with legs spread far apart, or the oratorical pose, with feet planted at studied angles, is conspicuous and contrived. Make good posture habitual, and you will be free to direct your attention to more important matters.

■ SHOULD I MOVE AROUND WHILE SPEAKING?   By all means, if you have some place to go. Moving around may help maintain contact with all your listeners. A few steps break the monotony of one position, indicate a transition in thought, and also relieve tension. Roaming restlessly like a caged tiger distracts the audience.

■ WHAT SHOULD I DO WITH MY HANDS?   When you make your first few speeches, you may discover that your hands have suddenly become as large as violin cases hanging at your side. This is just one sign of exaggerated self-consciousness.

Beginning speakers are often told to drop their hands to their sides when they are not gesturing. But this may look artificial and may make them seem more conspicuous. There's nothing wrong with thrusting a hand into your pocket—but don't forget where you left it. If you are standing near a lectern, feel free to rest your hands on it naturally, without clutching it like a shipwrecked passenger clinging to a floating log. After you get into your speech, your hands will stop being a problem and you will find good use for them.

■ How SHOULD I USE THE SPEAKER'S STAND?   During the first few minutes of a talk, it's comforting and reassuring to have a good, solid speaker's stand as a base of operations. It can, however, become an obstacle instead of an aid. Speakers who grimly attach themselves to the lectern, hide behind it, or drape themselves over it are a familiar and dismal sight. Make a point of moving to one side or out in front from time to time. You will find that your audience is much more interested in you once you come out of hiding.

Sometimes, of course, you have to stay close to the speaker's stand, as when you read from a manuscript. And when you are talking into a microphone fixed to the stand, you must remain relatively stationary. But it is still possible to gesture without pounding the lectern or rattling the mechanism.

Points to Keep in Mind

1. Develop and control your physical behavior in speech to:
    a. Capture and hold your audience's attention.
    b. Lodge favorable impressions of yourself as a person.
    c. Supplement your words in narrative, descriptive, and expository discourse.
    d. Give added impact to your convictions and feelings.
    e. Reduce muscular tensions.
2. Work especially for action that is:
    a. Vital and stirs up responses.
    b. Flexible and varied.
    c. Coordinated.
    d. Integrated with thoughts and feeling.
    e. Timed to fit the point you are making.
    f. Under control.
    g. Appropriate to the occasion.
3. In conducting yourself on the platform, try to:
    a. Walk easily and firmly to and from the platform.
    b. Stand where it is easiest to communicate with your audience.
    c. Make natural and comfortable adaptations that will relieve initial strain.

Exercises

1. Select two sites, one a building on campus, the other a building in your home town or city. Devise a one or two-minute report to in-

struct a stranger on how to get from one building to the other. Use bodily action and blackboard sketches to supplement verbal description.

2. Prepare a "how-to-do-it" talk on directing an orchestra, interpreting the gestures of football officials, or administering aid at the scene of an accident. Use bodily action as an aid to communication.

3. Prepare a report on a process, an operation, or an institution. Tell how stage sets are built; explain the structure of the United Nations Organization; describe the layout of your college library; report on prospecting for oil. Use visual aids, but also use gestures to suggest height, width, distance, direction, movement, relationships.

4. Recall an exciting event you witnessed firsthand—the finals of a tennis match, a rescue, a parachute jump, fighting a fire or a swollen river, climbing a mountain, a mock political convention. Try to recover the excitement you felt at the time. Make use of bodily action to depict the event and to communicate your excitement.

5. Pick a short story with lots of action in it. Make a cutting of it, and read it to the class. Make it come alive.

6. Choose a subject about which you have strong feelings. Make up your mind that the time has come to speak out. Deliver your talk with force and energy that do justice to your convictions.

7. Listen to comments about other people. Do any of them express stereotyped judgments based on appearance and physical behavior? Write up the results of your observations and present them to the class.

CHAPTER FIFTEEN

Inquiry

Sound method is an important means to good speech and one of the tests of good speech. In any speech, the best approach is largely dictated by the purpose of the speech. So far, we have been considering methods that serve the

purpose of all speech—*response*. We now begin four chapters dealing with the special methods associated with the four primary purposes of speech—inquiry, reporting, advocacy, and evocation. Logically, the method of inquiry comes first.

The Role
of Inquiry

Inquiry is a search for meaning, understanding, and guidance. In this respect it is unique among the purposes and methods of speech. In our other capacities as speakers we make use of insights and understandings, but first we must discover them. Speech performs one of its most important services in aiding in this search and discovery.

We are impelled toward inquiry by the problems we face in our daily lives and the larger problems of the society in which we live. But sensitive, thoughtful people raise questions in all areas of human experience, even to the nature of man and his ultimate destiny. The will and the capacity to explore these questions reflectively and creatively are among the highest marks of maturity.

The Nature
of Inquiry

Inquiry may be a solitary venture, or it may take place when two or more people meet to think together. There is no such thing as "group thinking," of course, except in a metaphorical sense. Only individuals think. But individuals within a group do think and often they think more gainfully than they would if each were by himself. By sharing information, exchanging views, and trying out ideas, we find our way to new vantage points and to a higher level of creative thinking.

An everyday conversation with a friend may contain some, most, or all of the elements of organized inquiry. You tell him about a problem that is worrying you. He responds with interest. He draws you out. He asks questions that focus on aspects of the problem you haven't considered. Together you ponder various answers, discard some, and ultimately settle on the one that seems to fit the case. This is inquiry in action in its simplest form.

We are carrying out inquiry when we talk with friends, teachers, fellow-workers, neighbors, and counselors on problems arising out of personal affairs, our college, our community, or in the larger arena of state, national, and international affairs. The most favorable setting for inquiry is a small group of interested, congenial people. Even large conferences and legislative assemblies refer most questions to committees for preliminary study. In small groups, everyone has a chance to participate. Roles shift from speaker to listener and back again. In large meetings, this kind of give-and-take usually yields to public speeches of inquiry followed by an open forum. Even in small groups, though, it is often wise to let a person talk himself out on a point without interrupting him. Such miniature speeches contribute most when they fit the spirit and pattern of inquiry.

The Pattern of Inquiry

Inquiry is both an analytical and a creative process. At its best, it combines rigor and freedom. Sometimes it resembles loosely organized chaos, and there is much to be said for letting ideas tumble forth before trying to sort them out. Although inquiry cannot be put into a strait-jacket, neither should it degenerate into aimless conversation.

But what is the best pattern of thinking to follow when we try to find the answers to a problem? People who have studied this question have identified six steps in such reflective thinking. Used flexibly and imaginatively, these steps provide a sound guide for inquiry.

■ 1. IDENTIFY THE PROBLEM.   Reflective thinking is triggered by a problem. Begin by stating and describing the problem as specifically as you can.

Phrase the problem as an open question that will invite a variety of answers. It is better to ask, "How should I invest my savings?" than "Should I buy Goods, Inc.?" The second question tends to limit answers to a simple "Yes" or "No." Put your question objectively. "How may we get rid of our worthless physical education requirement?" is a loaded question that is likely to block discussion at the outset. "How may we best insure a student's physical fitness?" opens the question objectively.

Explain the problem so that others can identify it. Then get them to share your concern so they will seek the answer as eagerly as you do.

■ 2. ANALYZE THE CAUSES.   The next step is to discover the causes of the problem you have identified. The causes of most problems that generate discussion are numerous and complex, some close at hand and others deepseated and obscure. Your job is to put your finger on those causes that seem most vulnerable to attack and most intimately related to an ultimate solution of the problem.

If you discover that one reason for the failure of students to turn out for football games is the fact that they have been assigned one of the least desirable blocks of seats in the stadium, you may have spotted an answer to the problem. But before you jump to this conclusion, it might be well to ask why they have been assigned to these seats and whether any other causes are operating to keep them away.

■ 3. CLARIFY YOUR VALUES.   Before you take up various solutions to the problem, you must first establish standards by which to judge them. These standards or criteria are your values—what you want the solution to do, the specifications that it must meet. Faced with the question "How may we improve our college newspaper?" students might agree that any forthcoming suggestions will have to (1) fit within the fixed budget, (2) be consistent with a balanced coverage of college news, and (3) not make excessive time demands on the student staff.

■ 4. SUGGEST SOLUTIONS.   Here you are after solutions that promise to correct the causes of the problem and meet the values you have laid down. Try to turn up one or more answers and then judge each proposal on its merits. Spare no effort at this stage to draw forth as many suggestions as possible. Even seemingly far-fetched ideas should be welcomed and given a hearing, for no one can be sure in advance that a novel approach won't turn out to be the best.

■ 5. WEIGH THE ALTERNATIVES.   Treat each proposal as a working hypothesis, as a guide to further exploration. Discuss its pros and cons, but avoid committing yourself prematurely. Superficially attractive answers may not stand up under exposure. Ask questions such as these: Does this proposal get to the root of the problem? Does it fit our criteria? Can it be made to work? Will it cost too much? If it solves the problem at hand, will it introduce new problems in the future? The solution that you ultimately agree on may be one of the suggested solutions, an integration of two or more of them, or a compromise.

■ 6. TEST THE SOLUTION.   Once you reach consensus, re-check your thinking before you make the decision binding. This is imperative if the decision is to be irrevocable. Often it is wise to keep the decision tentative until everyone has had a chance to sleep on it or to talk it over with others. Or you may decide to experiment with the proposal on a limited scale.

Inquiry Through Group Discussion

■ PREPARING YOURSELF.   Nothing is gained by pooling ignorance and misinformation. Most of the suggestions given in Chapter 6 will help you explore your subject in preparation for discussion. Following the six steps in reflective thinking, work up a discussion outline that records your information, organizes your thinking, and directs your questions. You may or may not refer to your outline during the discussion. Under no circumstances should you try to force the discussion to follow your outline. Good discussion combines the thinking of all. Your outline should merely sharpen your own preparation and enable you to bring your best efforts to bear.

Cast your discussion outline in the topical or logical pattern or some combination of the two (see Chapter 7). And present your topics or premises as questions designed to bring about a full and satisfying exploration of the problem.

The sample discussion outline that follows does not record the facts and expert opinions that you would consult and use, but it does trace out the lines of thought in each phase of the reflective thinking process. The facts, quotations, and examples that undergird your thinking may be included in your outline, recorded on file cards, or stored away in your head. But don't try to get along without them!

HOW SHOULD OUR COLLEGES HANDLE FINANCIAL AID TO STUDENTS?

I. *What is the problem?*
  A. What is meant by financial aid?
    1. Are scholarships included?
    2. Are student loans included?
    3. Are grants-in-aid without specific grade requirements included?
    4. How about tuition rebates?
    5. Should board, jobs, and the like, provided by the college, be regarded as a form of financial aid?
  B. What are the present provisions for financial aid to college students?
    1. How much aid is given?
    2. What kinds of aid are given?
    3. Who gets this aid?
    4. On what basis is it granted?
    5. What are the sources of the funds?
  C. How adequate are the present provisions for financial aid to students?

    1. Are worthy students denied a college education because they cannot afford it?

    2. Are needy students in our colleges forced to give too much time to jobs in order to stay in college?

    3. Are colleges using financial aid funds to best advantage?

II. *What are the principal causes of the problem?*

    A. Do the colleges face increasing demands for financial aid? From what sources? Why?

    B. Is financial aid more easily obtained in certain educational fields than others?

    C. Are the budgetary provisions for financial aid too limited?

III. *What should our objectives be in granting financial aid?*

    A. A college education for every worthy student regardless of financial resources?

    B. An equitable distribution of the available funds?

IV. *How can this problem be solved?*

    A. Should colleges appropriate larger sums for student aid in their operating budgets from the sources now available to them?

    B. Should colleges seek aid from outside sources: Private foundations? The federal government? Industry?

    C. On what bases should aid be given: Scholastic ability? Need? Service to the college?

V. *What are the merits of these proposals?*

    A. Is it wise for colleges to appropriate more money for student aid?

        1. Do they have the money to use for this purpose?

        2. How would an increase in funds for student aid affect other items in the budget?

    B. Should colleges seek student-aid funds from outside sources?

        1. How available are funds from these outside sources?

        2. Is there any danger that these outside agencies would exercise objectionable control over these funds?

        3. Will student-aid funds from outside sources force the colleges to pay hidden costs not covered by these funds?

    C. Should student-aid funds be granted on the basis of scholarship, need, or service?

        1. Should good students be denied scholarships because their parents can pay the bills?

2. Whose need should determine the assistance? The student's need? Society's needs? And what constitutes need?
3. Should students work for the financial assistance they receive from the college?

VI. *How sound is the proposed solution to the problem?*
   A. Does it attack the causes of the problem?
   B. How well does it achieve the objectives?
   C. Is it workable?

■ TAKING PART IN GROUP DISCUSSION. Inquiry at its best is "thinking out loud." You submit your ideas in a spirit that encourages others to assess their merits, to agree or disagree, and to point out why they agree or disagree. Sometimes you are not at all certain just where your inquiry will lead you. Other times, you will have formulated a tentative conclusion and will invite others to examine the thinking that has led you to it. You ask your listeners questions such as these: How do you react to this idea? Am I right? Where have I gone wrong? Your listeners may answer you with an account of their own thinking. Out of these exchanges emerge a clarification of the problem and new insights that enable you to move on together.

The spirit of inquiry is essential to the success of inquiry. You are engaged in a cooperative undertaking to find the best answer. Once special interests come into play, once participants become more concerned with selfish, private gain than with group purpose, the level of inquiry quickly sinks. Inquiry demands *cooperation among people* and *competition among ideas*. Ideas need to stand on their merits—not on the personality or prestige of their defenders.

Inquiry, then, calls for ideal attitudes—attitudes that are seldom perfectly realized. It is a fact that people do have special interests and prejudices. It is also a fact that people can and do learn to act maturely. When they do, they will be able to engage profitably in group discussion.

Let's say you fall into a dormitory discussion on whether or not your college should require at least two years of mathematics for graduation. You let it be known that you are absolutely opposed to such a requirement. You may give your real reasons, or some trumped-up arguments that sound better than your real reasons, or you may simply refuse to give any reasons at all. But as the discussion shapes up, you begin to realize that not everyone has had the same sad experience with mathematics that you have had. Your opinion begins to waver a bit, but you are afraid that if you reverse your position you will be suspected of retreating under fire. And after all that bright guy who snickered about your mathematical background is no friend of yours anyway.

If you haven't behaved this way on occasion, you are something less than human. But make no mistake: This kind of behavior denies you the full benefit of discussion. And if you persist in it, sooner or later you may find yourself with no one who is willing to enter into a serious conversation with you. The doors of discussion may be bolted against you.

An objective attitude toward people and their ideas leads to the most rewarding inquiry. Check yourself to see how well you measure up to these tests: Do you show a lively interest in ideas? Are you willing to suspend judgment until you have heard the other fellow out? Can you accept fair criticism of your ideas without taking it as a personal affront? Are you willing to give up or modify ideas that have proved untenable? Can you criticize poor ideas without attacking the person who proposed them? Do you assume that others are acting in good faith until they prove otherwise? Do you try to make it easy for people to back away from weak positions?

■ How to lead discussion. The leader of a discussion may be someone who is formally appointed or elected, or else someone who assumes the job with the approval of the group. In fact, leadership often shifts as one person after another temporarily assumes the responsibility.

The essential duties of the leader are to stimulate, guide, and integrate the group. He *stimulates* the members of the group by arousing their interest, by focusing their attention on relevant matters, and by encouraging them to contribute their ideas. He *guides* the members of the group by helping them think through the problem together, but without forcing them to follow any preconceived pattern. And he *integrates* the group by helping members resolve differences, recognize areas of agreement, and come to some kind of understanding. These duties are best performed by a democratic leader who helps each participant to make his greatest contribution.

The two most useful skills in leading discussion are the ability to ask good questions and the capacity to sum up a matter clearly and succinctly. Skillfully worded questions, asked at the right time and directed to the right people, are the leader's first responsibility. He builds his questions around the words *what, why,* and *how.* What is the problem? Why is it a problem? How can it be solved? Such questions help the group to identify the problem, to discover its causes and effects, and to work out a solution.

If you are leading a discussion, try to ask questions that will draw out the members of the group—What is your position? Why do you feel that way? How would you handle the matter? Keep the discussion moving along by raising a new question as soon as each successive point has been handled adequately. Use questions to probe into important aspects of the problem, to introduce phases of the problem that might otherwise be overlooked, and to explore the bases of agreement and disagreement.

Questions evoke discussion, and summaries pull together what has been said. Make short, tentative summaries when agreements have been reached and when disagreements have been fully explored. Use summaries to rephrase a position that needs clarification, to state the points at issue, to remind the group of the ground that has been covered, and to pin down conclusions. If your summary is acceptable, the group can move on to new ground; if it is not, it will open the way to further discussions of a controversial point.

Inquiry Through Public Speech

▪ PUBLIC SPEECH AS A VEHICLE OF INQUIRY.   Public speeches of inquiry are open-ended, and in this respect they differ from other forms of public address. A report transmits information. A speech of advocacy urges acceptance of a predetermined conclusion. An evocative talk inspires or entertains. But in inquiry you remain a seeker. Your goal is to find a solution to a problem by enlisting others to join in the search. If circumstances permit, your audience may enter into the discussion after you have finished your talk. In other situations, the most you can do is to send your listeners away intent on continuing the search you have initiated. But whether or not the audience has an opportunity "to think aloud," the speaker achieves his purpose only if he can induce his listeners "to think with him."

Here are typical examples. A president confronts his board of directors with the unhappy news that the company's business is slipping. Why? He explains the reasons as he sees them. Then he goes on to suggest alternative ways of recovering the lost business. His speech sets the stage for a general discussion by members of the board of directors. At a chapter meeting, a sorority girl analyzes rush methods, raises doubts about the efficacy of present practices, and stirs other members to consider new ones. An instructor in philosophy analyzes the moral issues of war, discloses various ethical theories that come to grips with these issues, and challenges the class to assess the merits of the theories.

"Now that our speaker has raised the questions—are there any answers?"

You are not likely to find speeches of inquiry in anthologies any more than you are to find pictures of a house under construction among photographs of model homes. Such speeches are "thought in process" rather than the finished "outcome of thought." And they should always be judged by standards appropriate to their unique purpose.

■ DEVELOPING A SPEECH OF INQUIRY.   As in group discussion, the six steps in reflective thinking offer a natural sequence for a speech of inquiry. Just how many of the steps you should try to take depends on the situation. Under some circumstances, it is enough to establish the validity and urgency of the problem itself. Here is an actual instance in which most of the speeches were limited to problem analysis.

A community grew up around an airbase that was originally planned for small military training planes and later was converted into a base for jet planes. Many residents felt threatened by the switchover and called a mass meeting. Anyone who wanted to speak was given the opportunity. Some speeches called for immediate action, but most were exploratory. The speakers addressed themselves to questions such as these: Does the conversion to jet planes threaten lives and property? What is the magnitude of the threat? Do we have a problem that is serious enough to investigate further? Out of such probing, consensus was reached that a problem did exist and that a committee of citizens should plan an extended study of all possible ways to deal with it.

Whether you choose to develop your talk through one, two, three, or all of the steps in reflective thinking depends upon the nature of the problem, your present knowledge and insights, the time at your disposal, and the background of your listeners. Student speakers often are challenged by topics that are too big and complicated to be carried through all the six steps in reflective thinking. They may perform a distinct service, however, simply by creating an awareness of the topic *as a problem* and by stimulating thinking where there has been none before.

Private inquiry may lead you to a tentative conclusion of your own. When you speak, you invite your audience to examine the steps that led you to your conclusion. Mind you, this should not be an *ex post facto* report of your private struggles with a problem. You must remain open-minded and be prepared to modify or abandon your conclusion if the thinking you provoke in others justifies a revision in your own thinking. The sample outline on financial aid for students is applicable to a six-step speech of inquiry as well as to group discussion. Let's say you have tentatively concluded that federal funds provide the best source for extending aid to worthy college students. You know this conclusion is highly controversial and you wish to share the thinking that led you to this conclusion— the same thinking you would introduce if this were a group discussion. Such a speech might then become the basis for an open-forum or group discussion.

Points to Keep in Mind

1. Speech that serves the purpose of inquiry is investigative and exploratory in nature.

2. The six steps in reflective thinking provide a useful pattern for speech of inquiry: *Identify the problem; assess the causes; clarify your values; suggest solutions; weigh alternatives; test the solution agreed upon.*

3. Good discussion results from careful preparation, effective participation, and skillful leadership—all accompanied by objective attitudes, reflective thinking, and speech that complements and reveals the thinking of the group.

4. A public speech can serve the purposes of inquiry in larger groups if it takes one or more of the steps in reflective thinking in the same spirit that motivates the best discussion. Such speeches may be given to stimulate the private inquiry of others or to lay the basis for cooperative group deliberation.

Exercises

1. Adopt a question worthy of discussion during two or more class meetings. Develop discussion outlines and come to class prepared to work through the six steps in reflective thinking. Take up each step systematically and carefully. Your main purpose here is to gain mastery of the reflective thinking process and experience in applying the process in discussion.

2. Use the subject you have worked up in Exercise 1, or some other problem of your own choice, for a speech of inquiry. Read the sample speech of inquiry on pages 324-327 before tackling this assignment.

3. Plan a discussion in which each member of the class comes prepared to act as leader of the discussion. Appoint someone to begin as leader and then pass this responsibility around to others as the discussion progresses. Be prepared to ask questions that evoke discussion and to provide short, terse summaries that pull the discussion together.

4. Divide the class into groups of five or six, adopt questions for discussion, appoint a leader for each group, and prepare discussion outlines. Then seat the panel in front of the class. The audience may be invited to present questions at the conclusion of the panel discussion. The leader of the panel may preside over this question period.

5. One way of conducting an inquiry is through interviews. Choose a person you would like to interview, select a problem, and prepare questions that follow the six steps of inquiry. Conduct your interview on the basis of these questions.

CHAPTER SIXTEEN

Reporting

One of the primary purposes of speech is to inform or to instruct. This is your job as a reporter—to communicate information accurately, clearly, and in ways that invite the attention and interest of your audience. You must

discover this information before you can report it, and you should report it without trying to persuade. In a sense, reporting occupies the middle ground between inquiry and advocacy. Your distinctive task as a reporter is to communicate information already in your possession.

Kinds of Report

Perhaps the most useful way to classify reports is on the basis of the audience to whom you are reporting—learning groups, policy-determining groups, the general public, your own friends and associates, and individuals to whom you want to give directions or other instruction.

The oral report is a familiar aid to learning. A teacher gives such reports when he lectures to his class. And you, as student, may be asked to report on your own studies, or on a special investigation, or on research that you have conducted. When you give such a report your purpose is basically the same as that of the teacher—to increase your listeners' knowledge and understanding of the subject.

Many reports are given to policy-determining groups such as boards of directors, councils, and legislative bodies. Such groups usually have standing committees to make reports at regular intervals and special committees to make reports on problems as they arise. In either case, your job as a reporter is to provide dependable information on which decision and action may be based. At a later date, you may be called on to survey the results of a policy thus determined and report your findings back to the group for review. If you make a career as a consulting engineer, a legal investigator, an auditor, or a diagnostician, reports of this kind will be an important part of your professional duties.

Other reports are made to the general public by news reporters and commentators. Most people who listen to radio and television have their favorite reporters—men and women who can be depended on to report reliably, clearly, and interestingly. Any report designed for the general public must necessarily take into account the broader interests of this audience and the many other sources of information competing for their time and attention.

Much of the reporting you do consists of conversation with friends, neighbors, and other close associates. You report experiences, give explanations and directions, and pass along news. There is no reason why this informal reporting should not be entertaining. But if your primary purpose is to inform rather than entertain, your first responsibility is to meet your obligations as a reporter.

How to Make a Report

There are five essential steps in the preparation and presentation of a report.

1. LIMIT YOUR SUBJECT

This first step is simple, but often one of the most troublesome. The beginning speaker, in particular, makes the mistake of trying to cover too much territory. As a result, his report is a string of generalities with neither depth nor impact. Limit the scope of your report so that you can observe the time limits imposed and still present a rewarding development of your subject.

In a recent report on "Who Are the Unemployed?" the speaker set up four distinct categories:

> About fifty per cent of our unemployed are unskilled or semi-skilled workers with limited education. A second group are those whose special skills are no longer needed because of technological advances in industry. A third group—increasing every year—are the older workers who have been retired from former jobs, but who remain in the labor market. And then we have the new workers coming into the labor force each year—some of them graduates of our schools and colleges—who have not yet been located.[1]

The speaker then built a tightly knit thirty-minute report around these four main points. If you were handling this subject with less time at your disposal, you would do well to limit yourself to some one aspect of this broad topic, such as "The Plight of the Unskilled

---

[1] Walter E. Parker, Superintendent of the Illinois State Employment Service, June 14, 1959.

Laborer," or "Automation and Our Skilled Trades and Crafts," or "Senior Workers in the Labor Market," or "How We Absorb New Workers into the Labor Force."

2. DIVIDE YOUR SUBJECT

Your subject, however limited, dictates the area that your report will cover. The next step is to divide this area into manageable units—the main points and sub-points of your report.

A good report breaks a subject down into its parts and shows the relationships of these parts to the whole and to one another. In other words, it is a process of analysis and synthesis. These parts or components might be steps in a process or operation, in an explanation of how to make out your income tax, how to treat the common cold, or how to use the library; they might be the working parts of a machine you are trying to explain, a classification of the parking regulations in your community, the formations most commonly used in professional football, the leading characters in a play; or they might be a list of trends, causes, historical periods, or basic principles. Actually, you may divide your subject into its parts on any conceivable basis or principle, so long as the division provides a useful organization for your report.

For example, a report on "The Accident Problem in Masonry Construction" was organized as follows: The speaker began by discussing the most dangerous operations in masonry construction; next he considered the most common types of injury; then he explained the incidence of accidents among workers of different age and experience; and he concluded with an explanation of a three-step plan of attack to reduce accidents. He discussed each of these topics in terms of the "parts" provided by the divisions—the *operations*, the *types*, the *incidences*, and the *steps*.[2]

No matter how you organize your report, always work for accurate, concise, sharp divisions. Mixed lists, long, unclassified lists,

---

[2] A report by Howard H. Warzyn, Senior Engineer, Construction Section, National Safety Council.

"Now, I want you just to sit there and pretend you're the American Society of Morticians."

overlapping topics, fuzzy distinctions, and intrusions of unrelated items are signs of faulty analysis.

3. PLAN ADAPTATIONS

The divisions and subdivisions of your subject provide the logical structure of your report. But remember that you may be presenting your report to people with different backgrounds, interests, and capacities. Somehow you must link what you have to report with the experiences of your audience. Learning proceeds from the known to the unknown, from the perceived to the unperceived, from the understood to the less well understood. You have to begin where your listeners are and relate the new to the old.

The best adaptive devices for the reporter are examples, comparisons and contrasts, illustrations, and stories. These devices translate the general and the abstract into the specific and the concrete. And they provide bridges from the familiar to the unfamiliar, if the illustrative material is well within the experience of your listeners. They also give life, color, and touches of human interest to your report.

Notice the use of these adaptive devices in this short excerpt from a student report on "Raising Dogs for Fun and Profit."

Bernie is one of our best kennel dogs—a Kerry Blue Terrier. This breed was brought to this country from Ireland in 1920 and was recognized by the American Kennel Club in 1932.

Bernie was one of a litter of seven pups, with good breeding

233

on both sides of his family. As a little fellow, he was coal black with tight curly hair, and a lively self-confident disposition which has always distinguished him in the show ring.

As an adult dog—the sire of a half dozen litters of his own—Bernie carries most of the better qualities of his breed. His coat is still a mass of tight curls, but now a shade between grey and blue. He is about two-thirds the size of an Airedale with alert brown eyes almost concealed by long terrier whiskers. His short, four-inch tail, docked to that length before his eyes were opened to the world around him, always stands at attention, and wags in friendly greeting as best a short tail can.

Bernie is *not* for sale! Not for any price—literally that! He is a champion dog—one of our best—but after all one doesn't sell a member of the family. Bernie will always have a home with us, long after his productive days are over.

Bernie illustrates the central theme of this report better than any dog we own. You can make a few dollars raising dogs if you know how to manage your operation, but the biggest dividend will be the trusting affection of a few almost human animals you never sell. If you get too commercial in this business, you are likely to lose both fun and profit.

This report was aided considerably by a few pictures of dogs and a brief analysis of the financial operations of the kennel. You will find that you can often use visual aids and statistics to good advantage in reporting. In reports that are primarily statistical analyses, you will discover that charts, diagrams, graphs, models, maps, and pictures are invaluable aids to clarity and understanding.

4. MAKE A TOPICAL OUTLINE

As we saw in Chapter 7, there are two general patterns of organization in speech: the topical pattern and the logical pattern. The topical pattern is best suited to reporting because it exhibits those divisions of a *whole* into its *parts* which we have seen to be characteristic of reporting. The sub-points are parts or explanatory divisions of the point to which they are subordinate. And the examples, illustrations, and other adaptive materials are listed under the sub-points to which they apply.

The sample outline that follows is an example of topical organization suitable for reporting. Such outlines may be tight and rigorous or relatively relaxed and informal, depending on the subject and the needs of the occasion.

THE WOMAN VOTER

Introduction

I. The woman voter is important in this election year.
  A. Over 104 million people in the United States are eligible to vote.
  B. Approximately 80 million are registered and therefore legally qualified to vote.
  C. Over 60 per cent of the eligible voters cast ballots in the last presidential election year.
  D. More than half of the eligible and registered voters are women.
II. I wish to analyze the woman's use of the vote, factors influencing the woman's vote, and some of the effects of the woman's vote.

Discussion

I. How do women use the franchise?
  A. Through the years voting records show that women are becoming increasingly active in political life.
  B. What women vote?
    1. A larger percentage in upper-income brackets vote.
    2. There are more in the upper educational brackets.
    3. A larger percentage vote in metropolitan areas than in rural areas.
II. These factors influence the woman's vote.
  A. Women vote more according to their interests and with an awareness of issues than do men.
  B. There is greater conservatism among women voters.
  C. Family influences affect their vote.
    1. In one case in twenty the husband and wife vote for different political parties.
    2. Parents and children vote differently in one case out of ten.

3. The proportion of disagreement among in-laws is one in five.
III. What are the effects of the woman's vote?
    A. What is its impact on political parties?
        1. Control remains in hands of men.
        2. Women are active on the precinct level.
        3. Women are given modest positions in party organizations.
    B. Women have greater influence on local elections and local is-
       sues than at the national level.
    C. There is enough difference between distribution of men's votes
       and women's votes to make women's votes crucial in close elec-
       tions.

Conclusion

  I. Women are making progress in using the franchise.
    A. They were given the ballot in 1920.
    B. The percentage of women exercising the ballot is increasing.
    C. The development of organizations such as the League of Women
       Voters tends to increase their influence.
 II. Parties and candidates cannot afford to neglect the woman voter.

5. USE EXPOSITION, DESCRIPTION, AND NARRATION IN DEVELOPING YOUR OUTLINE

Exposition, description, and narration are your principal
tools in reporting. Exposition gives an explanation; description
paints a picture; and narration tells a story. You will find that most
of your reports are primarily expository, with description and narration playing supporting roles.

Exposition classifies the data you wish to report and then identifies the more significant items in each category. For example, you
might report the operations of a corporation by explaining the several departments of the corporation and the essential activities of
each. The short exposition below reduces the principles of ele-
phant-stalking to a few simple steps and then tells you how to
perform each of these steps—at your own peril, we might add.

As an expert elephant stalker of 72 hours' experience, I now
elucidate to you the principles of elephant stalking.

First you must do it in a motor vehicle of instantaneous acceleration. You will find no difficulty in stalking by automobile, for the elephants like to walk on roads and frequently stay on or near them.

Next you spot your elephant, knocking down trees or dallying in a water hole. You find which way the wind is blowing by throwing a handful of dust into the air. You want to approach him in such direction that the wind blows from him to you. For if it is the opposite, it will carry your obnoxious odor to him and he will either charge you or run away in nausea.

The next thing to know is that the elephant has very bad eyesight. There is a legend that bull elephants sometimes show off in front of large boulders for hours on the mistaken assumption that the latter are potential mates. If you remain stock still, an elephant cannot see you at thirty yards distance. Even when you are moving, he loses sight of you at fifty yards distance.

Now . . . you spot your elephant, get the wind on the right side of you, then you back your vehicle up to the pachyderm slowly, the cameraman on the back shooting pictures. This is so that when he gets sight of you and charges, you can move forward, away from him, at top speed. Since he becomes blind to you at fifty yards distance, when you have put that space between you and him, you are safe, and the elephant will thrash around in the bush blindly and never find you.[1]

Description gives your listeners a picture of your subject by dividing it *spatially* and then listing the *qualities*—size, shape, color, texture, smell, feel, taste—of the several items produced by this division. When you focus your camera on a landscape, you can capture the entire picture with one click of the shutter. But if you want to describe the same scene in words, you have to begin with the cottage in the foreground, or the hills that form the backdrop, or the sunset, or the sheep grazing on the slopes. These spatial relations give your listeners perspective, and provide you with topics for description that you can put into clear, vivid word pictures.

[1] Reproduced by permission from a C.B.S. broadcast made by Howard K. Smith on November 17, 1954.

Narration tells how something happened, usually by giving the details of the event in chronological order. Here, *time* rather than *space* is the guiding principle in organizing your report. Description stops the clock and takes a still picture; narration keeps the clock running and takes a motion picture. For example, one speaker used narration in making a report on "Shipping by Freight." He gave a narrative account of the travels of a freight car in a single month— where it was loaded, the freight it carried, the switching terminals it passed through, the tracks it traveled, and the stops it made. He told a story—but in telling it he gave an informative report on the car pool maintained by American railroads and the purposeful wanderings of freight cars from one line to another.

Edward R. Murrow's report on Hurricane Edna (pages 327-330) combines exposition, description, and narration, but the basic plan is narration.

Points to Keep in Mind

In reporting, you present your information accurately, clearly, and interestingly without trying to persuade your listeners. There are five steps in preparing a report:

1. Limit your subject so that you will have time to develop it adequately.

2. Divide your subject clearly.

3. Illustrate your points specifically and concretely.

4. Prepare a topical outline to organize your report.

5. Develop this outline through exposition, description, and narration.

Exercises

1. Make a report on some process—how something is made, how something operates, how something is marketed, how you use a product.

Try to reduce the process to a series of steps. These will be your main points. Amplify each main point with specific, concrete materials. Make your report interesting as well as informative. In preparing this report be certain to draw up a careful topical outline as a basis for your speech. Discuss this kind of outline in class until you are sure you understand it.

2. Plan a short biographical report on a historical figure, a contemporary person, or an interesting fictional character. Make the subject of your report "come alive" for your listeners. Deal with two or three of the most interesting facets of the man's life. Here is a chance to use vivid description and narration.

3. Choose an important event that genuinely interests you—either a recent event or one that took place long ago. Steep yourself in information about it. Report it to your audience so that the event will live for them. Give your report the color and life and suspense that marked the event itself.

4. Plan a review of a book you have read or a play or movie you have attended. Your primary purpose here is to report rather than evaluate. Make the review interesting and vivid, but remain impartial and objective. We are interested here in *learning about* the book, play, or motion picture rather than in your opinion of its merits.

CHAPTER SEVENTEEN

Advocacy

The president of the Student Council is speaking to the student body: "As you know, the Council has voted to uphold the Board of Publications in their decision to replace Jim Meyers as editor of the *Daily Reporter*. Several of us sat in on the Board's discussion of the case. Later we took it up in Council meetings. Profes-

sor Smith, who has been chairman of the Board of Publications for years, gave us an unbiased report on the whole incident leading to Meyers' dismissal. Now, we've got nothing against Jim. We like him, and we respect his position. At the same time we're convinced that the Board's decision is right. We think you should support the action of the Board and Council because. . . ."

Here is an introduction to a speech of advocacy. The president of the Council has made an inquiry into a problem and has studied a report on it. He has reached a conclusion. He has committed himself to a position, and he now speaks to win support for it. This is advocacy in action.

Kinds of Advocacy

Some people are professional advocates—lawyers, salesmen, and public-relations men, to name a few. Men and women in many other occupations—clergymen, executives, and legislators, for example—often speak as advocates. But advocacy is not limited to these occupations. All of us speak to convince and persuade in family councils, community meetings, and even in the most informal social gatherings.

Advocacy may be presented in public speech or in conversation. And, in either case, other speakers may or may not be moved to express opposing views. If such opposition does develop, we have all the necessary ingredients of debate, no matter how public or private, formal or informal the occasion may be.

The Methods of Advocacy

An understanding of the methods of advocacy will enable you to present your views convincingly and persuasively. Basically, these methods consist of five clearcut steps. But how closely you follow these steps in any particular situation will depend on your specific purpose, the nature of the occasion, and the presence or absence of others who argue against your views.

1. DETERMINE WHAT IT IS YOU ARE PROPOSING OR ATTACKING

In the parlance of the debater, your proposal is your *proposition*. But whether you call it a proposition, a motion, a bill, or simply a statement of position, both you and your listeners need to know what you are driving at. You should always be able to state your proposition in clear, concise, unambiguous terms.

The matters you propose or attack will appear as statements of *fact, value,* or *policy.* Your proposition may be a *factual* judgment: "Air travel is the safest means of transportation." "Television reduces attendance at sports events." Or a *value* judgment: "The new Plymouth is the best buy in the low-priced field." "Alaska is the land of opportunity." Or a *policy* judgment: "State University should build a guest house for parents." "The voting age should be reduced to eighteen years."

2. DETERMINE THE ISSUES

Once you have phrased your proposition, you are faced with this question: What do I have to do to get my proposal accepted, endorsed, or favorably acted on? Or, if you are on the other side of the fence: What do I have to do to defeat the proposal? Whenever you are under some obligation *to prove* your proposition, you must look to the issues for the answer to this question. And you will always be on safer grounds if you know what the issues are. Otherwise you may deceive yourself as well as your audience.

The issues are the *inherent* and *vital* points on which the truth or falsity of a proposition hinges. The words "inherent" and "vital" are the keys to the matter.

The issues are *inherent* because they exist or inhere in the proposition quite apart from anyone's personal wishes or predilections. You discover issues. You don't invent them or make them up. Two or more persons analyzing a proposition independently should discover the same issues. If they do not, either their analysis is faulty or else the proposition is ambiguous.

The issues are *vital* because the life of the proposition depends upon them. If any one of them is opposed successfully, the proposition is lost, just as death results when a vital organ is destroyed. No point may be regarded as an issue simply because it is interesting, or even because it is important. To qualify as an issue it must be vital.

Suppose we say that the Jones farm, now up for sale, is a good investment. Here is a proposition of value. How do you know the farm is a good investment? In other words, what are the issues? First, is the farm *a good value*—in terms of agricultural production, future subdivision, or any other uses to which it might be put? Second, is the asking price *a fair price* on the current market? And third, are *real estate prices likely to rise* so that the investment will yield a significant inflationary increment?

Let's take our example one step further. Suppose a real estate agent offers the Jones farm to Mr. Davis as an investment. Now we have gone beyond a proposition of value—we have a proposition of policy. In addition to the first three issues, we now have three new ones: Does Davis have *the financial resources* to swing this deal? Will he get *a fair return* for his time and trouble in making the transaction? Is this the *best investment* he can make?

How would you use these issues if you were discussing the Jones farm as an investment? Or if you were trying to persuade Mr. Davis to buy the farm as an investment? These questions lead directly to the next steps in advocacy.

3. PLAN YOUR CASE

Your case is the sum total of the arguments, evidence, and any other inducements you offer to secure acceptance of your proposition. You stand or fall on how your case is regarded by the people you are trying to get to accept your proposition. You may present your case in a public speech. You may develop it in conversations with other interested parties. In any event, wherever circumstances permit, it is wise to plan your case carefully.

■ THE MAIN POINTS. The main points are the principal divisions or lines of argument in your case. These main points may or may not coincide with the issues.

Let's say that a village council is discussing the advisability of drilling a well to provide a central water supply. Up to now the villagers have had to scare up their own water by means of private wells, cisterns, or rain barrels.

There appear to be four issues involved here: (1) Will the proposed well reduce significantly *the inconveniences* imposed by the present arrangement? (2) Will the new well produce water in *sufficient quantity* to meet the needs of the village? (3) Will the new well deliver water of *good quality?* (4) Are *the costs* of this project reasonable?

Assuming these to be the issues, the case *for* the new well might be organized around four main points—convenience, quantity, quality, and cost. And the case *against* the well might be organized around these same points. In both cases, the main points would coincide exactly with the issues.

There is no compelling reason, however, for organizing either case in just this way. A speaker favoring the new well, for example, might decide to break the issue of inconvenience down into two main points, then handle the issues of quantity and quality under a single main point, and conclude with a final point based on the issue of cost. Or he might omit one or more of the issues completely. Or he might, for reasons of strategy, even introduce main points that have little or nothing to do with the issues.

Any advocate, whether he is for or against a proposition, should build his case with full knowledge of the issues. But how he *plans* his case—how he *uses* the issues—will depend on his analysis of his listeners and the known or potential opposition. The issues are impersonal logical considerations. The main points of the case represent the speaker's appraisal of the issues in terms of the occasion. A contention does not become an issue simply because some speaker chooses to make it one of the main points in his argument.

■ THE BURDEN OF PROOF. The burden of proof in any argument always lies with the advocate who is dissatisfied with things as they are. For example, if you propose a new high-school building for your community, you have the burden of proof. This simply means that you must initiate the argument and make a convincing case for your proposal before you can expect action on your proposal. Let's say your next-door neighbor is perfectly happy with the present high-school building. In these circumstances, there is no reason for him to offer a defense of the present building until you have made a case for a new building. And even then, it may be sufficient for him merely to refute your arguments.

Any proposition you choose to discuss, whether it is a proposition of fact, value, or policy, will fall into one of two categories: It will propose some *new* idea, policy, or way of looking at things—some *change* in the status quo. Or it will argue for the preservation of the status quo—for things *as they are now,* for our *present* institutions, values, and convictions. The burden of proof always rests on the speaker who is advocating change. He is the dissatisfied party. He is the one who stands to lose if nothing is done.

In advocacy of any kind, it always pays to know whether you have the burden of proof. This burden imposes two responsibilities: that of initiating the argument, and that of making a case that supports the issues. If you advocate any proposition that involves a change in existing policies, attitudes, and beliefs, these responsibilities are yours. On the other hand, if you support existing policies or attitudes and beliefs generally held, you have no reason to make a case for them until they are effectively challenged. And when you do make your stand, it is sufficient, if you choose, to defeat your opponent on any *one* issue—on any matter that is vital to his proposal.

This doctrine is simple common sense. Our example of the village council considering the advisability of drilling a new city well illustrates all the points we are making here. When the council is in session, quite obviously the people who want the new well will have to present their proposition and defend it. If they say nothing —make no motion and no case—the meeting will adjourn without even considering the matter. Certainly the people who oppose the new well aren't going to start the ball rolling. Why should they? They are satisfied with the present water facilities.

But let's say a motion is made that the new well be approved and a strong case is made in its behalf. Such a case, of course, calls for an answer from those who oppose the new well, because it threatens their position. They can no longer remain silent. They must counter this threat with a case that defeats the proposal on at least one vital count, at least one issue. The issues involved here, as we have seen, appear to be convenience, quantity, quality, and cost. The attack would be completely devastating if all issues were opposed successfully. Here the opposition would contend that the present water facilities are adequate, that the proposed well would not deliver enough water anyway, that what water it did produce would be of poor quality, and finally that the costs were prohibitive.

Actually any one of these points would logically defeat the motion. Why seek a new water supply if the present supply is fully adequate? Why drill a new well if it won't produce enough water? Why turn to a well that will deliver water of such poor quality that no one wants to use it? Or why give serious consideration to a proposal that you can't pay for?

The point is simply this: Wherever and whenever you speak as an advocate, you either have the burden of proof or you don't have it. If you understand the duties and the privileges that are yours in these different circumstances, you are in a position to behave much more persuasively and much more strategically than you would otherwise be able to do. The issues and the burden of proof prescribe your *logical* responsibilities in planning a case. You *may* win an argument without discharging these responsibilities, but critical listeners and informed opponents are likely to hold you to them.

■ REFUTATION.   When you are planning a case, try to take care of arguments that may be used against you or that may exist in the minds of your listeners. This is what we mean by refutation—replying to arguments that oppose your position. You may include a scheme for refutation as part of your planned case, or you may devise it to be used in replying to another speaker.

Your refutation may take the form of an *objection*—you may point out flaws in the other speaker's argument. Or it may take the form of a counterargument—you may present an argument of your own to support a conclusion that is inconsistent with the one you are trying to refute. For example, your opponent declares that Latin should be a required subject because a knowledge of Latin enables students to speak and write English more competently. You might offer the *objection* that he has presented no convincing evidence for his proposition. Or you might *counter* by showing that if the time given to Latin were spent on the study of English, better results would be achieved in the students' use of English.

There are four ways of dealing with arguments that are raised in opposition to your position:

1. Ignore them if they are unimportant.

2. Admit them if you can show that they do not damage your case.

3. Show that they are irrelevant.

4. Refute them: First state them clearly and correctly; then show why they won't hold up.

4. PREPARE A CASE OUTLINE

The outline you prepare for a speech of advocacy should reveal the structure of your case. It gives you a chance to organize all the materials—facts, expert opinions, and inferences—that you plan to present.

The logical outline (see Chapter 7) is ideally suited for speeches of advocacy, for here you present your main points as reasons in support of your proposition. You buttress your main points, in turn, with sub-points that serve as reasons to support the main points. You can carry this reasoning process down to points that can be supported directly by evidence (facts and expert opinions) or to points you believe will be accepted without further support.

This kind of rigorous, logical organization is useful in close argument, but you may find that it denies you the freedom to develop your case persuasively. And it is true that this organization, methodical and logical though it is, may be heavy-footed and dull if it is not brightened by description, narration, and exposition. Consequently the most skillful advocate combines logical and topical outlining in whatever pattern best serves his purpose. The three sample outlines that follow suggest some of these adaptations.

Here is a tightly drawn logical outline. Notice that complete sentences are used and that all sub-points, except those in the introduction, serve as direct support for the points under which they appear.

A HEDGE AGAINST INFLATION

Introduction

I. I should like to propose that now is the time to invest in common stocks.
   A. If you have any surplus funds to invest, I am convinced that common stocks are your best investment at this time.
   B. If you don't have funds to invest, you may know somebody who does.
II. The distinction between stocks and bonds is essential to an understanding of my argument.
   A. A stock certificate is evidence of ownership of one or more shares in a corporation.
   B. A bond is a certificate of ownership of a specified portion of the *debt* of a corporation.

Discussion

I. We face an inflationary period in the years immediately ahead, because
   A. Strong inflationary forces are at work, because
      1. There are heavy consumer demands, because
         a. There is a shortage of residential units.
         b. We are not keeping up with the demand in many commodity lines.

    2. Heavy expansion of manufacturing plant and equipment is in prospect.

    3. Government spending is increasing, because

       a. The international situation calls for heavy military expenditures.

       b. The philosophy of the present administration favors large governmental expenditures.

  B. The evidences of inflation are already at hand, for

    1. Prices have started up again.

    2. We have strong demands from labor.

II. Common stocks increase in value during periods of inflation, because

  A. The tangible assets of the corporation increase in value, because

    1. Plant and equipment are worth more.

    2. Commodity inventories on hand increase in price.

  B. The corporations are able to pay larger dividends out of increased profits.

III. The real value of bonds decreases during inflation, because

  A. They are paid off in cheaper dollars.

  B. The interest rate is fixed.

Conclusion

  I. Investments with fixed returns suffer in an inflationary period.

  II. Common stocks are your best hedge against inflation.

This next sample is another example of a logical outline. Here the speaker is urging action, and he develops his case with this purpose in view. Notice that he also includes some refutation.

VOTE FOR THE CITY MANAGER PLAN

Introduction

  I. I should like to open this meeting with a message from Mayor Brown.

  II. I join the mayor in urging you to go to the polls tomorrow and vote for the City Manager Plan.

Discussion

  I. The old Mayor-Council form of city government has outlived its usefulness, because

A. The system can't handle the growing complexities of city government.
B. It makes a political football out of city government.
C. The argument that the Mayor-Council system is more responsive to the will of the people is a myth.

II. More progressive cities everywhere are adopting the City Manager Plan—over 1000 of them—because
   A. It streamlines city government—it is more efficient, because
      1. It places a professional manager in charge.
      2. It fixes responsibility.
      3. It reduces the size of the council.
   B. It takes corruption out of city government.
   C. The contention that we will be unable to get a good city manager for the salary we propose is groundless, because
      1. We already have two applicants.
      2. We know where we can go for a man with an established record as a city manager.

III. Now is the time for us to act, because
   A. Mayor Brown, the best mayor we have had in decades, is retiring.
   B. Mayor Brown supports the new plan.
   C. With few exceptions, our community leaders are behind the plan.

Conclusion

I. I am not going to promise you that your taxes will be reduced, but I think I can promise more for your tax dollar.
   A. We'll get our garbage collected on time!
   B. We'll get the snow cleaned off the streets!
   C. We'll get better fire and police protection!
   D. And last, but not least, we'll let a little fresh air blow through the City Hall!
II. These things are worth voting for!

Our third sample is a topical outline using key phrases rather than complete sentences. This is an outline for a persuasive speech that draws on description, narration, and exposition.

A SUMMER ON TIPTOE

Introduction

I. Traveling to Europe in a vagabond spirit
   A. The high adventure of planning the trip
   B. Joining the green passport club
II. Watching the New York skyline recede from the deck of the *Liberté*

Discussion

I. First stop is Britain
   A. Glimpses of the countryside from the window of a boat train
   B. This is London
      1. City of medieval towns
      2. Excellent transportation plus the courtesy of the people make it easy to get around
      3. Queuing up for a day in Parliament
   C. Short journeys out of London
      1. The spires of Oxford
      2. On the banks of the River Cam
      3. The swans of Avon
   D. The moors of Scotland
II. From Dunkirk to the Riviera
   A. Making your fractured French work in the provinces
   B. Left Bank—Right Bank
      1. The live-and-let-live attitudes of the Parisians
      2. A city of art, superb cuisine, and gaiety
   C. A week end at Villefranche
III. The trek north from Rome to Amsterdam
   A. Crisis on the crest of the Apennines
   B. The tinkle of cow bells at St. Gotthard Pass
   C. Twilight specters in the historic city of Worms
   D. The land of green canals
      1. From the terrace of the Hotel Grand Gooiland
      2. Rembrandt's "Night Watch"
      3. The Peace Palace of the Hague
IV. Some quick glimpses of Belgium

Conclusion

I. Goodbye to the White Cliffs

II. Europe is within your reach

5. DEVELOP YOUR CASE PERSUASIVELY

Persuasion rests squarely on four basic concepts: attention, motivation, suggestion, and implication.

■ ATTENTION. Listeners respond favorably to speakers who capture their attention and hold it at a high level. An audience that listens only grudgingly and half-heartedly is unlikely to be stirred into action or into acceptance of a proposition. In giving speeches of advocacy, put to work what you learned about motivated listening in Chapter 9 and what you learned about developing your ideas in Chapter 11.

Plan an exciting opening. Make your listeners feel that you are talking to each of them as an individual. State your proposition arrestingly. Make abundant use of illustrative materials so that the bony structure of your case will be endowed with flesh and blood. Fresh language ignites interest; tired language snuffs it out. Show directness and vitality in your delivery. It is easy to accept the conclusions of an interesting speaker and just as easy to reject the conclusions of a dull one.

■ MOTIVATION. Make your listeners feel that their needs or desires will be satisfied by what you are recommending. Offer them a reward for buying your proposition. Some people respond most readily when the rewards are concrete and immediate. As they listen to you, they are asking, "What's in it for me?" But don't assume that everyone acts only for selfish purposes. Every day people are moved by calls to greatness. Every day they make personal sacrifices for the sake of justice, compassion, and the common good.

Effective motivation is not accomplished by working a few purple patches into your speech or by making a few isolated appeals. It must be part of the warp and woof of your argument. The reasons you use to prove your case should motivate your listeners to accept your conclusion. Ask yourself *two* questions about each reason before you use it in developing your case: Does it advance my argument logically and convincingly? And does it offer an incentive to my listeners to believe or act as I want them to believe or act?

In short, the key to effective motivation is first to identify the needs, interests, wants, and desires of your listeners and then to show them how your proposition will help satisfy those needs.

■ SUGGESTION.   Sometimes you can persuade listeners by dropping hints rather than by giving them a developed argument. You let them come around to your conclusion in their own way. In short, you don't spell everything out, although you should be able to do so if you have to. Present your listeners with an attitude, a word, an example, a story, or a gesture, and then let them interpret it for themselves.

A speaker who was urging a bond issue for a new school once said, "I'm going to vote for this bond issue even though I'm a taxpayer and haven't any children in school. And I'm not wholly altruistic in doing so either." He didn't have to spin out his argument. He simply suggested that if he was willing to pay higher taxes even though he didn't have children, those who had children should be much more interested. He merely hinted at the benefits the new school would bring to the community and the general increase in property values that would accompany it.

Another speaker, confronted with an incredibly stupid argument, simply shook his head slowly and said, "I pass." This action was more tactful and perhaps more eloquent than an extended reply would have been. It simply suggested that the silly argument had refuted itself. In effect, the speaker said, "Why go into it? We all see its weakness. Let's get on with the business."

■ IMPLICATION.   In using implication, you lead your audience to draw the conclusion that you want them to draw by explaining a matter to them, by describing a situation, or by telling a story.

You use description, narration, and exposition—the tools of the reporter—to present a picture that implies your conclusion. The argument is implicit in your explanation, but you don't state it outright.

Let's say you want to persuade a friend to accompany you on a short vacation to New Hampshire. You describe the brilliant foliage, the hills, the "Old Man of the Mountain," inviting trails, streams and lakes teeming with fish. You tell him about a lodge off the beaten path where "interesting" guests sit around a huge fireplace on cool evenings. You have certainly "worked on" somebody in this manner at one time or another. Maybe we're only giving an old "technique" a new name.

Points to Keep in Mind

1. Know what it is you are proposing or attacking and be prepared to phrase it as a concise proposition of fact, value, or policy.

2. Analyze your proposition to discover the issues.

3. Plan your case: Build it around main points calculated to win the response you are after; build it with full awareness of the responsibilities and opportunities arising out of the burden of proof; build it to counter arguments that may be used against you.

4. Prepare a case outline—a logical outline or some adaptation of it.

5. Develop your case persuasively by using attention, motivation, suggestion, and implication.

Exercises

1. Phrase five propositions of policy that you would like to defend or oppose in speeches of advocacy. State the issues in each proposition and be prepared to defend your analysis.

2. Plan a speech of advocacy on any one of the propositions you devised in Exercise 1. Make this a tight, logical speech in which your main points coincide exactly with the issues. Give special attention to cogency of argument and adequacy of evidence.

3. Plan a persuasive speech in which you urge your listeners to take a specific action. Make sure that the action is reasonable and that they are capable of taking it. For instance: Join an organization; read a particular book; eat at a certain restaurant; buy something. Give your speech with conviction and sincerity.

4. Divide the class into groups of five. Let each group adopt a proposition of policy that lends itself to debate. Two people will defend the proposition and two will oppose it. The fifth person will act as chairman and moderator. Then conduct a debate in which the positions of the several speakers are developed through conversation. Do *not* work as teams. Each speaker is on his own and it is up to him to get his ideas accepted as best he can. The moderator's job is to hold the reins on the debate, to draw speakers out, to give each speaker a fair chance, and to invite questions and comments from the class when the debate is concluded.

CHAPTER EIGHTEEN

Evocation

The purpose of evocative speaking is to inspire or entertain. It rewards listeners with emotional satisfactions ranging from the sublime to the ridiculous. Mind and emotions combine in all speech, but evocative talk gives *priority* to man's emotional needs.

258

Inspirational talk gives us a feeling of fulfillment, energizes hopes, reaffirms loyalties, stirs sympathy, stimulates appreciation. Its purpose is to awaken, quicken, and excite us. Entertaining speech, on the other hand, diverts and relaxes us. Listening to a pun, a joke, or a bizarre experience releases us from tension and tedium.

Although evocative speaking is commonly associated with sermons, lectures, ceremonial talks, and after-dinner speeches, it is by no means limited to public occasions. We seek diversion and fellowship through informal conversation with our friends. Inspiration and entertainment find their way into interviews, conferences, and all sorts of group meetings. What we have to say about evocative speaking, then, applies to all situations in which emotional stimulation or relaxation is appropriate.

Elements Common to Evocative Speaking

■ A HIGH DEGREE OF SPEAKER SENSITIVITY. All good speaking calls for sensitivity, but evocative speaking requires a particularly fine awareness of what is appropriate. A report or a logical demonstration of a proposition invites objectivity. Evocative speaking, on the other hand, ventures into intimate areas of personal experience around which we ordinarily throw a protective cloak—our fears, hopes, failures, whims, ideals, and caprices. Our guards are up until the speaker assures us that he is a sensitive and perceptive person. We want assurances, for example, that he knows the difference between sentiment and sentimentality, between warm humor and boorish jokes.

When we say that evocative speaking calls for special sensitivity, we are not suggesting that only a few, rare mortal beings have this capacity. All of us draw on our accumulated experiences and make intuitive judgments of what is fitting. You learn when to stifle the impulses to laugh and when to let go. If you're talking to someone who is in a panic over his grades, you withhold the joke about the fellow who was booted out of school. You choose the friends with whom you are willing to share your highly personal feelings.

The point is this: In evocative speaking, you must make full use of your sensitivities. No two situations are identical. Factors such as age, sex, and religion may be critical. Moods are evanescent.

Never assume that a joke or appeal that was successful in one situation will be suitable to the next.

■ A HIGH DEGREE OF AUDIENCE INVOLVEMENT. You want your listeners to do more than agree with you. You want them to *feel in* with you and what you are saying. You must create or recreate *specific experiences* with which your listeners can identify their own emotions.

Our minds assent to praise for Albert Schweitzer, the great humanitarian, but the winsome story of a boy's admiration for Schweitzer *moved* thousands to follow his lead. When thirteen-year-old Robert Hill, son of an army sergeant stationed in Italy, read of Schweitzer's hospital in Africa and its continuing need for medical supplies, he wanted to help out. He bought a bottle of aspirins and then asked an Allied Air Force Commander if he'd drop it off when he flew over the hospital. By chance an Italian radio station carried the story. It caught on, and donations of $400,000 poured in. Subsequently, Robert and four and a half tons of medical supplies were flown to Africa in planes provided by the Italian and French governments. Said a grateful and astonished Dr. Schweitzer, "I never thought a child could do so much for my hospital."

The story of Robert Hill suggests both the impact of empathy and the means of creating it.

■ A HIGH DEGREE OF CREATIVE IMAGINATION. Do you cringe a little when you hear the word "inspiration"? You have been drenched with corn-soaked exhortations to "buck up, old boy" and to strive upwards and onwards. Does "speaking to entertain" seem fatuous to you? You're probably still groaning at musty after-dinner jokes of the Pat and Mike variety. We all borrow ideas and materials, of course, but we should never be tempted by embalmed platitudes and decayed jokes. Some approaches have been worked to death. "When I was a boy, I walked five miles through snowdrifts to get an education"—however honest and sincere the speaker is, this opening probably leaves you a bit cold too.

"Oh, I don't remember what he said, but it certainly was inspirational."

Avoid hackneyed formulas. Inject fresh insights and your own individuality into what you say. Nobody else has had exactly the same experiences as you. No matter how ancient your theme, your listeners will find new inspiration and new delight if you endow it with authentic freshness and individuality. And match the freshness of your approach with freshness of language. Use words that are rich in associations, words that conjure up images. Notice the difference between these two passages:

> Abraham Lincoln was a complex man. He was unmovable when he was convinced that he was right. On the other hand, he was a very human sort—gentle and charitable when these qualities were demanded.

> Not often in the story of mankind does a man arrive on earth who is both steel and velvet, who is as hard as rock and soft as drifting fog, who holds in his heart and mind the paradox of terrible storm and peace unspeakable and perfect.[1]

Speaking to Inspire

Although there is no single, all-purpose method for you to follow in speaking to inspire, you will find that you can choose one of four master-plans, and perhaps use one or more of the others in subsidiary ways.

[1] Carl Sandburg's tribute to Lincoln before a joint session of Congress, February 12, 1959. *Vital Speeches,* March 1, 1959, p. 293.

THE IMPLICATIVE METHOD

When you follow this method, you *imply* more than you state explicitly. You know exactly where you are going, but your approach is oblique. Along the way, you give your listeners hints as to what your destination is, but you don't spell out everything for them. You energize their imagination with a succession of subtle observations and images.

The implicative approach is particularly effective when you are speaking to sophisticated audiences about ideals, ethical standards, or moral conduct. Recounting an episode that implies a virtue induces greater response than does a thumping homily.

The implicative method is also a congenial way of inviting people to re-examine their values, and to take their bearings in the midst of perplexities. In the life of a man or a nation, the times are often out of joint. Events take over and push us in bewildering directions. In our quandaries, we welcome talk that helps us help ourselves, that stimulates new insights or encourages us to revive old visions.

Notice how Eric Sevareid exposes a perplexity generated by the tensions of our times, how he guides us to new awarenesses, how he points the way out of our perplexity. He implies far more than he says as the speech moves through a succession of allusions and metaphors that surprise and stimulate.

"The Dark of the Moon"

Good evening . . . This is not only Friday night, thank goodness, but the first warm and balmy night of the year in these parts; the first frogs are singing; altogether this is hardly the night for whispering sweet sentiments about the reciprocal trade act, the extension thereof. But since we are confined, by tradition to the contemplation of public themes and issues, let us contemplate the moon. The lovely and luminous moon has become a public issue; for quite a few thousand years it was a private issue; it figured in purely bilateral negotiations between lovers; in the incantations of jungle witchdoctors and Indian corn planters; poets from attic windows issued the statements about the moon, and they made better reading than the mimeographed handouts now being issued by assistant secretaries of defense.

The moon was always measured in terms of hope and reassurance and the heart pangs of youth on such a night as this; it is now measured in terms of mileage and foot-pounds of rocket thrust; children sent sharp, sweet wishes to the moon; now they dream of blunt nosed missiles.

There must come a time, in every generation, when those who are older secretly get off the train of progress, willing to walk back to where they came from, if they can find the way. We're afraid we're getting off now. Cheer, if you wish, the first general or Ph.D. who splatters something on the kindly face of the moon. We shall grieve for him, for ourself, for the young lovers and poets and dreamers to come, for the ancient moon will never be the same again. Therefore, we suspect, the heart of man will never be the same.

We find it very easy to wait for the first photographs of the other side of the moon; for we have not yet seen the other side of Lake Louise or the Blue Ridge peak that shows through the cabin window.

We find ourself quite undisturbed about the front page talk of "controlling the earth from the moon," because we do not believe it. If neither men nor gadgets nor both combined can control the earth from the earth, we fail to see how they will do so from the moon.

It is exciting talk, indeed, the talk of man's advance toward space. But one little step in man's advance toward man—that, we think, would be truly exciting; let those who wish try to discover the composition of a lunar crater; we would settle for discovering the true mind of a Russian commissar or the inner heart of a delinquent child.

There is, after all, another side, a dark side to the human spirit, too. Men have hardly begun to explore these regions; and it is going to be a very great pity, if we advance upon the bright side of the moon with the dark side of ourselves, if the cargo in the first rockets to reach there consists of fear and

chauvinism and suspicion. Surely, we ought to have our cre
dentials in order, our hands very clean and perhaps a prayer
for forgiveness on our lips as we prepare to open the ancient
vault of the shining moon.[2]

THE METHOD OF COMPARISON AND CONTRAST

You can create a mood and heighten appreciation by pointing out dramatic similarities and differences between ideas, events,
people. You might spark a new response to our rich, diversified
heritage, for example, by contrasting the stark, crude frontier life
suggested by the restoration of New Salem, Illinois, with the gen-
tility and elegance of Mount Vernon, Virginia. In his speech, "The
New South," given in 1886, Henry Grady developed his theme
by unfolding a succession of comparisons and contrasts. He opened
with, "There is a South of slavery and secession—that South is
dead. There is a South of union and freedom—that South, thank
God, is living, breathing, growing every hour." As Grady continued, he used contrast and comparison to soften the bitterness
between the sections and to emphasize their common culture and
common ideals.

THE CHRONOLOGICAL METHOD

Carrying your audience through successive periods of time
is particularly appropriate on occasions that call for tribute, dedication, and commemoration—speeches in which you evaluate human
experience. A notable example is the Gettysburg Address. Lincoln
opened with a reference to the past ("Fourscore and seven years
ago . . ."), moved on to the immediate occasion ("We are met on
a great battlefield of that war. We have come to dedicate . . ."),
and ended by holding up the goals of the future (". . . that this
nation, under God, shall have a new birth of freedom—and that
government of the people, by the people, and for the people, shall
not perish from the earth.").

---

[2] CBS News broadcast presented over the CBS Radio Network, March 28,
1958. Reprinted by permission.

Naturally you don't have to stick slavishly to one order of events. You might want to open with the present, look ahead to the future, or flash back to the past.

THE METHOD OF CUMULATIVE DEVELOPMENT

You give an idea impact by restating it in new contexts. You impress the idea on your audience by weaving together example after example, illustration after illustration, quotation after quotation.

Suppose you speak to affirm some principle drawn from human experience, such as the only thing constant is change itself, or imagination is the power behind all creative effort. You might open by stating your theme and then give examples and illustrations that reveal the range of its truth and applications. But your speech will be even more arresting if you open with a well-chosen example that suggests the theme, and then offer additional instances that carry your principle forward into ever-widening circles of human experience. Note this emerging pattern in the introductory passage of a sermon by Ernest Fremont Tittle:

Opening example suggesting the universal principle to be developed

Once there was a young man in Anathoth, a small town not far from Jerusalem, who was called of God to be a preacher. He began his ministry in his home town and was not well received. Quite the contrary. A group of influential people, taking umbrage at the things he was saying, determined to get rid of him. In fact, they went even so far as to plot against his life. When the young preacher learned of this, not unnaturally he was upset. In his anxiety he turned to God for some word of encouragement, and the word that came was this: "If you have run with men on foot, and they have tired you out, then how will you keep up with horses?" Strange comfort! Like the whimsical admonition: "Cheer up, the worst is yet to come." Yet in Jeremiah's case it availed. Life for him did become more strenuous, more difficult and dangerous. But learning to run with men on foot and not get all tired out, he won the power to keep up with horses.

That life's demands increase with the years is a fact of human experience. In high school you may think the assignments are pretty stiff, and so they are; but how relatively easy in comparison with what is required of you if and when you get into college! When the first baby comes, you may think: Oh my! What would I do if I had two or more to care for? And presently you may find out. When you try to get started in business or in a professional career, you may take comfort from the belief that the first years are the hardest. You will, however, be mistaken. The first will presently appear easy in comparison with what you are now up against. You may even look back upon them with a feeling of nostalgia, wishing that life were now as relatively simple and undemanding as it then was. It is indeed a fact that burdens and responsibilities increase with the years.

Application of principle to a variety of personal situations

This holds true of human history as well as of the individual life. Life for us is easier in some ways than it was for those who came before us. Streets are lighted and paved. Houses have bathrooms, electric lighting, central heating. . . .

Extension of principle to wider areas of human experience

But technological advance, if it in some respects made life easier, has at the same time created new problems and dangers. Those who came before us knew the meaning of privation and hardship but not the meaning of mass unemployment or of widespread want in the midst of plenty. They were confronted with the problem of winning fundamental freedoms from reluctant kings, emperors, and czars, but knew nothing of the problem of how to *preserve* freedom in a world situation become so complex as to make necessary an increasing measure of government control. They knew the meaning of war but not of total war waged with absolute weapons against whole populations. Science and technology have brought it to pass that, whereas those who came before us ran with men on foot, we have got to keep up with horses.[3]

Outlining
Inspirational Speech

In working up an inspirational speech, use the topical outline. Organize and state your points with finesse lest you blunt the fine edge of your purpose. The following outline is drawn from a speech by Raymond Fosdick, "The Challenge to Knowledge," delivered at the dedication of the giant telescope on Mount Palomar, California. You will find the text of the speech on pages 336-339.

Introduction

I. In 1843, John Quincy Adams helped dedicate the Cincinnati Astronomical Observatory.
   A. He deplored the neglect of science in the United States.
   B. His speech did not foreshadow today's gap between advancing science and social control of it.
II. Today, knowledge and destruction have joined in a Grand Alliance.

Discussion

I. Our dilemma is that we can't foresee the uses to which knowledge will be put.
   A. Knowledge itself can't be classified into safe and unsafe categories.
   B. We can't predict how the instruments of knowledge will be used.
      1. The University of California's cyclotron, which was used to further the atomic bomb, was originally conceived of as an instrument of pure research.

[3] *A Mighty Fortress.* New York: Harper & Brothers, 1950, pp. 19-21. Reprinted by permission.

       2. Who knows to what purposes this telescope may be converted?
    C. We may elect to use any segment of knowledge for destructive purposes.
  II. How should we deal with our modern dilemma?
    A. We can't fix the boundaries of intellectual adventure.
       1. This would certainly lead to retrogression.
       2. We can't suppress man's innate and insatiable desire to know things.
    B. We need to anchor knowledge to sound moral purposes.
       1. Man's towering enemy is his own moral inadequacy.
       2. Man's survival hinges on the moral use he makes of his new knowledge.
 III. Modern man may well face his final choice.
    A. He can use his knowledge to build a rational world.
    B. Or he can put his knowledge at the disposal of his untamed passions.

Conclusion

  I. This telescope holds the promise of a healing perspective.
    A. Through it man confronts the order and beauty of the universe.
    B. It will dramatize the unsolved mysteries of his universe and existence.
    C. It will help man to see himself in proportion.
  II. There is a real sense in which Mount Palomar is Mount Everest.

Speaking to Entertain

The range of topics suitable for an entertaining talk is almost unlimited. The subjects grow out of your experiences, interests, observations, and imagination. On the surface, this statement may not strike you as very helpful. But there are no categories of entertaining talk as such. Almost anything can be treated entertainingly if you have an intimate acquaintance with it, look at it from a fresh point of view, and present it engagingly.

Call to mind experiences and interests your listeners might consider unusual. Recall out-of-the-way places where you have lived or visited, extraordinary events you have witnessed, a novel hobby you pursue, a curious institution you know about, a cult you have studied, a celebrity you have met, a harrowing experience. Here are some examples of novel subjects that students have used successfully for entertaining talks: life in a ghost town; my fractured French in Quebec; face-to-face with a bear in the woods; my interview with the Vice-President; my summer as a ballet dancer; a restaurant where you pay what you think the meal is worth; working my way through Europe; fighting a forest fire; outwitting a thief; a parrot that talked too much; playing in a bagpipe band; hurricane panic; I was there when my father was married; a summer on a sheep ranch; the deep-freeze I won.

But novelty is not a requisite. You know from your own listening that people talk engagingly on ordinary, prosaic matters. They give these everyday occurrences a unique twist, a wry interpretation, a comic slant, or a suspenseful development. Remember too that a subject may seem ordinary to one audience and extraordinary to another. These subjects, for example, have yielded delightful speeches: A night on a day coach; an acre of tri-levels; pets that have known me; mannerisms of teachers; a TV commentator who speaks as the Voice of Destiny; frantic behavior during exam week; traffic snarls; the ideal parent; my thirty seconds of play in a football game; a broken fiddle string; summer brings poison ivy and Aunt Maud; profile of a Good Humor man; blind dates; a fifty-year-old teenager.

Keys to Effective Entertaining Talk

■ 1. RE-CREATION. As you plan your talk, re-create it in your imagination so vividly that once again you hear, see, touch, taste;

so realistically that once again you feel fear, panic, rhythm, or whatever sensation you wish to convey.

■ 2. SEQUENCE.   Line up your steps or points so that you won't stumble or backtrack. Avoid interrupting yourself with, "Oh, I forgot to mention. . . ." True, you need to keep your material flexible enough for easy adaptation to your audience. But you can plan without putting your speech into a strait jacket.

■ 3. SUSPENSE.   An element of suspense and surprise picks up interest. Don't model every speech after a whodunit, but keep your audience guessing whenever you can. This calls for close attention to details that build toward your punch line or climax. Suspense depends on subtle blending of composition and delivery.

■ 4. VIVIDNESS.   Give enough detail to establish mood and action—but don't use a dump truck. Let concrete language and images work for you. "The man dressed oddly" doesn't help us to see him. But suppose you say he wore a Homburg hat, a rumpled plaid shirt, a dinner jacket, gray flannel slacks, and a pair of sneakers. Now we see what you mean.

■ 5. DRAMATIZATION.   If it's conversation you are recounting, let the participants speak for themselves. Use actual dialogue. If you have a knack for mimicry, go right ahead. Suggest mood and action through posture, gestures, and pantomime.

■ 6. TIMING.   This is tricky. Droll incidents can be annihilated by machine-gun delivery. On the other hand, action-loaded material needs to be presented at a good tempo. Fit the pace to the nature of the materials and the mood of the occasion. Bear in mind too that subtle touches are conveyed by well-placed pauses and skillful phrasing.

Humor

Humor is useful (1) in helping you to get on good terms with your audience quickly; (2) in making serious points painlessly; (3) in providing comic relief from concentrated mental effort and tension; and (4) in affording mutual delight by uttering and hearing nonsense.

Humor arises out of a spirit of play and out of a surprising or incongruous turn of events.

CHARACTERISTIC FORMS OF HUMOR

■ 1. PLAYS ON WORDS. These include boners, slips-of-the-tongue, misused words leading to confusion, and puns. A lawyer is questioning a witness in police court. "Will you testify to the driver's sobriety?" asks the lawyer. "Well, now I dunno," replies the witness, "but my guess is that he ain't so bright."

A pun is more likely to be intentional. If it is perfectly timed and tuned to the situation, it will get the laugh it deserves. Two men driving along barely miss a collision when a Cadillac cuts sharply into their traffic lane. One of the men says, "You never know how a cad'll act." Whether or not you find this pun funny, remember that it takes its humor from the event and emotions of the moment. But a pun can never be quite sure of itself. One man's pun may be another man's punishment.

■ 2. OVERSTATEMENT AND UNDERSTATEMENT. Overstatement leads to a broad, open kind of humor. Work in some element of plausibility, though, unless you can put your story across with such dexterity that your listeners will delight in your ingenuity. Usually exaggeration succeeds best when your manner underplays your words. The comic effect of Will Rogers' outrageous comments was heightened by his dry, mischievous manner. Mark Twain perfected a deadpan delivery.

Understatement is a more sophisticated form of humor. "Waiting to be whipped," said Josh Billings, "is the most uninteresting period of boyhood life." *Uninteresting,* as any boy who knows will testify, is hardly the word. It surprises by saying too little. Mark Twain was a master at combining overstatement and understatement. Note the abrupt switch in this passage from a speech on widespread property damage, injuries, and death caused by Fourth of July celebrations.

> I have suffered in that way myself. I have had a relative killed in that way. One was in Chicago years ago—an uncle of mine, just as good an uncle as I have ever had, and I had lots of them—yes, uncles to burn, uncles to spare. This poor uncle, full of patriotism, opened his mouth to hurrah, and a rocket went down his throat. Before that man could ask for a drink of water to quench that thing, it blew up and scattered him all over the forty-five states, and—really, now this is true. I know about it myself—twenty-four hours after that it was raining buttons, recognizable as his, on the Atlantic seaboard. A person cannot have a disaster like that and be entirely cheerful the rest of his life.[4]

■ 3. CARICATURE. This is humor through distortion. A ridiculous subject is treated with mock seriousness; a serious subject becomes absurd. Under suitable circumstances, almost anything may be caricatured—individuals, events, groups, manners, and customs. As one of America's most popular lecturers, John Mason Brown knows well the types of people who live to be heard.

> . . . Before the hall has been cleared and the chairman has asked for any questions, their full lungs have ballooned them to their feet. When they do leap up, they do so with the vigor of salmon headed upstream.
>
> "Mr. Chairman!" they call, their eyes rolling with frenzy, their voices a cross between Daniel Webster's and Willie Stevens', and their notes tucked behind their backs. "Mr. Chairman!"

---

[4] *Mark Twain's Speeches.* New York: Harper & Brothers, 1923, p. 347. Reprinted by permission.

But the chairman, knowing them all too well from previous sessions, looks the other way. To him they seem not men and women but dreaded ectoplasms. He no more sees them than Macbeth's guests spied Banquo at the banquet. "Mr. Chairman," they continue, eyeing the audience as Danton must have surveyed the Convention. The audience mutters, sometime going so far in its forgetfulness of Emily Post and the Bill of Rights as to cry, "Sit down," "Throw him out," "Shut up."

"Mr. Chairman, is this the United States of America or is it not?"

The Chairman, well aware of his Rand McNally, is sorrowfully compelled to admit it is.

"Oh, you, Mr. Ventrelibre," he says, much as a judge might recognize an old offender. His tones would have chilled anyone else, but not Mr. Ventrelibre.

"Mr. Chairman," continues Mr. Ventrelibre, whose name is legion, "as an American citizen I demand the right to be heard."

And heard he is, while you and the chairman get so tired of standing that finally you have to sit down, and while those in the audience who have remained for the question period begin to run, not walk, to the nearest exits.[5]

■ 4. SATIRE AND IRONY. Although not identical, these two forms of humor are closely related. *Satire,* which often bears a trace of irony, is trenchant wit laced with a spirit of ridicule. Commonly this ridicule is directed against specific human blunders, stupidities, vanities, and vices. In *irony,* we say one thing and mean another. What we say is so preposterous that we alert the audience to look for meanings below the surface. Both satire and irony backfire if their barbs are so sharp that they puncture the spirit of play and create sympathy for the victims. After long suffering at the hands of maladroit program chairmen, Stephen Leacock had won the right to satirize them:

---

[5] *Accustomed As I Am.* New York: W. W. Norton & Company, 1942, pp. 52-54. Reprinted by permission.

When any lecturer goes across to England from this side of the water there is naturally a tendency on the part of the chairman to play upon this fact. This is especially true in the case of a Canadian like myself. The chairman feels that the moment is fitting for one of those great imperial thoughts that bind the British Empire together. But sometimes the expression of the thought falls short of the full glory of the conception.

Witness this (word for word) introduction that was used against me by a clerical chairman in a quiet spot in the south of England.

"Not so long ago, ladies and gentlemen," said the vicar, "we used to send out to Canada various classes of our community to help build up that country. We sent out our laborers, we sent out our scholars and professors. Indeed, we even sent out our criminals. And now," with a wave of his hand towards me, "they are coming back."

There was no laughter. An English audience is nothing if not literal; and they are as polite as they are literal. They understood that I was a reformed criminal and as such, they gave me a hearty burst of applause.[6]

Note the vein of irony in this passage from a speech by Mark Twain. After commenting on the great number of people killed in railroad accidents, he added:

. . . But, thank Heaven, the railway companies are generally disposed to do the right and kindly thing without compulsion. I know of an instance which greatly touched me at the time. After an accident, the company sent home the remains of a dear distant relative of mine in a basket, with the remark, "Please state what figure you hold him at—and return the basket." Now there couldn't be anything friendlier than that.[7]

---

[6] Reprinted by permission of Dodd, Mead & Company from *Laugh With Leacock,* Copyright 1930 by Dodd, Mead & Company, Inc.

[7] *Mark Twain's Speeches.* New York: Harper & Brothers, 1910, p. 415. Reprinted by permission.

SUGGESTIONS ON YOUR OWN USE OF HUMOR

■ 1. ORIGINAL HUMOR IS BEST.   Don't hesitate to try your own brand. You may have more ability than you have yet discovered. Given a mellow mood, listeners enjoy the sly comment, the quick come-back, banter, raillery, a play on words. Remember, you don't always have to work for the big laugh. There are many states of amusement short of the guffaw.

■ 2. BE SURE THE HUMOR IS APPROPRIATE.   Adapt your humor to the sophistication of your listeners and the tone of the occasion. Humor may be too subtle or not subtle enough. Low humor is dubious.

■ 3. PLAN HUMOR WHEN IT IS INTEGRAL TO YOUR SPEECH. Good humor may be spontaneous or it may only appear to be so. If you are forewarned that your audience will be expecting you to talk with a light touch, you will want to make careful preparation just as you do for any other type of speaking. Contemporary big-name humorists seldom depend on the inspiration of the moment.

■ 4. HANDLE HUMOR EFFORTLESSLY.   You can't drive an audience to laughter. You have to lead it. It's pretty painful to watch a speaker struggling with his audience to make them laugh.

■ 5. DON'T ADVERTISE YOUR HUMOR.   Avoid comments such as "You'll die laughing at this one," or "Let me tell you a very funny story." If it's funny, your listener will discover it for himself.

Outlining
Entertaining Speech   In outlining a speech of entertainment, use the topical form. Your outline need not be so detailed or tightly drawn as outlines for other types of speaking.

The example below is based on a speech Mark Twain gave to the students of Barnard College, called "Morals and Memory." [8] Though a casual, light-touch speech, it has a design and order of its own.

Introduction

I. Here are two things common to our human experience.
  A. Everyone has a memory, however capricious.
  B. Everyone has morals though I won't inquire into yours.
II. I want to tell you about some freaks of my own memory that may teach you some kind of a lesson.

Discussion

I. I always considered myself a model boy.
  A. Oddly, I seemed to be alone in this opinion of myself.
    1. People around me seemed to think this estimate lacked something.
    2. Even my mother in her old age had forgotten everything about me except this youthful self-prejudice.
  B. There's a moral here if you search for it.
II. Once I "extracted" a watermelon from a farmer's wagon.
  A. I was overcome with remorse—when I discovered the melon was green.
    1. I returned it to the farmer and made him replace it with a ripe one.
    2. I also upbraided him for peddling green melons.
  B. My timely action helped to reform this farmer.
III. I learned something from another boyhood event I can vividly recall.
  A. This is what happened one day when I went fishing without my parents' knowledge or consent.
    1. A stranger in town was killed in a brawl.
    2. My father, who was the coroner, laid out the corpse in our living room.
  B. I came home after dark, not knowing what had happened.
    1. I decided to sleep on the sofa so I wouldn't disturb my parents.

---

[8] *Ibid.*, pp. 224-237.

    2. By stages I came to know who was in the living room with me.

    3. My exit was sudden.

IV. A theatre date with "a peach" made a lasting impression on me.

    A. I slipped off my boots and couldn't get them on again.

    B. The trip home was miserable.

V. Once I rudely dismissed a "peddler of etchings" who called at our house.

    A. He turned out to be a friend of the family.

    B. I had to make amends.

Conclusion

I. I hope I taught you some inspiring lessons.

II. I know I enjoyed you more than I enjoyed that "peach" of fifty-three years ago.

Points to Keep in Mind

    1. Speaking to inspire and speaking to entertain are the two principal types of evocative speech. Both require:

    a. A high degree of speaker sensitivity.

    b. A high degree of audience involvement.

    c. A high degree of creative imagination.

    2. Follow one basic method in developing inspirational speech—the implicative, comparison-contrast, chronological, or cumulative method. Others may be used helpfully in a subsidiary role.

    3. The keys to entertaining speech are re-creation of the event, careful sequence, suspense, vivid details and language, dramatization, and good timing. Skill with humor contributes much to this type of speaking.

    4. Use the topical outline on occasions when you speak to inspire or entertain.

Exercises

1. Select a great speech or sermon whose ideas stir you. Consult the Bible, Shakespeare's plays, or anthologies of speeches. Open your talk by reading portions of your selection. Then in your own words carry forward the ideas expressed.

2. Use this speech to stimulate interest in and appreciation for some person who is unknown or little known to your audience, but whose life in some way has affected theirs. He may be a founder of your college or university, a donor, a teacher who is only a memory to the alumni, an alumnus who has conferred distinction on alma mater.

3. Prepare a "This I do believe" type of speech. Begin with a concept such as democracy, education, happiness, courtesy, brotherliness, worship. Formulate a theme that crystalizes your credo. Develop the speech by means of the most appropriate pattern of the four listed in this chapter.

4. Make a cutting of an entertaining speech or piece of writing by Mark Twain, Artemus Ward, Robert Benchley, Will Rogers, Stephen Leacock, James Thurber, E. B. White, or someone else whose works you enjoy and would like to share. Prepare an introduction of your own.

5. Work up an entertaining talk based on a personal experience or an imaginative commentary on human behavior. Before you give it, check over the keys to entertaining talk and the suggestions on humor given in this chapter. Use as many of them as you can.

CHAPTER NINETEEN

Reading
Aloud

You already know that under certain circumstances it is a good idea to write out a speech beforehand and then read it to your audience. And you know, too, that many extemporaneous speeches benefit by quoted passages. This chap-

ter will help you as a public speaker, but it will also give
you insights into oral reading as a form of communication
—reading that will give your listeners more of the meaning and feeling of the original author than they would
get by reading the same passage silently.

Oral Reading
and Communication

The purpose of reading aloud is to communicate with your listeners. This is true whether you are reading from a book, a news story, a market report, a sonnet—or any other kind of material. The reader has a dual obligation—both to his audience and to his material.

When you read silently, you are the only person who is "listening." You skim, and you slow down. If the meaning of a passage escapes you, you go back and read it again. You pick up the meaning of a new word or phrase from its context. As you read along, you adjust yourself to the writer's sentence structure and punctuation.

But when you read aloud, your audience must depend entirely on you to convey the meaning. Hence, reading aloud is a more complex act than reading silently. As a reader, you must make the written word immediately intelligible, meaningful, and vital. You discharge your obligation to your material and to your audience through sensitive interpretation.

What we have said may strike you as obvious. But how many readers show *by their reading* any real competence to interpret the written word? The plain and painful fact is that good readers are rare. Absurd as it may seem, some people read lyric poetry in much the same way that they read the minutes of the last meeting of their club. Even remarkably fine speakers frequently lose their audience when they begin to read. They fence themselves off with wooden words. At the other extreme are the people who look on every opportunity to read as a chance to give a dramatic performance. They're out to make a show of it, and they go about it in the spirit of a prima donna. Listeners may be either amused or embarrassed by such histrionics, but they respond not at all to the writer's message.

Good reading, like good speaking, requires special preparation before you face your audience.

Explore Levels
of Meaning

■ FAMILIARIZE YOURSELF WITH THE INTELLECTUAL CONTENT.
Successive private readings of a selection may reveal new meanings.
If it's your own composition, you may be surprised to discover as
you read it aloud that it conveys meanings you hadn't intended.
If the selection was written by someone else, first read it for the
general sense. As you do so, look up unfamiliar words and allusions.
And while you are at it, learn to pronounce the words you're not
sure of.

In subsequent readings look for answers to these questions: What
is the writer's purpose? What is the central idea or theme that holds
the work together? What are the subsidiary ideas? Does the thought
lie at the surface, or is it difficult to follow? Even if you plan to
read only a small passage, know how it fits into the whole work.
Answers may be easy to come by, or you may have to dig for them.
When necessary, consult outside sources such as commentaries,
reviews, and reference books.

■ INVESTIGATE THE BACKGROUND OF YOUR MATERIAL. You
will acquire a deeper understanding and appreciation of your selection if you know something about its background. By way of illustration, consider two quite different types of material. The first is
J.B., a play by Archibald MacLeish. If you are guided solely by
the contemporary circus setting of the play, you will miss the pro-
found and timeless problem with which the poet deals. When you
compare this play with the Book of Job, from which MacLeish drew
his inspiration, you will appreciate more fully man's search for an
answer to the meaning of his afflictions. An awareness of this background will heighten your respect for a modern treatment of an
ancient theme, and will enable you to bring to your reading greater
breadth and depth of knowledge. In short, understanding establishes both the desire and the right to communicate the writer's
message.

Thomas Jefferson's First Inaugural Address offers a second illustration. Take this paragraph:

> During the throes and convulsions of the ancient world, during the agonizing spasms of infuriated man, seeking through blood and slaughter his long-lost liberty, it was not wonderful that the agitation of the billows should reach even this distant and peaceful shore; that this should be more felt and feared by some and less by others, and should divide opinion as to measures of safety. But every difference of opinion is not a difference of principle. We have called by different names brethren of the same principle. We are all Republicans, we are all Federalists. If there be any among us who would wish to dissolve this Union or to change its republican form, let them stand undisturbed as monuments of the safety with which error of opinion may be tolerated where reason is left free to combat it.

True, the general sense of Jefferson's remarks is not hard to figure out. His call for amity and his stand for civil liberty are familiar. But it is precisely because readers are too often content with such off-the-top-of-the-head reactions that their reading adds nothing to the listener's understanding or appreciation.

As a reader, you are somebody else's representative by your own choice. It would be a desecration to accept and read Jefferson's lines as if all he had done was to strike off shopworn platitudes, pious and empty generalizations wholly detached from the age in which they were written. Look at the passage again. It is filled with oblique references to past events and unsettling ideas. It carries intimations of the French Revolution and its impact on American politics, of bitter domestic struggles over the Alien and Sedition Laws, of the abusive political campaign of 1800, of Jefferson's persistent work in behalf of civil rights. Here is a distillation of Jefferson's faith in the free mind. No one can expect to communicate to others the inner meaning of the speech until he is steeped in the circumstances of its origin. And while we're on the point, note that the eighteenth-century expression "it was not wonderful" should be interpreted as "it was not remarkable" or "it is to be expected that."

■ ESTABLISH THE PREVAILING MOOD OF THE WORK. As you pursue your analysis, you will discover that some materials have little or no emotional content, and that others pulsate with feeling. We want factual reports to be interpreted with lucidity, precision, and just enough highlighting to bring out the essentials. It's a mistake to inject emotion into materials that were free from emotion when they were written. But aside from strictly factual reports, in most prose compositions the writer's emotions are in some way involved. Often he makes a deliberate effort to involve your emotions too.

First of all, then, discover the *nature* and *intensity* of the writer's feelings. It would be hard to miss the fervor of Patrick Henry's peroration in his famous speech on the eve of the Revolutionary War:

> It is in vain, sir, to extenuate the matter. Gentlemen may cry, Peace, Peace—but there is no peace. The war is actually begun! The next gale that sweeps from the north will bring to our ears the clash of resounding arms! Our brethren are already in the field! Why stand we here idle? What is it that gentlemen wish? What would they have? Is life so dear, or peace so sweet, as to be purchased at the price of chains and slavery? Forbid it, Almighty God! I know not what course others may take; but as for me, give me liberty or give me death!

Henry's appeal is directed to elemental emotions. His vivid words and jabbing sentences excite strong, sensory responses. Put the speech in its historical context and you will sense how inflammatory it was when it was first delivered. This doesn't mean that you should read the passage as if it were a pyrotechnic display; neither should you read it as if you were reciting the multiplication table. Discover the authentic emotion and then suggest it to your listeners.

Now let's look at a passage from Lincoln's Second Inaugural Address:

> With malice toward none, with charity for all; with firmness in the right, as God gives us to see the right, let us strive on to finish the work we are in; to bind up the nation's wounds; to care for him who shall have borne the battle, and for his widow, and his orphan—to do all which may achieve a just and lasting peace, among ourselves and with all nations.

Both Henry's and Lincoln's words have an emotional tone. But that's where the similarity ends. Henry was animated by and tried to arouse a combative spirit; Lincoln was moved by and sought to move others to compassion. Once again, your appreciation of the mood of Lincoln's speech will be strengthened if you understand the moment in history at which he spoke. Here was a soul-tortured President presiding over the destiny of the Union during the only civil war that has ever afflicted it. The agony of Lincoln and his age is an essential fact in the poetry of his speech.

Poetry vividly illustrates variety in kind and intensity of mood. A poem may express rapture, whimsey, melancholy; it may be pensive, contemplative, ecstatic, despairing, triumphant. You will develop and refine your perception by selecting poems for reading that exhibit these differences. A few selections will suggest what we mean. You will recognize at once the whimsey in these stanzas from Lewis Carroll's "Father William."

> "You are old, Father William," the young man said,
>   "And your hair has become very white;
> And yet you incessantly stand on your head—
>   Do you think, at your age, it is right?"
>
> "In my youth," Father William replied to his son,
>   "I feared it might injure the brain;
> But, now that I'm perfectly sure I have none,
>   Why, I do it again and again."
>
> "You are old," said the youth, "as I mentioned before,
>   And have grown most uncommonly fat;
> Yet you turned a back-somersault in at the door—
>   Pray, what is the reason of that?"

"In my youth," said the sage, as he shook his gray locks,
    "I kept all my limbs very supple
By the use of this ointment—one shilling the box—
    Allow me to sell you a couple?"

"You are old," said the youth, "and your jaws are too weak
    For anything tougher than suet;
Yet you finished the goose, with the bones and the beak—
    Pray, how did you manage to do it?"

"In my youth," said his father, "I took to the law
    And argued each case with my wife;
And the muscular strength which it gave to my jaw,
    Has lasted the rest of my life."

Move now to John Keats' poem "On the Grasshopper and the Cricket." Here is a contemplative comment on the ceaseless rhythm of nature's music.

The poetry of earth is never dead:
When all the birds are faint with the hot sun,
And hide in cooling trees, a voice will run
From hedge to hedge about the new-mown mead;
That is the Grasshopper's—he takes the lead
In summer luxury,—he has never done
With his delights; for when tired out with fun
He rests at ease beneath some pleasant weed.
The poetry of earth is ceasing never:
On a lone winter evening, when the frost
Has wrought a silence, from the stove there shrills
The Cricket's song, in warmth increasing ever,
And seems to one in drowsiness half lost,
The Grasshopper's among some grassy hills.

Now contrast the poems by Carroll and Keats with the last stanza of Matthew Arnold's "Dover Beach." Here you confront complex emotions—darkness and melancholy leavened by the affirmation of an enduring value.

Ah, love, let us be true
To one another! for the world, which seems
To lie before us like a land of dreams,
So various, so beautiful, so new,
Hath really neither joy, nor love, nor light,
Nor certitude, nor peace, nor help for pain;
And we are here as on a darkling plain
Swept with confused alarms of struggle and flight,
Where ignorant armies clash by night.

Finally, we perceive stark, unrelieved despair in these lines from Shakespeare's "Macbeth."

Tomorrow, and tomorrow, and tomorrow,
Creeps in this petty pace from day to day
To the last syllable of recorded time,
And all our yesterdays have lighted fools
The way to dusty death. Out, out, brief candle!
Life's but a walking shadow, a poor player
That struts and frets his hour upon the stage
And then is heard no more; it is a tale
Told by an idiot, full of sound and fury,
Signifying nothing.

Sometimes the authentic mood of a poem is not easy to discover. It may be half-concealed and elusive. It may lurk in a word or a metaphor, in the music and rhythm of the language. Should you find that the essential feeling eludes you, either consult somebody who can help you or choose something else that is within the range of your understanding.

■ KNOW THE STRUCTURE OF YOUR SELECTION.   Meaning and mood will emerge more clearly if you analyze the design of a work. Lincoln's Gettysburg Address offers a classic example. On this occasion, Lincoln wanted to do two things: to honor the heroic sons, husbands, and fathers who had been killed; and to state the case

"Of course, to get the full effect you should be sitting on a folding chair and drinking cold coffee."

BURR SHAFER

for democracy. In order to blend these two purposes into one unifying theme, he developed his haunting metaphor of birth, death, and rebirth—in the life of man and in the life of a nation. Thus Lincoln suggested not only the historical parallels between the life of a man and a nation, but he projected his faith in eternal democracy by linking it with man's aspirations for eternal life.

We gain a sharper perception of a writer's or speaker's purpose and meaning by exploring the structural artistry of his work.

Read Experimentally Before You Read to an Audience

Having analyzed the thought, mood, and structure of a work, test the results of your study by reading the work aloud to yourself. Listen critically to your reading, and, if possible, make a tape recording or get the reactions of a friend. You may discover a great gulf between the way you want to read and the way it actually comes off.

First read through your selection without stopping, to catch the swing of the author's style and to locate trouble spots. A sentence that gives no trouble to the eye may prove sticky on the tongue, such as this one: "Complex statistical statements excite us less than sensitively selected examples." Other things come to light—long, winding sentences that need to be punctuated by inflections; a patch of choppy phrases that needs to be smoothed out orally; a switch in the rhythm to which you must adapt.

Work on the specific problems you turn up. Slow down as you move through tongue-tangling sentences, and sharpen your enunciation. Pay attention to the way you group words. Stammering, illogical groupings break the thought and drive listeners to distraction. For example, "It has / been said / that / the Russians / have / given to science / some of / the aura that / they have denied / to religion." A more natural grouping would be, "It has been said / that the Russians have given to science / some of the aura / that they have denied to religion." In addition to natural grouping, spot the sentences and passages that need to be highlighted, and experiment with several ways of giving them prominence. An increase in volume of voice is not the only way to gain emphasis. A change in rate or pitch, or a pause, may be a better way.

Reading smoothly, of course, is not enough. As you experiment, concentrate on communicating faithfully the facts, ideas, and images of your material. Factual material calls for clarity, accuracy, and objectivity. Be especially careful to avoid injecting personal attitudes into reportorial reading. "The governor suggested that the budget for the next fiscal year will require a slight and temporary increase in the sales tax" is a simple, straightforward statement. But if phrases such as "the governor" and "slight and temporary increases" are doctored with inflections, the meaning is colored by the reader's attitudes of admiration or derision.

Give ideas the stature they deserve. Suppose you were to read these lines from John Milton's *Areopagitica:* "Though all the winds of doctrine were let loose to play upon the earth, so Truth be in the field, we do ingloriously, by licensing and prohibiting, to misdoubt her strength. Let her and Falsehood grapple: Who ever knew Truth put to the worse in a free and open encounter?" Here is a ringing declaration of faith, not a mundane statement of fact. When sentiment and ideas are majestic, your reading should endow them with impressiveness. Conversely, avoid giving an idea an importance greater than it warrants.

The imagery of a work will be more vivid if you re-create sensory experiences that are similar to those indicated by the writer. You may not have had the identical experience he describes, but you can approximate it by drawing on your memory and imagination. Let your mind's eye see "a crowd, a host, of golden daffodils . . . tossing their heads in sprightly dance," about which Wordsworth writes. Let yourself see, touch, and smell "the strong crust of friendly bread," about which Rupert Brooke writes. And "the cool kindliness of sheets," "live hair that is shining and free," "the musty reek that lingers about dead leaves." Consider the extreme distress that Coleridge describes in these lines:

> And every tongue, through utter drought,
> Was wither'd at the root;
> We could not speak, no more than if
> We had been choked with soot.

It's unlikely that you have ever had such a desperately parched feeling, but you do know what it's like to be thirsty. Recall the circumstance, and re-create accurately the specific sensations you felt at the time. Heightening your own empathic responses to a writer's imagery enables you to read with a vividness that is likely to stimulate listeners to re-create comparable sensory experiences of their own.

Some Practical Considerations

■ PREPARING COPY. Even under ideal conditions it is hard to read small print set in lines tightly squeezed together. The problem is compounded when you read to an audience. Avoid trying to read aloud from the crowded pages of newspapers and magazines. Whenever the printed page is unsatisfactory, take the time to type up the material for the occasion. Typed copy, double-spaced, is preferable to copy that you write out in longhand.

■ ESTABLISHING A CONTEXT FOR YOUR READING. When the material you are reading is just a small part of your whole speech, work it in through easy transitions. But when the reading is the main business at hand, work up a short extemporaneous introduction that identifies your selection and its author, stimulates interest in the selection, and establishes a congenial mood for your reading. You may or may not need to develop a conclusion of your own. Much depends on the material, your purpose in reading, and the circumstances.

■ INTERPOLATING COMMENTS.   If you are reading instructions or obscure technical material, stop and clarify the important points as you go along. Sometimes you may want to interrupt your reading momentarily to underscore your author's point in your own words. In short, feel free to interpolate your own comments whenever they will add significantly to your audience's interest, understanding, and appreciation. Ordinarily, however, refrain from intruding with comments of your own. You can ruin the fine edge of a poem, story, or a particularly well-written article with a running commentary. If your audience needs background, say what you need to say in your introduction.

■ HANDLING YOUR MATERIALS WHILE READING.   If you plan to read here and there in an article or book, always mark your places beforehand. You will be embarrassed and your audience will grow anxious if you have to fumble around while trying to find your place. These awkward moments dissipate any success you may have won up to that point.

The clumsy handling of a book, magazine, or manuscript may be enough to spoil an otherwise effective reading. The ideal is to manipulate these materials so that your listeners are hardly aware of them. If you are using a speaker's stand, you may want to place your materials there and leave them there. If you like more freedom and mobility, then hold your magazine or book in one hand. Hold it high enough so that you can read it easily, and a bit to one side so that you can see your audience readily. Avoid holding it up so high that it covers your face, or so low that your body looks like a question mark. If you are well prepared, you should be able to free your eyes from the page now and then.

In short, don't let your materials block your line of vision. Look up and out as much as you can without interrupting the fluency of your reading.

Points to Keep in Mind

> **1.** The purpose of reading aloud is to communicate faith-fully an author's meaning and feeling.

> **2.** Prepare by familiarizing yourself with the intellectual content of your selection, its background, its mood, and its structure.

> **3.** Before you read to an audience, practice reading your selection experimentally to test your preliminary analysis and to acquire skill.

> **4.** Prepare and handle your text so that you can communicate easily when you read to your audience.

Exercises

1. Make a brief report on the content of an article or a book you have read recently. Read aloud selected passages that point up the writer's ideas in a way that will bring them home to your listeners.

2. Take a somewhat technical piece of writing that you understand and think you can explain to your audience. Skillfully weave in enough interpolations to make it clear.

3. Write out a speech or report of your own. Maintain your best oral style in your writing. Read it aloud to the class. Be as communicative as you can. See if you can make the audience forget you are reading from a manuscript.

4. Choose one of the sample speeches that appear at the end of this book for reading aloud to the class. Analyze it and practice reading it beforehand.

5. Poetry that deals in values people live by offers fine opportunities to combine reading and speaking. Robert Frost's "Mending Wall" is a good example. Prepare your own introduction to such a poem. Give your introduction extemporaneously and then read the poem.

6. Choose a play, speech, poem, or story that has been read aloud by someone else and has been recorded. Familiarize yourself with the work before you listen to it. Then listen several times to the recording. Evaluate the skill of the reader. Did your reactions to the way the work was read change after successive listening experiences? Could you suggest ways in which the reading might be improved?

CHAPTER TWENTY

Speaking
in
Public

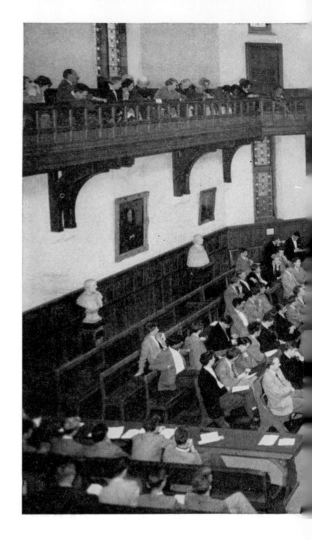

We have been talking about the principles and methods of public speaking all through this book. But now we shall deal with some of the special forms and the conventional procedures and amenities associated with them. This

information will help you apply what you already know about public speaking in situations that call for special adaptations.

In this chapter we discuss public deliberation, public policy-making, and speeches for special occasions.

Public Deliberation

Dealing with public questions in a way that will induce learning and understanding is one of the most important functions of public speech. Inquiry, reporting, and advocacy serve this function. Here are some adaptations of these basic methods that are useful in public deliberation.

■ PANEL DISCUSSION. This is an ingenious device for conducting group discussion in the hearing of an audience. We are all familiar with the unique values of give-and-take discussion in small, intimate face-to-face groups. Panel discussion attempts to achieve these same values for larger groups.

The members of the panel, four to eight people, sit in a semicircle facing the audience, preferably around a table on a raised platform. The panel leader opens the discussion and acts as chairman. He tells the audience what the panel is going to discuss, introduces the members, and starts the ball rolling by throwing out a question or two to the panel.

The panel discusses the subject in conversation among themselves much as they would in private discussion, but they must never forget that they are talking for the benefit of the audience. They must speak clearly and loudly enough to be heard easily and they must keep the discussion moving along at a brisk pace. The steps in reflective thinking explained in Chapter 15 provide a good general pattern for the discussion.

This kind of public conversation requires speakers who are both articulate and well informed. At its best, it is a lively interchange among knowledgeable people who hold different points of view and are prepared to explore their differences cooperatively.

■ THE SYMPOSIUM. A symposium is made up of three to five persons who deliver short speeches on a problem in front of an audience. Its chief difference from the panel is that it uses public speeches rather than group discussion. And it differs from public debate in that it uses the methods of inquiry and reporting rather than the methods of advocacy. The purpose of a symposium is to instruct and to increase understanding, not to persuade.

A symposium opens up a problem and gives it a thorough airing. The best way to do this is to have each speaker explain his point of view on the problem as a whole. Another way—though usually less effective—is to divide the problem up and assign one phase to each speaker. The first speaker defines and lays out the problem, the second analyzes it, and the others suggest various solutions.

The leader of the symposium simply acts as chairman. He introduces the speakers; makes a few opening remarks; fills in between successive speeches; winds things up after the last speaker has finished; and takes charge of the question-and-answer period.

■ DEBATE. Debate is a familiar method of public deliberation in which speakers oppose each other on propositions of public interest. The debater uses the methods of advocacy. Admittedly partisan, he tries to win support for his position. Listeners benefit from the chance to hear different points of view advanced and defended—an experience that helps them to extend their own knowledge and thinking on the question being debated. In addition to these educational values, a good debate often provides stimulating entertainment.

Ordinarily, the opposing debaters speak from the same platform on the same occasion, and the debate is conducted according to procedures agreed upon in advance. Often, however, there are many public debates in which the opposing speakers never meet each other face-to-face. In a sense, a national political campaign is a running debate that stretches out over several weeks or months. The candidates take sharp issue on public questions and pursue their interests in speech after speech, reply and counter-reply, before audiences all over the nation.

The essentials of a good debate are a carefully worded proposition or resolution, one or more speakers who support this proposition (the affirmative), one or more speakers who oppose it (the negative), and arrangements that permit opposing speakers to develop their cases and reply to each other. In a properly planned debate, the proposition is phrased so that the affirmative has the burden of proof (see page 245) and has the opportunity to open and close the debate. Here are some suggestions for arranging debates.

The Two-Speaker Debate

Affirmative constructive speech . . . . 10 minutes
Negative rejoinder (reply and constructive case) . . . . 14 minutes
Affirmative rebuttal . . . . 4 minutes

The Team Debate

Constructive Speeches		Rebuttal Speeches	
First affirmative	10 minutes	First negative	5 minutes
First negative	10 minutes	First affirmative	5 minutes
Second affirmative	10 minutes	Second negative	5 minutes
Second negative	10 minutes	Second affirmative	5 minutes

The Cross-Question Debate

The first affirmative presents the entire affirmative case . . . . . . 20 minutes
The first negative questions the first affirmative . . . . 10 minutes
The second negative presents the entire negative case . . . . 20 minutes
The second affirmative questions the second negative . . . . 10 minutes
The first negative presents the negative rebuttal . . . . 10 minutes
The second affirmative presents the affirmative rebuttal . . . . . . 10 minutes

In a good debate, no matter what arrangements are prescribed, the debaters hold close to the issues, and make adaptations and replies to the arguments of their opponents throughout the debate. This requires a thorough knowledge of the ins and outs of the subject, analytical and tactical skills, and, above all, competence in extemporaneous public speaking.

■ THE OPEN FORUM. Every panel discussion, debate, and symposium requires an audience. Ideally, the members of the audience should be more than a group of passive onlookers. They should be brought in as active participants. The best way to let the listeners have their say is to arrange for an open forum after the regular program. This is a question-and-answer period conducted by the discussion leader or chairman.

One way to conduct an open forum is to have members of the audience write out questions on slips of paper and send them up to the chairman. During a brief recess, the chairman can sift through the questions and arrange them in logical order. Written questions cut short the cranks and the frustrated orators who have their own little speeches all prepared.

But a better way is to invite questions from the floor. This makes for livelier, more spontaneous discussion. One question suggests another, and the audience has a chance to hear each question as it is presented. The chairman should keep the proceedings as informal as possible and should have the questions put directly to speakers on the platform. He should intervene only to clear up confusion or misunderstanding, or to decide which member of the audience has the floor when several speak at once.

Most audiences take a lively interest in the question-and-answer period. But if the leader suspects that an audience may be slow to respond, he may sum up the discussion in a way that throws the spotlight on vital and controversial issues. He may toss out a few questions of his own that will suggest others to the audience. Or he may put the first question to one of the speakers to start the ball rolling. But he must never hint that he expects to have a hard time in getting questions from the audience. Once the forum is under way, the leader should be content to repeat questions that are in-

"And don't just sit there at the end of my speech—ask questions!"

audible, help clarify ambiguous questions, and keep each question and answer within reasonable time limits.

Public Policy-making

Policy-making goes beyond deliberation for educational purposes. Any policy-making body must express the will of the group in the form of specific decisions. It must come up with a firm conclusion on which other people can act. The policy-making groups with which you are most familiar are committees, boards, councils, and legislative bodies. Actually, any organized group or public assembly can adopt resolutions and take whatever actions their needs and interests may dictate. Many of these groups have their own procedural rules. Here we shall simply give you some tips on committee procedure and parliamentary debate that will help you in most of the situations you are likely to face.

■ COMMITTEE PROCEDURE. Large legislative assemblies seldom talk through problems in full session, for too many participants make the discussion unwieldy. Instead, legislatures usually refer problems to committees for investigation and recommendation.

In the early stages of its work, at least, it is wise for a committee to proceed as a discussion group. If the discussion leads to a solution on which the members agree, their job is done; all they have to do is report their findings to the larger group. Very often this is exactly what takes place in a committee, especially where the members are accustomed to cooperative procedures and united in their desire to find the best answer to the problem.

If disagreement develops and persists, however, then the chairman of the committee should call for motions and conduct debate on these motions until a majority decision is reached (see below).

A committee uses formal debate only as a last resort after making every attempt to keep the discussion informal and co-operative. If the chairman calls for formal motions at the very outset, he runs the danger of crystallizing differences of opinion that might have been resolved in the opening discussion. An even greater danger is that the group may fail to analyze the problem carefully, because it has been hurried into a decision before developing the information and understanding it needs.

▪ PARLIAMENTARY DEBATE.   Parliamentary debate is the most useful method of determining policy in any large assembly. Recommendations for consideration may come from committees or be initiated by any member of the assembly. In either case, these recommendations are presented as motions for debate and action. Often, agenda are worked out in advance to determine the order of business.

Most policy-determining groups use the standard rules of parliamentary procedure to govern debate. You are already familiar with some of these rules. They are used in class meetings, clubs, fraternities, and wherever business is conducted in public meetings. If you are hazy about these rules, it will be worth your while to get them firmly in mind. There are many excellent manuals on parliamentary law, but the brief résumé below will suffice for most occasions.

The *principal motion* is used to introduce a proposal when there is no other motion before the assembly. The maker of the motion states his proposal and may, if he chooses, explain the motion. The motion itself should be a clear, unambiguous proposal that the secretary can record in his minutes. If the motion is seconded, it is then thrown open to debate. During debate, *subsidiary motions* may be applied to the principal motion. For example, someone may move that the principal motion be amended; then the motion to amend becomes the subject of the debate. If this amendment is carried, then the principal motion as amended is before the house. Merely passing an amendment does not mean that the principal motion has been passed.

Each of the six *subsidiary motions* in the accompanying table takes precedence over those above it and yields to those below. Of

TABLE OF PARLIAMENTARY MOTIONS*

Motions	Need a Second.	Amendable?	Debatable?	Vote Required	May Interrupt a Speaker
I. Principal Motion					
1. Any main question or any independent matter of business before the meeting....	yes	yes	yes	maj	no
II. Subsidiary Motions					
2. To amend	yes	yes	yes	maj.	no
3. To postpone indefinitely ...	yes	no	yes	maj.	no
4. To refer to a committee	yes	yes	yes	maj.	no
5. To postpone to a certain time	yes	yes	yes	maj.	no
6. Previous question	yes	no	no	⅔	no
7. To lay on (or take from) the table	yes	no	no	maj.	no
III. Incidental Motions					
8. To suspend a rule	yes	no	no	⅔	no
9. To withdraw a motion	yes	no	no	maj.	no
10. Question of consideration ..	no	no	no	⅔	yes
11. A point of order	no	no	no	Chair†	yes
12. Appeal from decision of chair	yes	no	no	maj.	yes
IV. Privileged Motions					
13. To make a matter of business a "special order" for a given time	no	no	no	⅔	yes
14. Questions of rights and privileges	no	no	no	Chair†	yes
15. To adjourn (unqualified) ..	yes	no	no	maj.	no
16. To fix time for next meeting	yes	yes	no	maj.	no

* Quoted with some changes from Gregg's *Handbook of Parliamentary Law* (Boston: Ginn and Company, 1910) in J. M. O'Neill, ed., *Foundations of Speech,* p. 395. New York: Prentice-Hall, Inc., 1941.

† Require only decision of Chair; no vote unless appealed.

the subsidiary motions, "the previous question" is puzzling to some people. Its purpose is to stop debate. In most assemblies, all you have to do is call for the question if you want to halt debate and get a vote on the resolution before the house. But if somebody objects to this method of stopping debate, you may then offer a formal motion to have the previous question brought to a vote. If your motion is seconded and carried by a two-thirds vote, the chairman must then put the question itself to a vote.

Incidental motions arise out of other motions. Their purpose is to make it easier for these motions to be considered. The order in which they are listed in the table is not significant.

Privileged motions have to do with the general conduct of the meeting. They arise independently of other motions and take precedence over them. However, any incidental motion or subsidiary motion that is properly applied to the privileged motion itself takes precedence over the privileged motion to which it is applied.

For speed and convenience in using the table of motions, we have listed below the specific purpose or object of each motion in the table.

Objects of Motions[1]

1. Main motion—to bring original business before the assembly.

2. To amend—to modify a question that is before the assembly.

3. To postpone indefinitely—(a) to dispose of a question for the session without voting on it directly; (b) used by the opponents of a question, to determine their strength.

4. To refer to a committee—to secure the advantage of action by a smaller group, or of greater freedom in debate in dealing with a question.

5. To postpone to a certain time—to defer action on a question to some future time.

6. Previous question—to suppress debate and bring the assembly to a vote.

7. To lay on the table—(a) to postpone a subject so that it may be taken up at another time during the same session;

---

[1] O'Neill, *Foundations of Speech.*

(b) to stop debate and suppress a question for the session, provided a majority cannot be secured to take the question again from the table.

8. To suspend a rule—to make temporarily possible an action contrary to the standing rules or rules of order of an organization.

9. To withdraw a motion—to expedite business in case of a changed opinion by the maker of the motion.

10. Question of consideration—an objection to the consideration of a question to enable the assembly to avoid irrelevant, unprofitable, or contentious questions.

11. A point of order—to correct a breach of order or an error in procedure.

12. Appeal from decision of chair—(a) to invoke a rule that the chairman has ignored or misinterpreted; (b) to appeal to the assembly to overrule the chairman on any rule where an opinion or a judgment may be exercised.

13. Special order—to set a specific time to consider a certain matter of business when all other things will be set aside.

14. Questions of rights and privileges—to secure to the assembly or any of its members some right with respect to safety, comfort, dignity, reputation, or freedom from disturbance.

15. To adjourn—to bring a meeting to a close.

16. To fix time for next meeting—to fix a time or place for reassembling.

Debate for the purpose of determining policy follows the methods of advocacy described in Chapter 17. Even though it follows the formal rules that we have outlined here, it is still debate. If you make a motion, you must state it clearly and assume the responsibility for defending it. Any motion is vulnerable unless you can present a convincing defense of it when the opposition raises objections. Opponents of the motion will defeat it if they can attack it successfully on one or more vital counts.

"Now, something about our guest speaker. Weighing six pounds, three ounces at birth, Mr. Hastings developed normally until at four months of age, requiring a formula change, he . . ."

Speeches for Special Occasions

Some speeches are designed primarily to recognize special occasions and to strengthen our ties with our fellow men. Often you are under something of an artistic obligation in handling these courtesies. Poise, graciousness, and appropriateness in style and manner are especially important on such occasions. The methods of evocation (Chapter 18) are appropriate to speeches for these occasions.

■ SPEECHES OF INTRODUCTION.   When you introduce a speaker to an audience, your job is to establish good speaking relationships between him and his listeners. Think of yourself as a go-between, a situation-maker, not as a principal in the show.

Find out all you can beforehand about the person you are introducing. If possible, talk with him and with people who know him. Track down some reliable biographical sketches, but don't try to use everything you gather together. Don't make your introduction sound like a paragraph from *Who's Who*. If the audience doesn't know much about the speaker, choose information that will identify him, establish his qualifications to speak, and make him liked as a person. If you can, let the audience see for themselves what kind of a person he is by telling an anecdote that puts him in a favorable light. If he is already well known, keep your introduction short and concentrate on the warm sentiments the audience feels toward him.

Above all, be accurate You may have heard introductions in which the speaker's name was mispronounced or completely garbled. Not every speaker can transform a blunder into a pleasantry, as Rabbi Stephen Wise did when he was introduced as Rabbi Mann. "These days," he retorted, "it's a wise man who knows his own name."

Avoid a long speech. Remember, the audience came to hear the main speaker, not you.

■ SPEECHES OF WELCOME AND FAREWELL.   You are a member of an organization or a community that is playing host to visitors, and you are selected to represent the host group. Make your greetings cordial and try to use a little originality. Most speeches on these occasions are dismally trite and are delivered in an inflated or perfunctory manner. Be direct, sincere, and brisk.

Make it clear that you really know whom you are welcoming, what they stand for, and what they have contributed. If the visitors represent a group dedicated to an ideal or to a program of public service, give your talk an inspirational note. Make your visitors feel at home. Show your hospitality by pointing out the services and facilities at their disposal, and the attractions and special events that will add to their pleasure. End by wishing your guests a pleasant and profitable stay.

Speeches of farewell are given at dinners or other ceremonies honoring someone who is leaving the group. When you make such a speech, feel free to reminisce about the past, express the esteem in which the departing person is held, and extend the group's good wishes.

What if you are the person who is departing? Here you have a chance to show publicly your affection and respect for the friends you are leaving, and to express appreciation for the pleasant associations you have had with them. If you have a personal philosophy that you want to share, this is a perfect occasion to put it into words.

In short, show that you have responded warmly to your friends' sentiment.

■ SPEECHES OF COMMEMORATION. Every society has certain anniversaries that it commemorates with special speeches. For example, we celebrate the Fourth of July, Memorial Day, United Nations Day, and the birthdays of distinguished men and women. Ordinarily, you will key a speech of commemoration to the immediate occasion, unless it is understood that you are free to use the occasion as a springboard to some related subject. If you are dedicating a park, talk about the work of the people who made it possible, about its values and uses for the community. If you are commemorating United Nations Day, build your talk around the history, purposes, work, and accomplishments of the organization. If you are offering a tribute, invite your listeners to look again at the life and career of the person whom you are praising.

But don't make your speech of commemoration a bloodless catalogue of facts. Go about it in an inspirational manner. Stir your listeners to contemplation and help them to look at the event, deed, or life as a symbol.

■ SPEECHES OF PRESENTATION AND ACCEPTANCE. These talks reflect the prevailing mood of the occasion. They put into words what everyone is feeling. A football banquet at which varsity letters are awarded invites lightness and gaiety. When the senior class presents a gift to the college, dignity is the order of the day. Occasions of this sort are often charged with sentiment. But if you are making a speech of presentation, you must keep a nice balance between what you are feeling and what good taste permits. Suggest the appropriate sentiment, but don't parade it.

Bring out the reasons that have prompted the gift or award. For example, assume that you and your associates are honoring the school physician for long and faithful service. First, suggest the group's feelings toward him. Then supply the reasons for these feelings—reasons that grow out of his years of service to the group.

6. Prepare a tribute to some person. Choose someone from one of the following fields who is already well known to the class and whom you admire.

Politics	Science	Social work
Literature	Entertainment	Education
Art	Industry	Religion
Medicine	Agriculture	Communications
Engineering	Law	Sports

CHAPTER TWENTY-ONE

Microphone
and
Camera

We live in an age of electronics—of public-address systems, radio microphones, and television cameras. Doubtless, you will be called upon to use one of these devices at one time or another. So it is worth your while to learn how to get the best results from them. Good speech remains

314

good speech whether or not you are speaking before a microphone or camera. *But there are important differences.* This chapter will tell you about the adaptations you need to make in your regular speech habits if you are to speak before the microphone and the camera with assurance and competence.

The Public-Address System

Amplification of your voice is often helpful, and when you are speaking in large auditoriums or out-of-doors it may be essential. On such occasions a public-address system in good working order with an experienced operator at the controls is often the only means of getting through to your audience.

But don't use a public-address system if you can make yourself heard easily without it. Without a microphone you are freer to move around the platform, and you avoid erecting a physical barrier between yourself and your audience. If you can speak without strain and be heard without strain, you will establish closer rapport with your audience without an amplifying system.

The principal advantage of a public-address system, apart from simple audibility, is that it enables you to talk to a large audience more intimately than you could without it. It lets you speak with exactly the same volume and inflections you would use in talking to a small group. In fact, you will get very poor results if you depart from the conversational level of speaking. Don't forget that you are using the system and begin to shout into the microphone as if you were trying to project your voice to the last man in the top balcony all by yourself. Nothing will put a listener's nerves on edge faster than a distorted voice that comes screeching out of a loudspeaker.

When you use a public-address system, then, let it work for you. Keep your lips about 18 inches from the microphone, and avoid moving your head abruptly. Talk as though you were addressing a group of 10 or 15 people in a small room. Keep your hands off the microphone and avoid coughing or laughing explosively into it.

Radio Speaking

Most radio speaking takes place in acoustically designed studios under the control of trained personnel. An engineer or producer will position the microphone and show you how to use it. On all technical matters, put yourself in the hands of the experts.

ADAPTING TO THE RADIO AUDIENCE

Radio audiences vary with locality, station, time, and program. But one factor remains constant: Most of the people listen by themselves or in small groups under informal circumstances. You can't talk to two or three people sitting in their living room or driving in their automobile as you would to a big audience assembled in an auditorium. The best radio speaking is man-to-man conversation. By and large, radio discussion programs have been successful because the participants speak as though they were talking directly with each listener in his own home. If you are confronted with a good-sized studio audience as well as a radio audience, to which audience should you accommodate your style, voice, and manner? To the audience that is more important to you or to your sponsors. Here we shall assume that you are interested in adapting to your radio audience.

A good way to learn the technique of effective radio speaking is to ask three or four people to sit in the studio with you. Then talk directly to them. Talk into the microphone, but concentrate on communicating your ideas *to the listeners who face you*. If you keep this technique in mind when you are actually on the air, your radio listeners will receive your message almost as if they were actually in your presence.

VOICE AND ACTION IN RADIO SPEAKING

Since radio listeners can't see you, you will have to pack your voice with meaning and feeling. You will have to depend on variety in force, pitch, time, and quality to convey fine shades of sense and attitude. What we have said in Chapter 13, on the use of your voice, applies directly to the radio speaker.

Many speakers sound stiff and wooden when they speak on the

radio. The reason is that they become muscle-bound before a micro-phone. They forget that bodily action is part of normal speech. Whenever you suppress the movements of your arms, hands, body, head, and face, you cramp and impoverish your speech—and that goes for radio speech too. Most good radio speakers use just as much bodily action in the studio as they would if they were carrying on a spirited conversation with a friend or giving a public address. They find that bodily action reduces tension, makes their voice sound spontaneous and fresh, and adds variety. Don't pound the table or go streaking off out of the microphone's range. But remember that engineers in the control room are remarkably clever at adjusting their equipment to fairly active people.

NOTES, OUTLINES, AND SCRIPTS

When you can see and hear your listeners, you can sense how they are responding and adapt your speech to their shifting moods. Extemporaneous speaking is your best method on such occasions. But when you are sealed up in a studio, the only faces in sight may be those of the engineers—and they probably won't be paying much attention to what you say. In these circumstances, you may want to write out your talk and use a manuscript. It certainly helps you to stay within set time limits. Be sure to write your manuscript in your best oral style and to read it as if you are talking to a few people seated directly in front of you. Again, having two or three interested listeners in the studio helps you to come through to your radio audience with warmth and directness.

If you are preparing a radio round-table discussion, get the participants together for a preliminary meeting and agree on a short discussion outline. Give each speaker a copy of the outline on which he can make notes. But when you go on the air, be sure that everyone speaks extemporaneously and uses the outline only as a working guide. A script kills the lively give-and-take that is the life blood of an effective discussion program.

Television Speaking

Television offers greater possibilities for speech than any other medium of mass communication that man has devised.

ADAPTING TO THE TELEVISION AUDIENCE

As with radio, most people who watch television are sitting comfortably at home—alone or in a small group. The total television audience is huge, but it is made up of individual viewers.

The best television speaker is the one who talks directly to his viewers rather than to the studio audience. If you want to get the most out of this medium, talk—don't shout or orate—with your listeners in a conversational manner. As with radio, your speaking should reveal the same warmth and vitality that you show in man-to-man communication at its best. Be as informal as the situation permits.

Television is ideally suited to panel discussions and interviews. The cameras can cover three or four people at fairly close range, and can give close-ups of individual speakers. The best setting for television discussion programs suggests a living room or a study or a conference room. Such a setting invites discussion and helps both speakers and viewers to forget about the cameras and the technical equipment.

VOICE AND ACTION IN TELEVISION

You are seen as well as heard on television. And your audience gets a much closer look at you than it would in a public auditorium. The camera brings your eyes, mouth, facial muscles, and the movements of your head and shoulders into painfully close focus. If the picture on the television screen tells a story that is out of keeping with your words, your audience will dismiss the words as false, affected, or ridiculous. Television is hard on fakes. It is kind to honest and sincere people who speak with the confidence of their convictions. Your voice and actions must agree. Both must reveal in you a genuine desire to communicate.

NOTES AND SCRIPTS IN TELEVISION SPEAKING

Scripts and clumsy notes raise havoc. An ingenious gadget called the teleprompter has been devised to overcome just this difficulty. It enables you to read from enlarged type suspended before you, so that you look as though you were gazing directly into the camera. But in most cases this proves to be a poor substitute for directness. It often leads to a preoccupied, glassy stare or to furtive attempts to keep up with the moving script. Moreover, the teleprompter is one more mechanical device to be adjusted to.

It comes down to this: If you are a good extemporaneous speaker, you will have a tremendous advantage in television. If you must use brief notes or a short outline, don't try to disguise them. But avoid making them the center of your attention. Be so well prepared that you won't be at the mercy of your notes. Handle them unobtrusively and maintain direct contact with your audience.

PROPERTIES FOR TELEVISION SPEAKING

Television enables you to use visual aids that are out of the question on radio and often difficult to handle in public speech. It sends out a private copy of charts, pictures, diagrams, maps, and models to every member of your audience. But don't feel that you have to use visual aids because you are being televised. Use them only when they serve a real purpose.

Points to Keep in Mind

Here are the key suggestions:

1. Speak before microphone and camera just as you do when you are talking effectively to another person or a small group in your home.

  a. Maintain the best elements of conversational speech.
  b. Use bodily action even if your audience can't see you.

2. Speak extemporaneously whenever possible. Reading from a manuscript may be a satisfactory substitute in a radio studio.

3. Stay within close range of a public-address microphone. Engineers will tell you what to do in a radio or television studio.

4. Television is ideally suited for visual aids—but don't drag them in unless they serve a real purpose.

Exercises

1. Choose several subjects suitable for panel discussions on radio or television programs. Assign four to eight students to each panel. Have one member of each group serve as chairman or moderator. Each panel will work as a group in preparing an outline for the program. When the panel "goes on the air," try to simulate actual studio conditions.

2. Have each student prepare a short talk suitable for a radio or TV program. Record the talk and play it back during a class period. Listen to each talk with these questions in mind: If I were dialing for a program, would this speaker and his speech invite my interest? Would his voice attract me? Is his language arresting? Are his ideas challenging? If time permits, have the students rework their talks in the light of the criticisms offered.

3. Devote a class period to a report, persuasive speech, or discussion on a radio or TV program. Immediately following the program or at the next class period, conduct a class discussion of what you heard. Did all the listeners derive essentially the same impressions as to what was said? Did the speech or discussion exemplify the standards and principles set forth in this book? To what audience was it directed? Did the speaker or speakers adapt to the medium of communication?

4. If facilities permit, present a short talk with the benefit of a public address system. After the talk, have the class make suggestions for improving your presentation. Repeat part of your talk in an effort to follow through on the suggestions.

Sample
Speeches

The speeches that follow are examples of the four main types of speaking: inquiry, reporting, advocacy, and evocation. Read them critically. Notice how each speaker puts into practice the advice we have given you throughout this book.

322

A Speech of Inquiry:
"What's Happening Downtown?"

One hundred million Americans live in metropolitan areas, and over half of them live in our twenty-three largest cities.

For these people "going downtown" is a trek to the heart of the city —a compact area of ten or twenty or more city blocks that contain the principal interests of the city. Downtown is the City Hall, the biggest department stores, the biggest office buildings, the biggest movie houses, the biggest medical centers, theaters, museums, libraries, hotels, restaurants, and an amazing array of shops and entertainment facilities of every kind and description.

Downtown is busy, bustling, crowded, exciting. It is the political, social, cultural, and economic center of the city. White-collar workers pour into the city in the morning and out at night. Shoppers dominate the midday flow, and pleasure-seekers the night hours. There is always somebody going downtown, or coming back—a lot of somebodies— literally millions of them!

To the casual observer, at least, downtown appears to be thriving. But let's take a closer look. The Editors of *Fortune Magazine* took such a look and report their findings in a book entitled *The Exploding Metropolis*. This explosion appears to be leaving downtown with "fall ing retail sales, tax bases in jeopardy, stagnant real-estate values, impossible traffic and parking conditions, failing mass transit, and encirclement by slums." These are the words of one of the editors.

Does this picture sound exaggerated? Those of you who live in or near our big cities can probably answer the question for yourself. But an analysis of some of the basic forces at work in most metropolitan areas suggests pretty strongly that the core of the city is destined to lose some of its traditional strength unless action is taken to counteract these forces.

There is no question that millions of people are leaving the cities for the suburbs. The first to go vacate the old residences close to the core of the city for newer homes and greener lawns. The less fortunate move in behind them. Then the slums begin. And then the next layer moves out farther to escape the encroaching slums. This gives more room for slums. So on it goes—a powerful centrifugal force pulling people away from the heart of the city into a vast suburban sprawl. And the vacuum their leaving creates is filled by some 17 million Americans living in dwellings now beyond rehabilitation—"decayed, dirty, rat infested, without decent heat or light or plumbing."

There is a second force at work which bears examination. Urban dwellers appear to be enamored with two things: a house in the suburbs and a car—perhaps even two cars. And anybody who invests three to five thousand dollars in a car wants to operate the car. Especially is this true if the alternative is an outmoded, rundown public transportation system. So the inevitable happens: Downtown becomes so congested with automobiles without adequate parking facilities that Mr. and Mrs. Suburbanite begin to look for some more convenient place to work, shop, and play. And anyone who has had any experience with recent suburban developments knows that they do not have to look far. Slick new shopping centers dominated by acres of free parking are ready at hand. And many of them include office buildings for professional services, theaters, and even amusements for the kids.

Why go downtown? That is precisely the question most of our downtowns face. And there appear to be millions of people who are perfectly willing to let them worry along with their own problem. But before we settle for this attitude, let me raise a few questions: How much do the hearts of our cities mean to American life—to the culture and economy of the nation? And more particularly, what happens to the suburbs if the mother city loses its vitality? Are people abandoning the central city by choice or because circumstances force them to leave? In short, are the downtown areas of our cities worth rehabilitating and worth making more easily available to the people who want to use them? The keys to the problem appear to be imaginative planning and accessibility. Downtown must first be a place people want to go and, second, a place they can get to without paying too heavy a toll in time, energy, and patience.

Jane Jacobs raises this first question in her article *Downtown Is for People*. She asks, ". . . What make a city center magnetic, what can inject the gaiety, the wonder, the cheerful hurly-burly that makes people want to come into the city and to linger there?" She continues, ". . . Downtown's values are its by-products. To create in it an atmosphere of urbanity and exuberance is not a frivolous aim."

Jane Jacobs' thesis is that we must exploit the unique compactness of downtown by making an enormous variety of goods and services available to people in the compass of a few blocks. Here is where all sorts of highly specialized enterprises can exist—enterprises with markets so selective, they need exposure to hundreds of thousands of people. She sums it up this way, "A metropolitan center comes across to people as a center largely by virtue of its enormous collection of small elements, where people can see them, at street level." And, I might add, where they can get to them on foot without risking life and limb in city traffic.

Whether this or some other picture of downtown sums up its magnetic potential, we cannot escape the problem of getting there to enjoy whatever it has to offer. Here is where the battle lines are really drawn: Should we rehabilitate, modernize, and add to our facilities for public transportation to the center of the city? This question raises a whole brood of related problems: Will people ride the subways, elevated lines, and buses even if they are improved? Who is going to pay for these improvements? The riders—or the public, through subsidies?

Or should we make it easier for people to get downtown by private car? Build bigger and better freeways for through traffic and bigger and better parking facilities in or near the downtown area? In fifteen of the nation's twenty-five largest cities, 60 per cent or more of all riders entering the downtown business district arrive by automobile. If this trend continues, how long will it take to reach car saturation? As Francis Bello asks in his article "The City and the Car," if we attempt to provide parking space for all the motorists who want to come, will there be anything left worth coming to?

One solution to this knotty problem that is receiving considerable attention is a proposal to keep cars out of the central city and turn it into "a pedestrian mall." The architect Victor Gruen has proposed such a plan for the redevelopment of downtown Fort Worth. This plan recommends perimeter parking facilities around a limited downtown area and express bus service that would deposit its customers at even more convenient points than their own cars.

I see that my time is up, and I know I have not given you any neat answer to the question that motivated these remarks. As a matter of fact I didn't intend to, nor am I at all certain that I know the answer. In all probability there is no *one* answer. I am convinced, however, that downtown faces problems. I have tried to suggest some of the causes contributing to these problems and to suggest directions that solutions might take. If enough people value the unique density and variety of opportunity that the central city can offer, I suspect that these values can be conserved and that we can find ways of getting to them. But most competent observers appear to agree on one thing: There is no time to waste!

A Report:
"Hurricane Edna"

EDWARD R. MURROW

This is the news:

Hurricane Edna is moving north-northeast faster and with higher winds at her center. The latest from the Weather Bureau is this: Edna's speed has increased from ten miles an hour to between seventeen and twenty-two miles an hour. When last reported, she was centered eighty miles slightly "east of south" of Cape Hatteras, North Carolina. The center is expected to pass the Cape at midnight. Previously the highest winds near the center were one hundred and fifteen miles per hour. Now they are one hundred and twenty-five miles per hour. The weather-men expect the hurricane to step up its forward speed in the next few hours. Tonight hurricane warnings—a central white light with two red lights on each side—are displayed from North Carolina to Maine. Here in New York, the weatherman has told us: "It could be one of the most serious hurricanes in the city's history." There is a slight possibility that it may go out to sea, but we have all been adequately warned. The phone companies here and in New England are ready with their "master disaster plan." Military and naval planes have been flown inland from all shore installations. Civil defense agencies, the Red Cross, are ready. Coastal residents of Connecticut have been urged to move inland before midnight. Sandbags have been piled around buildings in Providence, Rhode Island, hard hit by Hurricane Carol. On Martha's Vineyard, bull-dozers are pushing up sand dikes to protect low inland areas. Ham radio networks have been set up to relay emergency messages. Three thousand National Guardsmen in New Hampshire have been ordered on a stand-by alert. Yesterday I flew into Hurricane Edna's eye, with the Air Force. I'd like to try to describe what I saw. . . .

We took off from Bermuda at 11:30 A.M. in a specially equipped B-29. The Air-Force boys were working for the taxpayers, going out to chart, measure, map and study the hurricane. We climbed to ten thousand, blue sky overhead, blue water without a single whitecap below, and headed West. For about an hour-and-a-half there was nothing to do except remember that flying is made up of many hours of boredom, interspersed with a few minutes of stark terror. Then there were a few whitecaps, but no clouds. Then the whitecaps grew in size—surface wind about thirty miles an hour; a few scattered cumulus clouds ahead. A big cloud seemed to summon its neighbors, and they built castles and lakes and cities on hillsides, all white against the blue of the sky. We bored through a few and skirted others. Then there was a big mountain of clouds ahead, and we went in. A few rain squalls, but little turbulence. The texture of the cloud changed, became a ghostly gray; we couldn't see the wing-tips of the aircraft. Twenty minutes later there was a little blue-gray light, but it seemed to come from all around us. Suddenly blue water again, no whitecaps, but the ocean was heaving as though a giant were shaking a rug. Into another cloud, out on the other side, and the ocean had changed its face.

Long irregular furrows, as if a drunken plowman had been plowing a field of blue velvet and turning up snow. We went down to seventy-five hundred—surface winds now estimated at sixty miles an hour; flew right along the top of a flat cloud, with the feeling that if the pilot let his wheels down he'd leave a track in it. The next time we saw water, the wind was cutting the top off the whitecaps, and there was a thin gauze of spray as far as we could see. Then into the cloud again, and that ghostly gray light that seemed to rub off on the faces of the crew members and to cause them all to look as if they were ill and hadn't slept.

Radar kept reaching out, looking for Edna's eye. It showed a high bank of clouds to the right and to the left. We were flying blind through that gray stuff in the valley between. Suddenly there was a hole in the cloud—maybe a quarter-mile across—and at the bottom there was sea-foam. It was as if we were looking down a deep well, at a huge egg-beater churning up milk at the bottom. We flew on and began the real search for the eye of the hurricane. There were sudden changes in temperature—more rain. Radar reported, the engineer reported, the navigator wanted to know if anybody could see surface wind. The radarscope didn't show anything. We were bounced around a little. The skipper said: "There's a storm around here somewhere. Let's find it."

The navigator asked for a turn to the left, and in a couple of minutes the B-29 began to shudder. It was a twisting, tortured motion. The co-pilot said: "I think we're in it." The pilot said: "We're going up"—although every control was set to take us down. Something lifted us about three hundred feet. Then the pilot said: "We're going down"—although he was doing everything humanly possible to take us up. Edna was in control of the aircraft. We were on an even keel but were being staggered by short, sharp blows. We then hit something with a bang that was audible above the roar of the motors, and more than one man flinched. It was a solid sheet of water. Seconds later brilliant sunlight hit us like a hammer; a little rainbow spun off the starboard outboard prop. Someone shouted: "There she is," and we were in the eye. Calm air—flat, calm sea below; a great amphitheater, round as a dollar, with white clouds sloping up to twenty-five or thirty thousand feet. The water looked like a blue alpine lake with snow-clad mountains coming right down to the water's edge. A great bowl of sunshine. Someone, I think it was the right scanner, shouted: "So help me, there's a ship down there." And there was—right in the center of the eye. We guessed her to be a ten-thousand ton merchant ship, moving very slowly in that calm water, with only a thin feather of wake behind her. She appeared to be in no trouble, but trouble was inevitable sometime ahead, because she was surrounded by those cloud mountains and raging water.

The eye was twenty miles in diameter. We went down to fifteen hundred feet and flew back and forth across it, making shallow penetrations into the storm area. The temperature went up fourteen degrees. The altimeter said four thousand feet, but we were actually at fifteen hundred feet. The civilian weather officer aboard looked at Edna with a clinical eye and said: "She's a copybook hurricane—beautifully formed." We took her temperature, measured her speed, threw overboard scientific gear that might help to chart her future movements, while we continued to fly around in the calm at the bottom of that funnel of white clouds.

The eye of a hurricane is an excellent place to reflect upon the puniness of man and his works. If an adequate definition of humility is ever written, it's likely to be done in the eye of a hurricane.

The engineer reported some trouble with the number three engine. We climbed to ten thousand feet and bored into the wall of the white cloud that surrounded the eye. It was not as rough going out as it was coming in because the navigator had picked his exit well.

Going back to Bermuda, we talked of hurricanes. One of the pilots said: "We certainly were disappointed in Carol; we just didn't think she would do what she did." He had flown through Carol so often that he regarded her as a friend who had committed a major misdemeanor.

These young men who fly the Air Weather Service are doing all that can be humanly done to provide information upon which adequate warning can be based. After all, the only thing you can do about a hurricane is to watch it and get ready for it.

After flying yesterday for only nine hours with these young men of the Air Force, on a routine mission, I think they deserve combat pay.

[Given over C.B.S. Network, September 10, 1954. Published by permission.]

A Speech of Advocacy: "The Intellectual and the Politician"

JOHN F. KENNEDY

It is a pleasure to join with my fellow alumni in this pilgrimage to the second home of our youth.

Prince Bismarck once remarked that one third of the students of German universities broke down from overwork; another third broke down from dissipation; and the other third ruled Germany. As I look about this campus today, I would hesitate to predict which third attends reunions (although I have some suspicion), but I am confident I am looking at "rulers" of America in the sense that all active informed citizens rule.

I can think of nothing more reassuring for all of us than to come again to this institution whose whole purpose is dedicated to the advancement of knowledge and the dissemination of truth.

I belong to a profession where the emphasis is somewhat different. Our political parties, our politicians are interested, of necessity, in winning popular support—a majority, and only indirectly truth is the object of our controversy. From this polemic of contending factions, the general public is expected to make a discriminating judgment. As the problems have become more complex, as our role as a chief defender of Western civilization has become enlarged, the responsibility of the electorate as a court of last resort has become almost too great. The people desperately seek objectivity and a university such as this fulfills that function.

And the political profession needs to have its temperature lowered in the cooling waters of the scholastic pool. We need both the technical judgment and the disinterested viewpoint of the scholar, to prevent us from becoming imprisoned by our own slogans.

Therefore, it is regrettable that the gap between the intellectual and politician seems to be growing. Instead of synthesis, clash and discord now characterizes the relations between the two groups much of the time. Authors, scholars, and intellectuals can praise every aspect of American society but the political. My desk is flooded with books, articles, and pamphlets criticizing Congress. But, rarely if ever, have I seen any intellectual bestow praise on either the political profession or any political body for its accomplishments, its ability, or its integrity—much less for its intelligence. To many universities and scholars we reap nothing but censors, investigators and perpetrators of what has been called "the swinish cult of anti-intellectualism."

James Russell Lowell's satiric attack more than one hundred years ago on Caleb Cushing, a celebrated attorney general and member of Congress, sets the tone:

> Gineral C is a dreffle smart man,
> He's ben on all sides that give places or pelf,
> But consistency still wuz a part of his plan—
> He's ben true to *one* party, that is himself.

But in fairness, the way of the intellectual is not altogether serene; in fact, so great has become popular suspicion that a recent survey of American intellectuals by a national magazine elicited from one of our foremost literary figures the guarded response, "I ain't no intellectual."

Both sides in this battle, it seems to me, are motivated by largely unfounded feelings of distrust. The politician, whose authority rests upon the mandate of the popular will, is resentful of the scholar who can, with dexterity, slip from position to position without dragging the anchor of public opinion. It was this skill that caused Lord Melbourne to say of the youthful historian Macaulay that he wished he was as sure of anything as Macaulay was of everything. The intellectual, on the other hand, finds it difficult to accept the difference between the laboratory and the legislature. In the former, the goal is truth, pure and simple, without regard to changing currents of public opinion; in the latter, compromises and majorities and procedural customs and rights affect the ultimate decision as to what is right or just or good. And even when they realize this difference, most intellectuals consider their chief function that of the critic—and politicians are sensitive to critics (possibly because we have so many of them). "Many intellectuals," Sidney Hook has said, "would rather 'die' than agree with the majority, even on the rare occasions when the majority is right."

It seems to me that the time has come for intellectuals and politicians alike to put aside those horrible weapons of modern internecine warfare, the barbed thrust, the acid pen, and—most sinister of all—the rhetorical blast. Let us not emphasize all on which we differ but all we have in common. Let us consider not what we fear separately but what we share together.

First, I would ask both groups to recall that the American politician of today and the American intellectual of today are descended from a common ancestry. Our nation's first great politicians were also among the nation's first great writers and scholars. The founders of the American Constitution were also the founders of American scholarship. The works of Jefferson, Madison, Hamilton, Franklin, Paine, and John Adams—to name but a few—influenced the literature of the world as well as its geography. Books were their tools, not their enemies. Locke, Milton, Sydney, Montesquieu, Coke, and Bolingbroke were among those widely read in political circles and frequently quoted in political pamphlets. Our political leaders traded in the free commerce of ideas with lasting results both here and abroad.

In these golden years, our political leaders moved from one field to another with amazing versatility and vitality. Jefferson and Franklin still throw long shadows over many fields of learning. A contemporary described Jefferson, "A gentleman of thirty-two, who could calculate an eclipse, survey an estate, tie an artery, plan an edifice, try a cause, break a horse, dance a minuet, and play the violin."

Daniel Webster could throw thunderbolts at Hayne on the Senate floor and then stroll a few steps down the corridor and dominate the Supreme Court as the foremost lawyer of his time. John Quincy Adams,

after being summarily dismissed from the Senate for a notable display
of independence, could become Boylston Professor of Rhetoric and Ora-
tory at Harvard and then become a great Secretary of State. (Those
were the happy days when Harvard professors had no difficulty getting
Senate confirmation.)

The versatility also existed on the frontier. An obituary of Missouri's
first senator, Thomas Hart Benton, the man whose tavern brawl with
Jackson in Tennessee caused him to flee the state, said:

> With a readiness that was often surprising, he could quote from
> a Roman law or a Greek philosopher, from Virgil's *Georgics*, the
> *Arabian Nights*, Herodotus, or Sancho Panza, from the Sacred
> Carpets, the German reformers or Adam Smith; from *Fénelon* or
> *Hudibras*, from the financial reports of Necca or the doings of the
> Council of Trent, from the debates on the adoption of the Consti-
> tution or intrigues of the Kitchen Cabinet or from some forgotten
> speech of a deceased member of Congress.

This link between the American scholarship and the American politician remained for more than a century. Just one hundred years ago
today in the presidential campaign of 1856, the Republicans sent three
brilliant orators around the campaign circuit: William Cullen Bryant,
Henry Wadsworth Longfellow, and Ralph Waldo Emerson. Those
were the carefree days when the "egg-heads" were all Republicans.

I would hope that both groups, recalling their common heritage,
might once again forge a link between the intellectual and political
professions. I know that scholars may prefer the mysteries of pure scholarship or the delights of abstract discourse. But, "Would you have
counted him a friend of ancient Greece," as George William Curtis
asked a century ago during the Kansas-Nebraska controversy, "who
quietly discussed of patriotism on that Greek summer day through
whose hopeless and immortal hours Leonidas and his three hundred
stood at Thermopylae for liberty? Was John Milton to conjugate Greek
verbs in his library or talk of the ancient Shunamites when the liberty
of Englishmen was imperiled?" No, the duty of the scholar—particularly in a republic such as ours—is to contribute his objective views and
his sense of liberty to the affairs of his state and nation.

Secondly, I would remind both groups that the American politician
and the American intellectual operate within a common framework—a

framework we call liberty. Freedom of expression is not divisible into political expression and intellectual expression. The lock on the door of the Legislature, the Parliament, or the Assembly Hall—by order of the King, the Commissar, or the Fuehrer—has historically been followed or preceded by a lock on the door of the university, the library or the printer's. And if the first blow for freedom in any subjugated land is struck by a political leader, the second is struck by a book, a newspaper, or a pamphlet.

Unfortunately, in more recent times, politicians and intellectuals have quarreled bitterly—too bitterly in some cases—over how each group has met the modern challenge to freedom both at home and abroad. Politicians have questioned the discernment with which intellectuals have reacted to the siren call of the extreme left; and intellectuals have tended to accuse politicians of not always being aware, especially here at home, of the toxic effects of freedom restrained.

While differences in judgment where freedom is endangered are perhaps inevitable, there should, nevertheless, be more basic agreement on fundamentals. In this field we should be natural allies, working more closely together for the common cause, against the common enemy.

Third and finally, I would stress the great potential gain for both groups resulting from increased political cooperation.

The American intellectual and scholar today must decide, as Goethe put it, whether he is to be an anvil—or a hammer. Today, for many, the stage of the anvil, at least in its formal phases, is complete. The question he faces is whether he is to be a hammer—whether he is to give to the world in which he was reared and educated the broadest possible benefits of his learning. As one who is familiar with the political world, I can testify that we need it.

For example: The password for all legislation, promoted by either party, is progress. But how do we tell what is progress and what is retreat? Those of us who may be too close to the issue, or too politically or emotionally involved in it, look for the objective word of the scholar. Indeed, the operation of our political life is such that we may not even be debating the real issues.

In foreign affairs, for example, the parties dispute over which is best fitted to implement the long-accepted policies of collective security and Soviet containment. But perhaps these policies are no longer adequate, perhaps these goals are no longer meaningful—the debate goes on nevertheless, for neither party is in a position to undertake the reappraisal necessary, particularly if the solutions presented are more complex to, and less popular with, the electorate.

Or take our agricultural program, for another example. Republicans and Democrats debate long over whether flexible or rigid price supports should be in effect. But this may not be the real issue at all—and in fact I am convinced that it is not, that neither program offers any long-range solution to our many real farm problems. The scholars and the universities might reexamine this whole area and come up with some real answers—the political parties and their conventions rarely will.

Other examples could be given indefinitely—where do we draw the line between free trade and protection, when does taxation become prohibitive, what is the most effective use we can make of our present nuclear potential? The intellectuals who can draw upon their rational disinterested approach and their fund of learning to help reshape our political life can make a tremendous contribution to their society while gaining new respect for their own group.

I do not say that our political and public life should be turned over to experts who ignore public opinion. Nor would I adopt from the Belgian Constitution of 1893 the provision giving three votes instead of one to college graduates; or give Harvard a seat in the Congress as William and Mary was once represented in the Virginia House of Burgesses.

But, I would urge that our political parties and our universities recognize the need for greater cooperation and understanding between politicians and intellectuals. We do not need scholars or politicians like Lord John Russell, of whom Queen Victoria remarked, he would be a better man if he knew a third subject—but he was interested in nothing but the Constitution of 1688 and himself. What we need are men who can ride easily over broad fields of knowledge and recognize the mutual dependence of our two worlds.

"Don't teach my boy poetry," an English mother recently wrote the Provost of Harrow. "Don't teach my boy poetry; he is going to stand for Parliament." Well, perhaps she was right—but if more politicians knew poetry, and more poets knew politics, I am convinced the world would be a little better place to live on this Commencement Day of 1956.

[Given at Commencement Exercises, Harvard University, June 14, 1956. Reprinted by permission.]

A Speech of Evocation: "The Challenge of Knowledge"

RAYMOND B. FOSDICK

A hundred and five years ago, John Quincy Adams, 77 years of age, journeyed from his home in Massachusetts to Cincinnati, Ohio, to lay the cornerstone of the Astronomical Observatory. It was a long and fatiguing trip by stagecoach, by canal boat, by steamboat, and part of the way by the newly invented railroad train. Much of Mr. Adams' dedicatory address concerned the neglect of astronomy in the United States. We have been, he said, "so absorbed in the toil of converting the wilderness into a garden," that we have been indifferent to the sciences, and "particularly to the science of astronomy."

To our generation, a hundred years later, the significance of his address lies, perhaps, not so much in what he said—although his comment is historically illuminating—as in what he failed to say. And what he failed to say was what nobody could have foreseen a century ago, because in 1843 there was no evidence that the time might come when the lag between advancing knowledge and social control would threaten the existence of society itself.

Twenty years ago, when the 200-inch telescope project came up before our group in New York, one of the Trustees raised an objection. It was in the form of a question—a question which finds an echo everywhere today. "What are we going to do with our new knowledge?" he asked. "Aren't we acquiring more knowledge than we can assimilate?" The shattering events of the last two decades have underscored the relevancy of his query. Knowledge and destruction have joined in a Grand Alliance that has made the history of our generation a history of deepening horror.

Obviously the difficulty lies in the fact that there is no way of foretelling what particular kind of knowledge is divertible to destructive ends. There is no method of classifying knowledge into safe and unsafe categories. All knowledge has become dangerous. Indeed, knowledge has always been dangerous; for knowledge means power, and power can be used to degrade as well as to ennoble the life of man.

Today in dedicating this telescope, we are face to face with the problem of the unpredictable consequences of knowledge. We cannot even guess what will come from this mighty instrument, or to what ends the fresh insights which we gain here will be employed. When the giant cyclotron was built at the University of California, nobody was thinking of the atomic bomb. The cyclotron was conceived as an adventure in pure research, as an attempt to advance the boundaries of understanding on a far frontier. It was a symbol of the human hunger for knowledge, an emblem of the unconquerable exploring urge within the mind of man.

And yet the cyclotron contributed materially to the development of one of the phases in the construction of the atomic bomb, just as this telescope may conceivably give us knowledge which, if we so choose, we can employ in the insanity of a final war. Years ago an Oxford professor working in the field of theoretical mathematics, remarked that he loved his subject because it could never be prostituted to any useful purpose. But he was wrong. There is no segment of knowledge, whether in the physical sciences or the social sciences, whether in medicine or economics or astrophysics or anthropology, which cannot ultimately be employed to the detriment of mankind if that is what we deliberately elect to do with it. Indeed, I believe that if the social sciences were developed as the physical sciences have been, we might have a weapon which, in unscrupulous hands, would be as deadly as the atomic bomb.

In the face of this dilemma, what is our proper course of action? Do we stop building telescopes? Do we close down our cyclotrons? Do we forbid the extension of knowledge? Do we retreat to some safe, underground existence where we can barricade ourselves against our fears and the unwelcome intrusion of new ideas?

The questions answer themselves. Any attempt to fix boundaries beyond which intellectual adventure shall not be allowed to go, even if it could succeed, would return us to an animal existence in which mere survival was the only goal. The search for truth is, as it always has been, the noblest expression of the human spirit. Man's insatiable desire for knowledge about himself, about his environment and the forces by which he is surrounded, gives life its meaning and purpose, and clothes it with final dignity. We are false to ourselves and to our best instincts only when we turn our backs on truth or close our eyes when it beckons.

And yet we know, deep in our hearts, that knowledge is not enough. This telescope is not enough. The vast enterprise of men that is pushing out the boundaries of knowledge in glorious adventure on a score of frontiers—all this is not enough. Unless we can anchor our knowledge to moral purposes, the ultimate result will be dust and ashes—dust and ashes that will bury the hopes and monuments of men beyond recovery.

The towering enemy of man is not his science but his moral inadequacy. Around the world today, laboratories supported by almost limitless resources are feverishly pushing their research in the development of physical and bacteriological weapons which overnight could turn this planet into a gigantic slaughterhouse. On what moral basis will the decision be made to use these weapons? What ethical restraints will have developed to curb the hysteria, fright and passion of men against such a blind paroxysm of destruction? For if this final Nemesis overtakes the pretensions of modern man, it will not be his science that has betrayed him, but rather the complete prostration of his moral values. It will not be this telescope and all that it symbolizes that have led him to the doorstep of doom; it will be the impotence and immaturity of his ethical codes.

There is a sense, of course, in which the problem we face is not new Over scores of centuries, man's progressive accessions of power have always outstripped his capacity for control, and the gap between his morality and the physical force at his disposal has always been uncomfortably wide. But never before have his curiosity and ingenuity led him within the space of a few years to weapons by which he could completely obliterate his own institutions and decimate the planet on which he lives.

This may seem too somber a note to be sounded at the dedication of a mighty instrument whose purpose is in line with man's noblest instincts; but in the twenty years that this telescope has been under construction, the human race has lived through its greatest tragedy. We know now that knowledge is not a gift; it is a challenge. It is not merely an augmentation of facts; it is a test of human character. And our generation is presented with what may well be the final choice between the use of knowledge to build a rational world or its use to arm, for one last, desperate affray, the savage and uncivilized passions of mankind.

And yet I believe that in the crisis which we face, this telescope can furnish our stricken society with some measure of healing perspective. This great new window to the stars will bring us into touch with those outposts of time and space which have beckoned from immemorial ages.

It will bring into fresh focus the mystery of the universe, its order, its beauty, its power. It will dramatize the questions which mankind has always asked and to which no answers have been found, and perhaps can never be found. Why are we here on this dwarf planet? Are there other planets that have burst into consciousness like our own? Is there an answering intelligence anywhere in space? Is there purpose behind the apparent meaninglessness and incomprehensibility of the universe? What is this divine spark of awareness which we call consciousness? And finally, in the words and spirit of the Psalmist, what is man?

In the face of these supreme mysteries and against this majestic background of space and time, the petty squabbling of nations on this small planet is not only irrelevant but contemptible. Adrift in a cosmos whose shores he cannot even imagine, man spends his energies in fighting with his fellow man over issues which a single look through this telescope would show to be utterly inconsequential.

We need in this sick world the perspective of the astronomer. We need the detachment, the objectivity, the sense of proportion which this great instrument can bring to mankind. This telescope is the lengthened shadow of man at his best. It is man on tiptoe, reaching for relevancy and meaning, tracing with eager finger the outlines of order and law by which his little life is everywhere surrounded. There is nothing which so glorifies the human race, or lends it such dignity and nobility as the gallant and inextinguishable urge to bring this vast, illimitable complexity within the range of human understanding. In the last analysis, the mind which encompasses the universe is more marvelous than the universe which encompasses the mind. "Astronomically speaking," said the philosopher, "man is completely negligible." To which the psychologist answered: "Astronomically speaking, man is the astronomer."

So we dedicate this instrument today in humbleness of spirit, but in the firm belief that among all the activities and aspirations of man there is no higher peak than this. There is a real sense in which Mount Palomar is Mount Everest.

[Given at the dedication of the 200-inch telescope on Mount Palomar, California, 1948. *Vital Speeches,* July 15, 1948, pp. 586-587. Reprinted by permission.]

Index